IN THE VALLEY OF MIST

IN THE VALLEY OF MIST

Kashmir's long war: one family's extraordinary story

Justine Hardy

RIDER

LONDON · SYDNEY · AUCKLAND · JOHANNESBURG

1 3 5 7 9 10 8 6 4 2

First published in 2009 by Rider, an imprint of Ebury Publishing
A Random House Group Company

The Random House Group Limited Reg. No. 954009

Addresses for companies within the Random House Group can be found at
www.rbooks.co.uk

A CIP catalogue record for this book is available from the British Library

The Random House Group Limited supports The Forest Stewardship Council (FSC), the leading international forest certification organisation. All our titles that are printed on Greenpeace approved FSC certified paper carry the FSC logo. Our paper procurement policy can be found at
www.rbooks.co.uk/environment

Map artwork by Rodney Paull
Printed and bound in the UK by CPI Mackays, Chatham ME5 8TD

ISBN 978-1-84-604146-4

For the people of Kashmir

CONTENTS

ACKNOWLEDGEMENTS

IT IS JUST NOT possible to thank people in a full enough way when a book is a story of people's lives, as this is. All I can do is acknowledge those whose story this is: Manzoor and all your family, you are *mashkur*, *dil se*, and to Maqbool, Salaama and Farouk on the boats and the lakes. Ramesh Halgali, for all that has been done and can be done. Dr Arshad Hussain and Parveena Ahanger, for all that you are doing for your people. To all the teachers of students at BEI school, for the future that you represent. Lovely Oberoi for your advice across the years. And beyond your Valley, Sudha Koul and Rafiq Kothwari. In Delhi Madhu, Krishna, RP Jain and C M Pie for being home. To Victoria Schofield and Alex Evans in friendship and conversation over time. In London and New York, my thanks to Elizabeth Sheinkman, my agent, to Judith Kendra at Rider and Amber Qureshi at Free Press for seeing into the heart of this story, and to Sue Lascelles, Kirsa Rein, Morag Lyall and Celia Knight, for elegant editing and assistance. Thank you Nitin Upadhye for the film of the story. And to Tamara, for your translations. To Johnny for listening and advising. And to Richard for unquestioning support through all of this. All of you have built this story. And my great thanks as well to all those who have given to the Kashmir Welfare Trust since 2005. For more information please see www.justinehardy.com

NOTE ON THE TEXT

As the situation in Kashmir continues to be fragile I have changed the names of some of the characters in this story, for the purpose of anonymity and protection.

Throughout the book I refer to the separated parts of Kashmir as Pakistan-controlled Kashmir and Indian-controlled Kashmir. In politicised parlance India refers to Pakistan Occupied Kashmir, or POK, likewise Pakistan uses the expression Indian Occupied Kashmir, or IOK. Pakistan also refers to the Pakistani controlled part of Kashmir as *Azad Kashmir*, or Free Kashmir. I have only used these terms in dialogue and reported speech.

Throughout the text there is transliteration from Kashmiri, Urdu, Arabic and Hindi. I have tried to combine accuracy with the most common usage in Kashmir of the various phrases, particularly the use of Arabic by non-Arabic speakers.

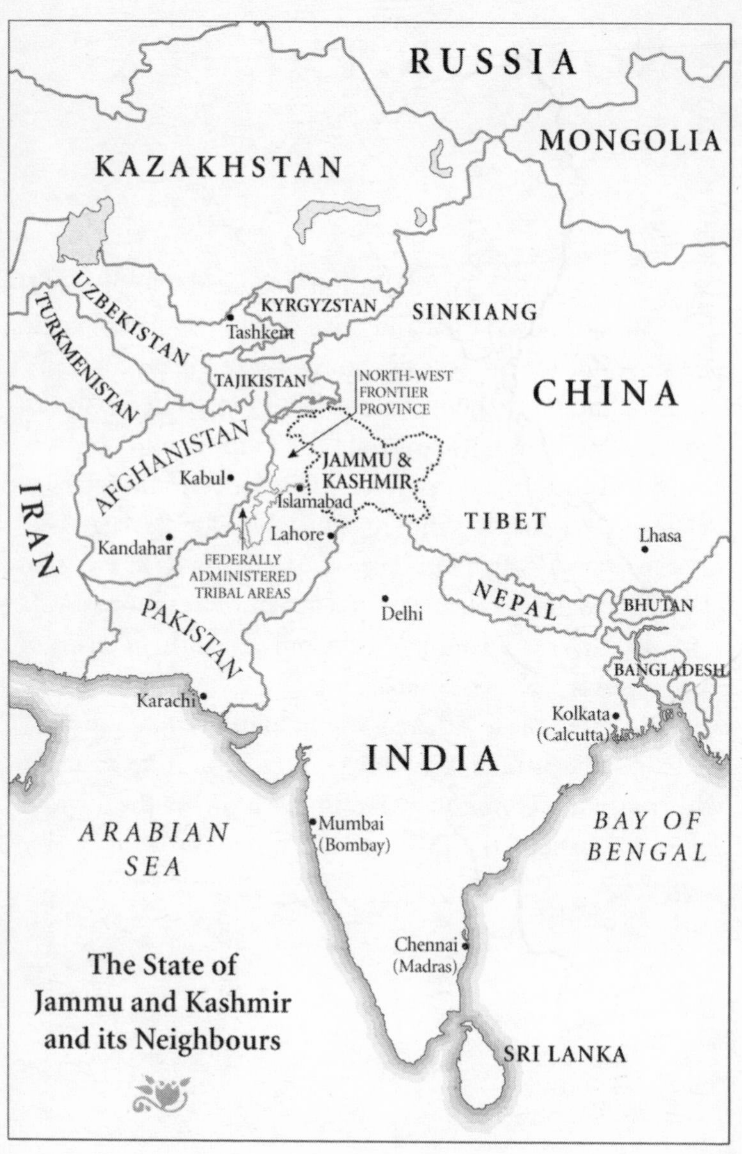

The State of Jammu and Kashmir and its Neighbours

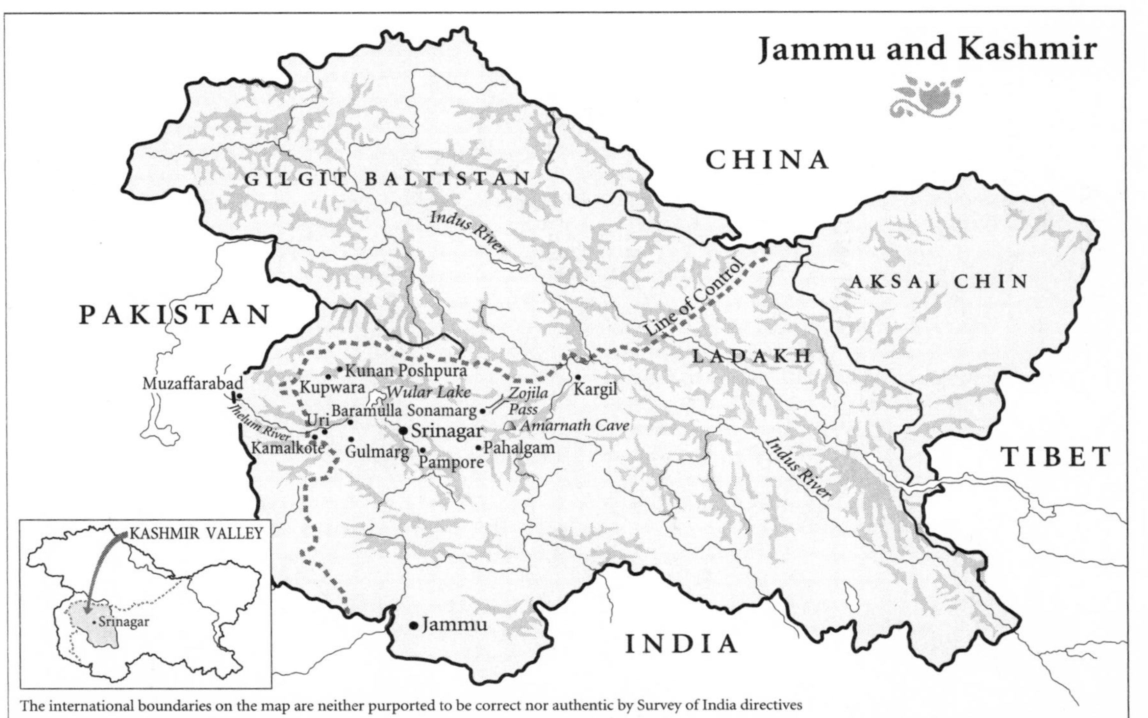

The international boundaries on the map are neither purported to be correct nor authentic by Survey of India directives

INTRODUCTION

Mohammad Dar is many men: patriarch, husband, son, houseboat-owner, carpet-seller, aid worker and conservationist. But he would not pick any of those to define himself. He talks of being a Muslim, and then a Kashmiri.

He was born on a wooden boat moored on a lake between a lotus garden and a white marble mosque that houses a hair of the prophet.

He was a water-boy, skimming the lakes of Kashmir with his three younger brothers, Imran, Ibrahim and Yusuf, hunched at the front of small boats with paddles carved in the shape of the leaves in the lotus garden, wooden hearts. In winter they walked on water, scudding between boats frozen in hard beneath the high peaks that mark the limits of their valley home.

And while the boys explored their world their sisters stayed at home, because that was how it went. But they grew up thinking of themselves as Kashmiris, above all else.

And then their world changed.

Mohammad, the adult, husband, father and carpet-seller, was sitting on the tree of life when I met him in Delhi, his bare feet stretched out across the silk of the carpet, the hair beneath his embroidered skullcap shaved close to the back of his neck, his hennaed beard as full as his hair was short.

It was still burning in Delhi though it was softer autumn in his valley. He talked of the tree line around his lake turning to earth, fire and blood. He ran one hand over the tree of life carpet as he spoke.

'You must come back soon, *Inshallah*. No matter how short a time you are away from Kashmir, it is always too long,' he said.

When Mohammad and his brothers speak it is with constant invocations to Allah. They punctuate their sentences with them: *Inshallah* (God willing, if it is God's will), *Bismillah* (in the name of Allah, the Merciful, the Compassionate), *Al-hamdulilah* (all praise belongs to God). For flow of dialogue I have mostly left these invocations out, yet I have endeavoured to capture conversations as they were spoken. As Mohammad said to me, when I asked him and his family permission to tell their stories, 'If you want people to know…tell them the truth. It is strong enough.'

I first met Mohammad and his brothers in 1997, a time when the situation in their valley had forced many Kashmiris to become itinerant salesmen, refugees, migrant workers or emigrants. I have known Kashmir for most of my life, and Mohammad, his brothers and the broad spread of their family for the past twelve years of that time. As daily life contracted in the face of conflict the Dars have become home to me, solid ground beside the lake where they were born.

Their home is a Himalayan state of soaring physical beauty divided between two nations, India and Pakistan. The desire to possess Kashmir in its entirety colours almost every aspect of the tension between these two countries. Because it has been lusted after by just about everyone who has found themselves amid its water and poetry, the people of the Kashmir Valley have long craved independence.

In full the state is called Jammu and Kashmir, and a broad stroke taken across its spread presents three very distinct regions on the Indian side of the Line of Control, the ceasefire line of 1949 that dates from the end of Pakistan and India's first military clash over the state, fought hard on the heels of Indian independence and the formation of the two nations of East and West Pakistan in 1947. To the north the High Himalayas cleave into the Kashmir Valley, a majority Muslim region. South of Srinagar is Jammu, the summer capital, and Hindu by majority. To the north-east is Ladakh, a high-altitude place of bare mountains stripped of vegetation, and home to a people following Tibetan Buddhism, both religiously and culturally. But this is a sweeping stroke for the sake of simplification so as to focus on the first of the three regions, the Kashmir Valley.

In the winter of 1989 tension between the Kashmiri people and the Central Government in Delhi finally erupted into the first stage of a generation of full-blown conflict. What began as a local uprising for *Azadi* – freedom and autonomy for Kashmir – was rapidly hijacked by 'foreign' fighters. The majority of these 'god warriors' had been battle-hewn during the Soviet-Afghan war, and they fought into Kashmir with the blessing and support of Pakistani intelligence.

The war that had honed these fighters lasted from 1979 to 1989 and it bred a new generation of *jihadis*, warriors of Islam, fighting against the godless condition of communism, forging new frontiers for Islam in the aftermath of the revolution of 1979 in Iran. This *mujahideen* army was backed covertly and overtly, armed and trained by nations as ideologically divorced as China and Iran, the USA and Egypt.

When the Soviet Union pulled out in 1989 the *mujahideen* concentrated their attention on 'the suppression and oppression of the peoples of Islam'. They turned towards the state of Jammu and Kashmir, or more precisely to the northern part of the state that India controlled, which was bordered by China and Pakistan – the Kashmir Valley, the beauty.

This divided region has become a flashpoint surrounded by nuclear-armed neighbours. Here, instability now carries the threat of affecting the whole world. Fearfulness sits in the landscape, and in the faces of the people.

I have watched the changes across a generation as militarily backed democracy and politically armed Islam have mauled each other. It was here that I first witnessed the concept soundbites that are now played across the headlines, throughout the Middle East and Afghanistan: fundamentalist Islam, *jihad*, Shari'a Law, enforced *hijab*, martyrdom, *Nizam-e-Mustafa* (the rule of Islam, Islamic law).

This story does not come from behind the barbed wire of government and military compounds. These are not the views and ideas of politicians, analysts, the powerful and manipulative. It comes from the streets, and from daily life. It is the story of a family, and those around them, trying to find a way of existing through the long, dark night of a twenty-year conflict.

Chapter One

THE PHERAN

MOHAMMAD WAS BORN on a lake that a capital curls around, a water city of canals and bridges. It is a place of quarters, of professions and religions: the laundry district, copper merchants' market, Sunni beside Shi'a beside Pandit, the Hindus of the Valley. In the merchant quarters tall wooden houses line narrow alleys, their carved casements and balconies staring blindly onto paved streets, burned out, black-eyed by conflict. But beyond the silence of curfewed markets and streets the sky opens to water, mountains and sky, to autumn Kashmir, a monsoon-rinsed blue above peaks where heavy August rains leave a deep new snowline. The earth, fire and blood of Mohammad's description surround the lake, the season burning in the tree line. Beneath the trees houseboats fringe the water, floating dreams, eight, ten rooms long, cedar-carved balconies of time slowed down.

Autumn is fire but the colour of winter in the Valley is grey, even under fresh snow.

From out of the faded colour the houseboats emerge, lying low to the freezing lake.

The cold air of winter brings a mist that makes people want to huddle together, and around each other. Except that here it can be a crime to do that.

In the thick heat of the hot season down in the plains,

through airless nights people dream of water, escape, open space and room to breathe. But in this high valley seeking out human warmth between November and April is logical, though only permissible within marriage, and in total privacy.

There is a garment that is the shape of winter in the Valley against the grey. It is formless, plain, a three-quarter-length thing, part sack, part woven woollen tunic. The *pheran* does not change that much in form between the male and female version. Yet among the black, all-covering, three-part *burqas*, now more common than the more traditional pale blue and white ones in the city of Srinagar, the *pherans* worn by women are proudly more elaborate, more intricately embroidered at the neckline and cuffs than those worn by men. They are a relief among the formlessness of all the black.

Pherans appear as the leaves begin to turn in that final colour show before winter's grey. Below the swell of the mountains the scurrying city ants pull out their *pherans*, even while the gold autumn days are still in the mid-twenties. By sunset the woollen rolls that have doubled as cushions, or been worn slung as a cross-belt, like ammunition, have been unbundled. Figure and form slip beneath them to disappear until the spring, but in an indigenous way, a practical and Kashmiri way that does not cause rage, spitting or stoning if not worn.

The *pheran*'s heavy tweed may engulf people but it does not stop them from doing things. This outer skin is constantly adapted, the wide sleeves often having slits halfway up that create a shorter sleeve, with the lower length pinned back to allow room for manoeuvre. And then there is the half-shoulder look favoured by the charioteers.

Carts still move much of the low-value freight between the

towns and villages of the Valley. Once the mist comes down they are heard before they are seen, the heavy-shod ponies clattering through the fog, a thrusting muzzle emerging from the gloom, beaded with condensation. Body, traces, cart and charioteer follow; a man standing tall at the front, feet wide apart to brace himself, reins held high, a whip in hand, the shroud of the *pheran* pulled up and over one shoulder, draped and glamorous.

That was what I had always wanted, to be able to wear a *pheran* draped up and over one arm, warm in its folds while still free to move. However, it took me several years of living and working in the Valley to find the confidence to go to a tailor and have one made. Of course anyone can wear one, wherever and however they like. The *pheran* is, after all, about as practical as it gets as an all-encompassing cold-weather skin, covering everything from the heavily pregnant to the old and bent over.

In my mind's eye the outlines of Mohammad and his three brothers, Imran, Ibrahim and Yusuf, are shaped by the *pheran*, each of them wearing it a little differently to mark themselves out in the crowd, and within the growing spread of their own family. Mohammad wears his straight, without detail or fuss. He is the eldest – this simplicity gives him authority. Then comes Imran who likes to wear his with his arms pulled inside, flapping occasionally against the fabric as he makes a point with his hands inside their tweed tent. Ibrahim usually has his charioteer-style, leaving one hand free to gesticulate as wildly as required. As the third brother he needs to make his mark. Yusuf is the youngest. He pulls a *pheran* on, wearing it in a way that seems more careless than really intended, just as teenage boys wear their trousers dragged down in defiance of having to pull up most things for the rest of their lives. However far in the distance one of the brothers may be, across a lake meadow, heading down the road to the mosque, partway around a corner into one of the market alleys, his shape within his winter skin is familiar.

When I first stayed with the Dar family, Mohammad asked why I did not have a *pheran*. I had been coming to Kashmir for so long. His voice swung up at the end in surprise. It made no sense.

'We must go to the tailor and have one made,' he announced.

The visit to Mohammad's tailor became an outing. We spent the afternoon at his shop in the market, comparing tweeds and wools while tea came in shifts from the *chai* stall across the road. I watched as the boy from the stall loped across, glasses of tea in a wire carrier swinging, as Mohammad and the tailor discussed the water-resistant qualities of various weaves. Both men rely on the looms of the Valley for their livelihood, Mohammad for carpets and shawls, the tailor for woollens and tweeds. As they spoke about warp and weft with the passion usually reserved for sport, I tried to work out how the boy from the tea stall managed not to spill a drop of *chai* in motion.

As we walked back from the tailor's small shop, through the streets of the market near the Dars' house, the meadow below, and the lake beyond, I told Mohammad about the *pherans* that I had already owned and then lost.

When I first came back to Kashmir alone as an adult in 1990 I had longed for an excuse that could get me into a tailor's shop with credibility, but I sidled away without crossing the threshold, unnerved in a nervous time for women. Even during easier times the commissioning of a *pheran* was no lightweight thing. This is what you will live in for the foreseeable future – it will be home. You do not just go about it as though popping into some local shop to pick up any old T-shirt.

Rafiq the tailor's shop was halfway down Lal Bazaar above one corner of Nagin Lake. He had been trained by a Pandit tailor, a Kashmiri Hindu, from the community that used to dominate the business and government sectors in the Valley. The Pandits, almost in their entirety, fled the Valley soon after it exploded into violence at the end of 1989. With their departure the romanticised and much vaunted secular ease of Kashmir came to an abrupt end.

Rafiq was just a teenager when he started cutting for his Pandit teacher, and they made only two things: *pherans* and English-cut tweed, wool and cashmere suits. Rafiq began as an apprentice to the Pandit in May 1947, three months before Indian independence. The hot season was burning up down on the plains, nudging people to the edge of madness as the lines were drawn that would divide Greater India into two nations, India and the two-winged states of East and West Pakistan.

Kashmir's lakes had always been a place of retreat from the lunatic grill that the capital city of Delhi becomes between April and October. Yet this little coveted slice of the Himalayas had never been an easy escape. Time in the pretty valley of water, walnut and almond groves, fruit orchards and trout rivers came with layers of deceit.

For young officers of the British Empire in India it was a place they could sneak to in order to consummate flirtations with the wives of senior officers of their regiments, often precociously pretty young women who had been parcelled up with much older men, officers who had reached a rank of seniority that required a wife. A colonel's dewy bride could be left alone for months at a time, her boredom making her easy prey for the idealistic lieutenants and captains. These were young men with enough boyish romantic poetry to take risks, and the road to Srinagar, the summer city of water, houseboats and slow-paddled lake taxis, custom-made for the leisurely flirtation of drawn-out, hot-season love affairs.

Keen but over-tired suitors needed respite. They would leave their pretty cheats on board houseboats to meet up with fellow illicit weekenders of the regiment for a round of golf, or a game of polo. The tailors were ready for them, their shops lined up along the roads bordering the Kashmir Golf Club and Polo View, the street beside the polo ground. There was usually just enough time between golf, polo and love-making for the requisite number of fittings for at least one good suit. Sometimes the newly besuited young men would have a *pheran* made as well: a souvenir of the Valley, of poignant secret sex, a tangible memento of a fleeting and sensual dream time.

I found one in the dressing-up box of a grand friend when I was about ten. I was in search of some hardcore tomboy gear. Richard the Lionheart was my pin-up at the time, mainly for his manly horsemanship. Therefore I was in search of something regal but I found what looked like an old horse-blanket. I wanted to be the king, not his horse, so it was discarded. It was not until more than a decade later that I realised I had rejected a *pheran*. I wrote to the friend with the dressing-up box to tell him. He wrote back that he had known what it was, but that he had never been quite sure where it had come from as his grandfather had 'covered off most of North India during his various postings'.

'Covered off' was used in a way that moved beyond

military geography, leaving behind a sense of hot skin and tugged muslin.

When the Raj withdrew in 1947 it left many calling cards, one of the least controversial being a whole tribe of tailors tutored in cutting to fit your average English officer's exercised and nipped physique with all the right flaps, vents and required overstitching. They did not have much of a tailoring hiatus as a myriad of embassies and high commissions opened for business in Delhi, the capital of newly independent India. With them came a new generation of diplomatic customers. They too quickly sought out the tailors in the bazaars and malls of the hill stations where the Raj had retreated to during the hot season.

The Pandit tailor and his young assistant Rafiq were busy again to the extent that, by the time independent India was only a few years old, they had moved to bigger premises and taken on two new full-time seamstresses, or rather seamsmasters. The artisan traditions of Kashmir are customarily male; another vestige from another empire, the Mughals. But the move had also been because independence for India had ignited a desire for independence in Kashmir. Cutting suits for foreigners was deemed unpatriotic to the state. Some of the busier tailors with foreign clientele simply added discreet back rooms or moved premises.

Within a few years, on the heels of the diplomats, came another new generation of customers to Kashmir, freewheeling into Srinagar on the hippie trail in pursuit of the haze of Afghan Black, and a different kind of lake trip.

They drove overland from Afghanistan with their hashish stashes packed into dust-caked Land Rovers that they had worked through many university holidays and school vacs to buy for 'the big adventure'. Through the Hindu Kush they came, jauntily cocked soft-rolled *pakul* hats jammed on dirty long hair. The boys, and they were mostly boys, set up camp on Kashmir's lakes, lying back and sighing in delight at the sweet prettiness of their surroundings after the brutal high altitude of the Pamir Mountains and the Karakoram Range. They turned the houseboats of the side-by-side lakes, Dal and Nagin, into modern opium salons. Like flies they came to over-ripe fruit. The Kashmiri boatmen nodded and tolerated the gap year and Afghan Black behaviour, and took the dollars and pounds with wide smiles.

Mohammad's family has been among the most highly regarded of the houseboat owners across two centuries. For the Dars this new era of travel meant that their business was also brisk again. Mohammad's father, Sobra, and his brothers took their glazed-eyed temporary tenants to see the Mughal gardens, the mosques and markets. They shrugged and encouraged the new round of travellers to buy from the lake salesmen who lined up beside the houseboats, their flower-fringed *shikara* boats bobbing in serried ranks as they waited their turn to pitch for business. Each would hop up the wooden steps of the back veranda of the boat, laden down with wicker baskets. The travellers lolled on mounds of cushions and watched the show: all things papier-mâché from pencil boxes to napkin rings with rabbit's ears; shawls of every weave and colour, some light enough to float on air, others as thick as blankets; every kind of carved cedar trinket; and carpets, carpets, carpets.

The wicker baskets were just not big enough so the carpet men came as emissaries of the great showrooms. They cajoled hard, and the travellers were malleable enough to be persuaded into *shikaras* for the ride to a 'carpet garden', to be settled back into more mounds of cushions, plied with

Kashmiri green tea until the thread count per square inch of silk and woollen carpets made their heads spin almost as much as the Afghan Black.

Mohammad and his family watched closely, overseeing the sales patter, and advising their guests on fair prices. Then they would offer better prices for their own carpets, shawls and papier-mâché, and so their business grew.

The 'hashish *sahibs*' as they began to be known, lay about on houseboat verandas, and in various artisan showrooms, complaining of being preyed on, of the constant hassling. However, they still wrote postcards home that they had franked at floating post offices, water lilies and kingfishers beyond the wooden casements behind the postmaster's desk. They wrote of the hedonistic Valley, its beauty and all-round hip desirability, and they recommended the Dars as trustworthy and high-calibre, just as an earlier generation of *sahibs* had.

So their friends came too, joining the swarm. For a while they would lose their balance on landing, confused by a new set of cultural signposts, but they soon found their way to the lakes and the houseboats. Days passed, salesmen came, and the next round of interlopers found their feet again, and began to complain too about the constant call of the salesmen, about being swarmed around, batting them away from the sides of the houseboats as *shikaras* lined up to pitch.

The salesmen did not mind. They were used to it. Several centuries of honing their sales pitch had stood them in good stead.

For a while the Pandit tailor plied his trade by *shikara* as well, until he began to get tired of the arguments with this new wave of tourists. They were polite enough until it came to the money and then they would try to beat down his prices.

Even if their hair was dirty and their clothes stained the Pandit tailor knew that they were educated, privileged and mostly wealthy: a new travelling elite, talking among themselves as though he did not understand English.

He had been educated at one of the English-medium schools in Srinagar. The headmaster had come from Cheltenham College and his pupils thought that he sounded like the Earl of Reading, the Viceroy of the time. So the Pandit tailor stopped going to the lakes but the customers did not stop coming, in part because he was very good and did not cut the seams as narrow as other tailors, partly because his assistant Rafiq was nearly as good as he was, and in part because the pupil did not tell his teacher but he continued to trawl the lakes for business when the Pandit was away from the shop.

By the late 1980s the Pandit tailor was in his eighties too. Even though his life had been successful he slumped into a deep depression. Rafiq believed that his teacher died of prescient despair, a sense that a day was near when the wearing of the *pheran*, the garment that he had made throughout his life, would be declared an act of *jihad* by an army that saw it only as a covering for weapons rather than as an outer skin.

'How could that be?' I asked Rafiq, when I had finally made up my mind to visit his small shop to have a *pheran* of my own made.

Rafiq sat on the floor, looking at bundles of tweed. He picked up a wooden measure, an old yard stick that he used for measuring off lengths of gabardine, linen, drill, flannel, herringbone, houndstooth, moleskin, needlecord, whipcord, tweed, cashmere and more. He shrugged into one of the many *pherans* that he had been showing me, and pulled his arms inside. The yardstick followed and disappeared. He turned it inside the *pheran* to point towards me as though it were a gun.

The tailor talked of the attacks on military posts by militants who hid their guns, or even small arsenals, inside their *pherans*. Measuring me from shoulder tip to shoulder tip he talked about his view of the beginning of the uprising.

For him it began in winter, the middle of December 1989, just before the beginning of *Chilla Kalan*, the deepest bite of Kashmiri cold that runs for over a month, the time when no one moves without a *pheran*.

So much can be hidden under its all-encompassing folds.

It was said that the police, paramilitary forces and the army sent in by the Indian Government to stamp on the uprising declared the *pheran* an illegal garment for men, unless it was worn with one side pulled up, in the same way as the cart charioteers of the Valley. The soldiers and police at check-posts could then see from a distance whether the wearer was armed. Still this did not stop people from wearing the *pheran* even though it had been declared an accessory to *jihad*.

'Couldn't they have just pushed their weapons down the back of their *pyjamas*, *salwar* or trousers, even if they had to have their *pherans* pulled up on one side?' I asked.

Rafiq went on measuring me and told me that I was talking like a man, like a *jihadi*, and that it was not a suitable conversation.

He did, however, allow me to choose a man's design, rather than one of the broader-sleeved and more ornate women's ones. He sniffed when I asked him if he minded.

'Not at all,' he said, with a gracious smile that I later learned to read not as an expression of pleasure but more one of submission. His real smile was gap-toothed and wide, lifting his whole face.

The tailor's brother-in-law had been one in the first round of people 'killed during an encounter' between Indian security forces and militants in the aftermath of the early uprisings in December 1989. Rafiq's sister believed her husband to have been heroic, a freedom fighter, a *jihadi* for *Azadi*, a warrior of Allah, a martyr killed fighting for Kashmir. Rafiq had not agreed. He had been taken to the police station to identify the body, and all that he had seen were the dark circles around the bullet punctures in the heavy sage green of the *pheran* that his brother-in-law had been wearing when he had been shot. He did not even use a familiar word for the colour of the *pheran* that he had made for his brother-in-law. He described it as being that moment when frost begins to melt off grass in winter sun.

The tailor did not find the sight of a line of corpses in stained *pherans* heroic. They were not dead warriors, just local men whom he had known, clothed in what had become their shrouds, not garments of *jihad*.

Conflict makes many very thin, and some fat. Rafiq lost perhaps a third of his bodyweight across the years of the conflict, judging from the photographs of him that I saw around the shop, posing through the 1970s and early 1980s with delighted customers. They sported newly made clothes, hands in jacket pockets so as to show off waistcoats beneath. Rafiq stood to one side, smiling his wide, lifting smile, one arm around a broad-shouldered and broadly grinning Australian diplomat; another in the same pose with a square-jawed Swedish man who had been in the Valley to work on a hydro-electric project. The tailor seemed a substantial man then, full-faced without being fat.

By the time I met him, a couple of years into the insurgency, he was losing weight. Even his eyes seemed to be getting thinner as they sank down into the dip that was opening up between the lower curve of his eye socket and the rise of his cheekbones.

When he was not measuring a body, or lengths of material, pinning or cutting, when he was just sitting, at ease, his hands fluttered as he spoke, rising from his lap as if they were going to take flight in gesture. But they never quite made it, as though each idea of an expression were pulled back down before it could be fulfilled. I did not even notice this until the hot season when the protective layers came off. While it was cold his hands were either working, or pulled into the body of his *pheran* and wrapped around the hot basketwork of a *kangri*, the little fire pots that complete the shape of the cold season in the Valley.

The *kangri* is as much part of the anatomy as the *pheran* is the skin of winter. These little earthenware pots hold hot coals, the swell of the pot's belly contained in wicker so that they can be carried around as a portable personal heater throughout the long icy months, creating tents of warmth inside *pherans*, clasped against bellies and between thighs. The *kangri* even has a cancer named after it because of the very high occurrence of a particular form of skin cancer of the stomach and inner thighs triggered by charcoal heat so close to the skin. But *kangri* cancer does not stop people from using them. They are indispensable.

As the tailor shrank he seemed to recede further into his *pheran*, hugging closer in around his *kangri* for warmth, but his wasting was not due to lack of food.

For so many in Kashmir this has been the constant struggle of a generation, finding enough to eat through the cold. With the stand-off between the Indian security forces and the militants the economy stalled. It had been plump on tourism and agriculture, shiny too with international co-productions headed up by such men as the Swedish engineer in the photograph on Rafiq's wall. When the conflict began the local economy crashed and the people on the city streets and in the villages could only dream of the time of *harisa*, a rich mix of rice and mutton that had once been daily fare.

Hunger was not the tailor's plague. It was another horseman of conflict.

He began to itch, all over, like a mangy dog. It stopped him as he walked in the street, making him scratch himself into a sweat. It woke him in the night, maddening him to itch and rub until his skin was raw and bleeding. At other times it would be localised, just his scalp, the palms of his hands, along his spine. He began washing several times a day, even though in winter the water was icy as the power was rarely on for long enough to heat up the geyser. He burned his mattress and bought a new one. He burned that one as well.

He described the itching as being like another person, a criminal or ghost, constantly on the lookout for a time to attack him, waiting for moments when he was vulnerable: on the way to the mosque, his back bent with worry; at the darkest point of the night when his mind was cramping with fear; during long stretches of the empty day in the shop when no customers were coming to order clothes, when his hands clutched in financial terror. Then it would pounce, sometimes pulling him to the floor with it, making him writhe on the ground as he tried to scratch more parts of his body at the same time. He said that the only thing that stopped the itching was going to the mosque to pray, or the time he spent with his children and grandchildren.

When I asked him how long he had been itching, he had not seemed sure, though he knew that it was around the time that the worst of the violence began, when the *pheran* had already been declared a garment of *jihad*.

While he was making a second, or even third *pheran* for me, there still seemed to be long periods when he did not scratch, when he could sit and just talk, take a cup of tea with me, his hands only moving in half gestures. Perhaps when he left the room to order *chai* from next door, or to tell his assistant stitching and cutting in the back room something, perhaps then he was also leaving the room so that he could perform what he called his dance of the *djinns*, the mad shuddering of the wild and wicked spirits of smokeless fire.

The *pherans* that Rafiq had made for me were somehow lost, packed away in boxes that never arrived in the round of moves between India and England. Each disappearance seemed much greater than just the loss of a piece of clothing.

As a foreigner it is more comfortable to live in the Valley in winter with a *pheran*. Of course clever microfibres, Thinsulate, fleece and all coverings unnatural do very well in creating warmth. They seal in body heat and whip away sweat. Yet in all their synthetic forms they make the foreigner stand out even further from the greys and browns of the local crowd, all bright, shiny and alien in colours punchy enough to seem rude. The *pheran* allows anonymity, freedom of movement, androgyny.

In November 1999, ten years into the conflict, tension was racked high as two newly nuclear-armed nations snarled at each other in the aftermath of a short summer war between Pakistan and India. This was swiftly followed by an autumn coup and counter-coup in Pakistan that deposed the incumbent Prime Minister, Nawaz Sharif, and brought General Pervez Musharraf to power. It was not a time to be wandering the streets of Srinagar in loud puffed-up jackets. The women of Kashmir were not seen by the security forces as a threat and, unlike the men, they were still largely unchallenged at check-posts for wearing *pherans* as they always had.

This was when Mohammad Dar said that it was time for me to have another *pheran*. He wanted me to go to his tailor but I told him that I would rather go again to the one I knew.

I had not seen Rafiq for over a year.

He was not at his shop.

The *chai-wallah* next door told me that he had died in the spring. He had been sixty-eight years old. Not so alarmingly young as to have been a conventional victim of conflict. He had weighed only forty-eight kilos when he died, far too little for a man who must have been at least five feet ten inches in his bare feet.

The *chai-wallah* said that he had died from a heart attack.

I went to Rafiq's house.

His family home is behind the bazaar, down a side alley beyond the mosque, close enough for him still to have been able to find the solace of prayer, even when he was at his weakest.

The welcome was unexpected.

I had only been to the house once before, while Rafiq was making the first *pheran* for me, eight years earlier. It had been just to have a cup of tea.

He had been so proud as his children paraded in front of me, his grandchildren as well, two of them already old enough to be married. One of his grandsons was engaged at the time, and a granddaughter was staying away from the family because she too was engaged, to a cousin, Rafiq's brother's youngest son.

It was this same granddaughter who met me in the alley in front of the house when I returned. Taking my hand, she led me through cold rooms at the back of the house, bedding rolled against the walls, damp woollen Kashmiri carpets on the floors. She called to people as she went and by the time we reached the kitchen most of the women of the house had come to see.

The room was warm, full of life, the heart of it a platform slightly raised up from the rest of the kitchen. A low wall around the edge of the platform, perhaps just a foot high, marked this out as the eating-place, the gathering point. The women turned to me, their faces wide, cheeks pink from winter chapping and the peach and hazelnut skin-colouring of the Valley, their heads covered with bright floral headscarves. The bowed faces of these women tell much of the Valley's story – their downcast eyes, small smiles and half-hidden gestures learned under the hard watch of patriarchal law. The women of today's Kashmir are not as exuberant as they once were.

Tea was made, the clatter of pans made louder by the lack of conversation. And then Rafiq's granddaughter began with some questions, the ones always asked by women whose role in society has been narrowed to the home and giving birth. Why was I still not married? Did I not want to have children? She pulled her two children apart, boys of about three and five who were rolling on the carpet, pinching each other. She picked tea-soaked breadcrumbs off their clothes and tidied their hair as she asked me more questions.

Rafiq's widow sat in the corner, curled into her *pheran*. She did not speak English or Urdu, and we exchanged only a greeting in Kashmiri. She nodded as she spoke and smiled with just her mouth before receding into the tweed of her neckline. The children playing near her left a space, her circle of grief.

When tea came they broke up small rounds of bread into their cups, not dipping but submerging them in the tea. We drank in silence except for the bubbling of hot tea on lower lips, and the slurp of sodden bread.

Even when the tea had been drunk we did not speak of Rafiq, though there were three photographs of him on the wall, lined up below an engraving on copper of the black solidness of the Kaaba at Mecca. The middle photograph was of Rafiq as a young man. He was wearing a *pheran*, his brow smooth under a black astrakhan cap. It must have been taken to mark some important date. His expression was without emotion, rigid in the formality of the moment.

It was not until his granddaughter showed me the way back out into the street at the end of the visit that she talked about him. She told me that at the end of his life the itching had been so bad that he had been unable to sleep at all. He had been tested for every allergy from dairy to dust, even for scabies possibly picked up from street cats and dogs, though there had been no mite threads to be seen under his frail, brutalised skin. There had been no answers.

War breeds depression, crippling, dehumanising nervous collapse. Many of those in Kashmir live with conflict depression. It manifests itself in two main types, fairly clearly divided by sex. Women became manic as the conflict moved from months to years. They pushed themselves beyond natural limits: keeping their families together, foraging for food, caring for children, trying to keep teenage boys out of the orbit of militant recruiters, struggling to keep their husbands alive and away from the attention of the security forces, attempting to keep their parents-in-law sheltered from the worst news of the daily rounds of violence. The well-being of their own parents was the duty of their brothers, it being the practice for a woman to go to the house and family of her husband. So the women drove themselves to breakdown, total physical and mental collapse, their nervous systems short-circuiting until they became hysterical or fell silent. The men slid into a state of extreme lethargy, almost to catatonia, incapable of the most basic decisions or simple actions, unable to provide for their families or themselves, given to weeping for extended periods of time, or sitting staring at blank walls. They too are looked after by the women.

Rafiq's symptom had been harder to diagnose.

It was a pallid, overworked doctor at the only psychiatric hospital in Srinagar, the Government Hospital of Psychiatric Diseases, who had an idea about the tailor's itching when I asked him about the symptoms after I had seen Rafiq's family.

The hospital's main psychiatric ward was a place of human waste at the height of the insurgency. It was more asylum than hospital with beds crushed almost on top of each other, bodies prostrate and humped, either limp and motionless, or caught up in some all-consuming manic activity: plucking threads from the sheets, hair from their heads, biting skin from around already badly bitten nails. The doctor told me that he had seen a few similar cases among the thousands and thousands that were passing through the wards. He considered it a stand-alone symptom of what he referred to as an MDD, a major depressive disorder. The nerve-endings become so fried that they keep sending SOS messages across the synapses, desperate neural cries for help that manifested themselves as extreme itching.

'They scratch themselves to death as much as anything else,' he said.

In 1985, four years before the beginning of the conflict, the hospital saw 775 patients. In 1998, nine years into the conflict, 80,000 patients passed through the hospital. There were 150 beds, and, at that time, it was the only psychiatric hospital in the state.

The face of the young man on the wall at Rafiq's house, upright in his *pheran* and astrakhan hat, had not been an image of *jihad* to come. He was simply a young tailor with no idea that his mind would not let him survive the long fight ahead.

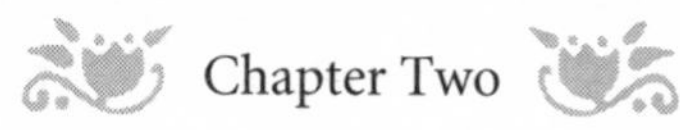

Chapter Two

EVERYTHING BEAUTIFUL IS BROKEN NOW

IT BEGAN WITH BEAUTY. And then it was about greed. It usually is.

Kashmir's beauty is the stuff of eulogy and big movies: a great sage who begged a god to strike a cleft in the Valley so that a demon could be slain. It was done, they say, and most of the water drained away leaving a fertile land, a soft green place in the midst of the world's youngest and crudest mountain range, lunatic peaks thrown up towards the high cloud strata when the Indo-Australian plate of the fragmenting super-continent of Gondwanaland is thought to have collided with the Eurasian plate. During the Time of Reptiles, an inland sea, the Tethys Ocean, is believed to have existed between the super-continents. Parts of it were hurled upwards in the collision that became the Himalayas, bringing marine life to be embedded in mountain walls. This is where the Kashmir Valley's beauty was bred, in the rich silt that was laid down in this high garden that was once an ocean floor.

Of course everyone likes to take credit for the formation of the fecund Valley. The Brahmins said it was because the holy man, Kasyapa, was so diligent in his devotions that he was allowed to call on a god to do his bidding. He called on Shiva, the Destroyer, one of the ruling triumvirate with Brahma and Vishnu in the pantheon of gods. Yet every regional community has its version, each laying claim to this place that instils a desire for ownership in all who live there, and among so many of those who pass through.

'When I am away from my family and my valley there are times when I am so sad that my eyes are filling up with tears,' Mohammad Dar once said, and his messages and emails usually end with the question of when I am coming back. 'You should not be away from here at this time,' he would say or write. And then there would be a list of reasons why: 'You cannot imagine how lovely the light is now on my lake,' and 'It gives me so much joy to be able to do something that is so simple as to walk across the meadow nearby to my house when I am making my way to the mosque.'

Mohammad is not alone in mythologising his home.

'We had it for so long,' a separatist told me several years ago, standing in the snow, looking down onto a huge military camp laid out across what once had been one of the most romanticised meadows of the Valley. 'And that is why we want it again, to be able to write our own fate.'

He too was a Kashmiri, a local man in a *pheran*, a separatist, a *jihadi*, a terrorist, a freedom fighter. He had been given many names.

The word that leapt from his statement was 'we'. Who did he mean?

His speech seemed to be made on behalf of all Islam.

'We' became another romanticised meadow, a place where all Muslims live, a global caliphate, the nation of Islam – it too has been given many names.

*

The poetry of the Valley's past is that it was a heaven on earth, a place of such gentleness that those who lived there did so in harmony, most particularly the Muslims and Hindus, the doors of their homes open to each other, their festivals shared, some of their saints interchangeable. A poetic term was created for it, one that marked the Valley as separate from its neighbours, even its Muslim ones. The dress, the Kashmiri language, the sing-song reply of prayer, the architecture, all made it different. A word was found for this way of being, a potent expression that implied a sense of kinship and togetherness that transcended the parameters of differing religions and rituals – *Kashmiriyat.* It became a word hung about with a history that it did not have, a call to arms from when it first came into common use when the Kashmiri people were calling for India to 'quit Kashmir', just as so many of the Indian nation were calling for the British to 'quit India'. *Kashmiriyat* had barely been in use before 1947.

In the spring of 1989 I came to Kashmir with my mother for the last time before the fighting really took hold. We knew the Valley well enough to be there just ahead of the hot season, while there was still enough air to breathe down in the plains. I was leaving England to train as a journalist in Australia. My mother came as far as India so we could spend some time there together before I travelled on and away. I had been ill in Karnataka a few weeks before, sick enough to have been scared. In the state of recovery everything was heightened: taste, smell, sight and hearing. On that first night back in the Valley I sat out on the veranda at the back of a houseboat. As the day dropped down behind the encircling peaks, evening mist slid in across the lake, blurring the lines of the *shikara* boats to smudges and the men who paddled them to quivering uprights against the horizontal strokes of their boats in the water. The stage turned to theatre: those wild peaks shifting from burnish to blush and lavender, before fading, as though bruised, through blues and greens to grey. The *shikaras* were diluted by the mist. I stared, trying to see through the haze to find them. All was irrelevant, a collision of time into one of those moments when everything is coloured with possibility, so exquisite, a lurch of infatuation.

It was late March. The nights were cool, the late afternoons and evenings still a time for *kangris* and *pherans*, but the days were hot in the mountain sun. We rented bicycles and rode around the lakes, picnicking in fields, borrowing horses from the palace stables near Dal Lake to ride through surrounding orchards. We looked out at apple, apricot, almond and cherry blossom through the heart shape made by the horses' ears where they meet in the middle with the curious paisley shape that their ears make when pricked.

Filmic it was, a Bollywood movie. But still we huddled around the main *bukhari* stove in the sitting room of the houseboat, the only one that did not smoke so much when alight that we would have to evacuate the room. We chattered away about what to do the next day, and whether to have Kashmiri chicken cooked in yoghurt spiked with ginger, cardamoms, almonds and cashew nuts for supper, or lotus root in a *masala* made hot with red chillies, tempered with curd. We wrangled in that meandering way that mothers and daughters sometimes do as the generations begin to shift.

Beyond our world of small decisions the city was plagued with strikes. A month before there had been a one-week-long anti-Indian demonstration over Salman Rushdie's book, *Satanic Verses*. Even though India had been the first country to prohibit publication of the book the banning itself created publicity, and further rage. Shopkeepers in Srinagar were told to close up. If asked afterwards who had told them to lock up they would look around and refer to 'them', flicking their heads in a direction of some other place, pushing the question away. There was an excited nervousness, an agitation. The Soviet army had pulled out of Afghanistan the month before. The *mujahideen* army had been victorious, and now parts of it were breaking off and re-forming into separate cadres that were on the move, crossing borders.

But still we carried on, my mother and I. We wore T-shirts in the city without thinking that it would cause offence. It never had before, not in Srinagar. Out in the villages it was different but the city had been host to the entire gamut of tourist excesses over the years, from Russian roulette to naked ice-skating. My young mindset was focused on appearing to be independent, even though I was travelling with my mother. I was not wondering whether people were passing moral judgement on our upper arms but whether I came across as interesting enough in my own right. This narrow focus meant that I missed a collective tension. In much the same way as many of the local people, indeed the vast majority, we were all just trying to ignore what was beginning around us.

Mohammad and I have often talked about the signs that we were attempting to ignore at that time. They were loud and often brutal ones, but everyone was used to the most obvious one of all. The Indian military had been a consistent presence in the Valley since 1947, a low-level constant in the background, its spreading security net widened by the police and paramilitary forces. We would see them in the narrow alleys of the Old City, moving among the shuttered wooden buildings whose casements almost kissed across the street, three- and four-storey tinder boxes. The people ignored the *jawans*, as the soldiers are called. And so, because we too wanted to pretend that we were like the people, we tried to ignore them as well. It is an odd word to choose for those who were being cast as the enemy. In many languages that stretch from Iran to Bengal *jawan* just means young. Now it had come to mean an infantryman, a soldier, a man with a gun, and now a man who was the enemy.

The round of strikes had become an accepted part of life. A third of the working days that year, 1989, were lost to these *hartals* and *bandhs*. On the days we wanted to go into town we would ask if there was going to be a *bandh*, a strike, and if we were told no we would set off. We had much to do in the Old City, searching for stainless-steel cups, plates and bowls in the copper market beyond Zaina Kadal, one of the city's nine main bridges. We were going to go trekking and my mother had bought into the view of the time that eating and cooking in aluminium contributed towards triggering Alzheimer's disease. Kashmiris who had become trekking guides did not take their valued copper cooking ware out and about. They trekked with lightweight aluminium instead, except for their samovars, the great silver tea carriers that went everywhere; but my mother's father had died of Alzheimer's a few years before, and so we went to the market to find stainless steel.

We wandered among the stalls, calling storekeepers out from behind their high stacks of Buddha-bellied copper pots. We asked them for stainless steel, and then tried to beat down the price, because it also made us feel as though we were doing the real thing. Not to bargain with a Kashmiri was to suck the breath from his lungs. And to us the Valley seemed flush, rich in tourism and agriculture, its children the most highly educated in the country because of the Central Government's attempt to buy the love of the Kashmiri people, spending more on state education than in any other part of India.

It meant that they had been sowing one of the main crops of rebellion themselves, producing thousands of graduates full of ambition but very little employment to temper their expectations.

Once we had our cups, plates and bowls we were ready to go. The days were clearing, the nights did not seem to be so cold. I would sit out on the back veranda of the houseboat in the late afternoons, drinking tea and eating macaroons that we had brought back from the city, from the best bakery on Maulana Azad Road, and I would try to persuade Shabir, our houseboat owner at that time, to take us trekking. We had all our equipment, even a double quantity of new hot-water bottles. It was still early in the season but we did not want to go high, and the last of the heavy snows had fallen over a month before. We hoped to go to some of the lower meadows, to camp by streams where we could try to catch brown trout to eat straight from the line, fried in a pan over a campfire, just with some butter and ground pepper.

I went on asking Shabir, and each time he would tell me that it was too early, and that there was still snow in some of the meadows.

I knew that he loved going in search of some of the lesser known Sufi shrines scattered around the Valley. He had told us that his uncle had been a poet and had written about some of the shrines, though we did not hear the poems. I tried to encourage Shabir to take us shrine-hunting as part of the trek. He would bow his head and say again that it was still too early.

Then he turned his attention to my mother. He knew how much she hated to be too cold, so he gave her lavish detail of how bitter the nights would be. He won. My mother does not sleep very much, and for her it is a form of heightened torture to lie awake and icy.

We dropped the plan for trekking.

Mohammad and his brothers took one of their last treks up into the hills later that spring.

'We had a good time,' he said, ten years later. 'It gave us a little time to be out in all the beauty of nature. We closed our eyes and did not think about what was happening for some time.'

Eight months later, as the wall came down in Berlin and the cold war released its grip on world order, the seeds of a new era of militancy took root in the Kashmir Valley.

It was a biting winter afternoon on 8 December later that year, 1989. A young medical intern got onto a city bus in Srinagar, near the only women's hospital, Lal Ded, named after a venerated fourteenth-century Kashmiri, a woman born into a Pandit family, who became a yogini, and then embraced the path of the Sufis as well, becoming a mystic and poet revered by both Hindus and Muslims. The young intern was making her way home. About twenty minutes later she was forced off the bus by three men who held guns to her head. They bundled the girl into a blue Maruti car. Those remaining on the bus watched as she was driven away.

People were unsure what to do. It is said that they sat for a while without moving.

The young doctor had been taken by the main separatist movement, the Jammu and Kashmir Liberation Front.

No one had believed that the boys of the Valley would really take up arms. People used to joke, 'Yes, yes, my brother is a militant now. He has a gun.' People used to laugh about it, a little proud of the notion of a freedom fighter in the family.

The men with the guns in the blue Maruti had a good bargaining chip in the young doctor. She was the daughter of the newly sworn-in Home Minister of the Central Government in Delhi. Mufti Mohammed Sayeed was the first Muslim to hold such a post in modern India. He had only been sworn in a few days before Rubaiya Sayeed was kidnapped. He was also a Kashmiri Muslim. The separatists did not like the idea of him working with 'the enemy'.

During the following six days the Central Government negotiated with the kidnappers. At first they communicated via a journalist at the Valley's main newspaper, the *Kashmir Times*, and a high court judge, a close friend of Rubaiya's father. Then the negotiations became more direct. The separatists wanted five of their imprisoned colleagues in return for releasing Rubaiya. On 13 December a message was passed to the separatists that the five men had been released in a downtown area of Srinagar.

The journalist at the *Kashmir Times* got a call. He was told that Rubaiya Sayeed would be back with her family soon. Within an hour she was home.

People did not particularly celebrate the return of the young doctor to her parents. But in the downtown area of the city thousands of young men gathered around Rajouri Kadal, the bridge near where the five jailed separatists had been set free. The crowd marched in a victorious procession, shouting a new slogan as they went. As quickly as they had gathered they melted back into the winding streets as police trucks reached the scene.

A few young men had been able to bargain with Delhi at the end of a gun. Among the hot, excited crowd at Rajouri Kadal freedom from India felt possible. The battle cry of the triumphant procession became the rallying cry of the people: '*Jo kare khuda ke khauf, Utale Kalashnikov!*' (All god-fearing men, pick up the gun!)

In the autumn of 1990 I returned to the Valley.

The houseboat that my mother and I had stayed on eighteen months before was closed up. They all were. I am not sure why I had expected them to be open. Even in the good times that point in the year was when people began to shut up their boats for the winter, but when returning to a place you know well only to find it utterly changed, in flames, whole sections deserted, firebombed, the charred remnants of family life littering the streets, a visceral instinct drives you to seek out the familiar. And so I walked down the wide boulevard beside Dal Lake, where the houseboats sit lined up for business. I went dressed very differently – not in the T-shirts of the previous spring. My head and face were covered, the sides of the road I walked were lined with soldiers, rifles raised, safety catches off.

To the right a line of hotels that look out onto the lakes, ones that had mushroomed during the tourist peak to take the overflow from the houseboats, were strung about with khaki and olive bunting. They had been requisitioned by the army and the paramilitary, their windows boarded up, the balconies festooned with lines of dark green socks, thermal underwear and T-shirts. A khaki turban sat at the end of one line, cocked merrily on a pole.

No one stopped or questioned me as I walked.

I was almost at the midway point, where the post office floats beside a wooden building on stilts that is the All J&K Taxi Shikara Owners' Association Office – Central, and opposite the *chai* stall where my mother and I used to sit drinking sweet milky tea, our bicycles leaning against the stall's wooden bench.

It was there that I was pulled out of the road and pushed down beside one wall of the Shikara Owners' Association building, my shawl pulled away from my face.

Gunfire has a small, tight sound when first heard at close quarters. It does not have the reverberating enormity of the film version. It has a popping, almost tinny quality.

Like a child, I put my hands over my ears, as though shutting it out might make it go away. I crouched while all around were the sounds of running, shouting and gunfire. It seemed to come from every direction, and every time a bullet hit something it made a different sound, whether it was entering timber, tarmac, a flak jacket or flesh. There are those that just continue, travelling without contact, while you wait to hear, your whole body cramped lest you are to be the contact point, as though your muscles believe that by tensing somehow the bullet will be deflected, or not penetrate so deep.

It was the first time I had been in any kind of crossfire. I had heard live gunfire before, but in controlled situations: on army ranges, on hillsides in Scotland, across fields of autumn stubble. This was another kind.

Everything becomes tight, and both fast and lead-weighted, as though movement is three times as hard despite the fact that every nerve is firing, the whole body coiled for reaction; but still it feels slow when what you require, or what

I most wanted, was the superhuman ability to be able to spring half a mile away, across the other side of the lake, just away.

I cowered, trying to duck lower all the time. A soldier was right in front of me, firing from the corner of the building. He was shouting something to someone. He was screaming at them to stop.

And then the gunfire ended. The soldier ahead ran out into the road. I still cowered, though it was now silent. I know I cried, in fear, and anger at my stupidity for having charged into this situation without knowledge or understanding of what was really happening, combined with the dangerous arrogance of knowing a place, and believing that would somehow protect me. I stopped when I realised that someone was coming towards me, telling me to stand up, in English. He was a captain, though he looked as young as I was, in his early twenties, baby-faced behind the statutory moustache. He was controlled but furious. I do not remember exactly what he said to start with. It was as though I could not hear him properly.

He could not understand how I had got beyond the checkpoint at the end of the Boulevard. He was shouting again, not at me now, but at the soldier who had been in front of me, firing from the corner of the building, the man who I think had pulled me out of the road as the gunfire started, though he did not seem to want the officer to know this. The captain called to another soldier to find out what was happening at the checkpoint.

As he asked me where I had come from, where I was going, where my passport was, another officer behind him was shouting orders to the soldiers in the road to line the alley where the shooting seemed to have started. I handed my passport over to the young captain while soldiers moved to fill the narrow alley. Two men were down, left behind, sitting in the road, a third man helping them. Their flak jackets seemed to have taken the impact. One of them was pulling at his jacket and his fatigues.

The captain asked me again where I was going as he flicked through my passport. The line of soldiers in the alley behind him parted and three soldiers came through dragging bodies. When they saw me one of them ducked down and pulled the *pheran* of one body over the face, and a scarf from around the other dead man's neck across his collapsed features.

The captain indicated that we should move further around the Shikara Owners' building. He asked again where I was going, and what I was doing in Srinagar. I think it was the first time that I had said anything when I asked him to give me my passport so that I could show him the journalist's visa. I told him the name of Shabir's boats, pointing further down the Boulevard. He told me that I could not go there as the area was sealed. I remember being oddly indignant, asking if someone could just escort me there so that I could see if I could find Mr Shabir.

Everything had become formal. He addressed me as Miss Hardy, I ended my answers with 'Captain', Shabir became Mr Shabir.

For some reason the captain allowed me to go with two soldiers to keep a check on me. As we started to walk I thanked the captain. For a moment I thought he was saluting me, but behind us there was a major getting down from a jeep that had just arrived. I walked on with my escort.

There was no one at the boats. I called out. One of the soldiers tried to stop me as I stepped onto the duckboard that went from the main houseboat to the *donga* boat behind, the smaller houseboat with its kitchen and sparse, unfurnished rooms. It was from here that Shabir had always come, crossing the shifting cedar planks, a hand raised to my mother or me. The second soldier let me go to see. I called out again. The *donga* was silent, the door to the kitchen padlocked.

A girl came to a window of a neighbouring boat, young and slight, her pale blue *pheran* a relief from the khaki. I asked her where Shabir was. She looked up at the soldiers and told me that he did not live there. As I turned away she began to recite an address. I asked her to repeat it as I crouched at the window searching for pen and paper. My hands were shaking and I could not write properly.

I am not sure whether the young captain had given the two soldiers any specific order beyond accompanying me to the houseboat. They seemed unsure what to do as we walked away from the girl. We stood facing each other in the road, my hands stuffed into my pockets so that they would not see how much I was now shaking. There was an auto-rickshaw stand further down, away from the houseboats and the alley where the shooting had been. I asked the soldiers if I could take a rickshaw from there. They still seemed unsure, but without orders to contradict this there seemed no reason not to let me go. They walked me to the stand.

The drivers turned away as we approached, a couple of them pushing their rickshaws back from the stand, as though they had somewhere else to go. One of the soldiers called to a driver and told him that he had to take me. The Kashmiri looked at the uniformed Indian with unconcealed disgust. The soldier pointed me towards the rickshaw, encouraging me to get in. He raised his hand, halfway between a salute and a wave, as the driver slammed the rickshaw's thin metal half-door shut.

I told the driver where I wanted to go but he argued that the road back to Dal Gate, where I had walked from, had now been closed by the army. I asked if we could go the other way, all around the lake and back into the city past Hazratbal mosque on Hazratbal Road. He asked for three times the usual price. I did not haggle.

The temperature was dropping but I was already cold as we drove around Dal Lake, a route that is perhaps fifteen times longer than if we had just been able to drive straight back to Dal Gate. The Boulevard disappeared and the mountains began to colour over Nishat Bagh, one of the Mughal gardens that sit above the lake amid patterned lawns, beds and waterfalls. The lake was utterly still, as it is so often just as the sun is about to set. All was reflected: the sky, the changing mountains and Rupa Lank, silver isle, one of the little islands, a few minutes' *shikara* ride from the shore, its four chinar trees as clear in their reflection on the lake as on the land.

It had been a place of picnics and flirtation. Generations of newly married couples have gone there to have their photographs taken. Families went to picnic at the weekends. Lovers made and broke promises there. The broad-girthed chinars looked down, shading all from the sun, their five-fingered leaves the symbol of the Valley, carved endlessly into filigreed balconies and the interiors of houseboats, painted on papier-mâché, embroidered onto shawls, woven into carpets. Now, between the trees, there were military installations, netting spread over lake check-posts, turning the tiny island into an ugly hump-backed place.

Nothing seemed to be moving on the lake now as the rickshaw driver bumped through every rut on the road. By the time we reached Shalimar Bagh, the next of the Mughal gardens, I was so cold I could not even look left down the elegant waterway that reached from below the garden to the lake, and out to a bridge beyond that arced in and out of the water.

When we reached Maulana Azad Road, in the centre of town, the driver told me to get out fast. It was only twenty minutes until the curfew, and he still had to get across town to Batmaloo, his *mohalla*, his neighbourhood, known as the laundry area, and increasingly as a militant safe-house district. He asked me if I was with the army. I told him no, that I had got through a checkpoint by mistake on the Boulevard while trying to find a houseboat owner I had stayed with the year before. He dropped the price of the journey as I reached to pay him, charging twice the going rate instead of three times. He was already driving away as I lifted a hand to him in thanks.

It was at night that the detail came back, as though the body had absorbed everything but the mind needed silence, and the isolation of the dark, for recall. It became a pattern that I would wake up in the night in pyjamas cold with sweat, because another image from the lakeside had resurfaced.

By then I knew the official report: a patrol of the Rajputana Rifles had been attacked by militants of the JKLF (Jammu and Kashmir Liberation Front). Two *jawans* had been injured, two militants killed, and several others had escaped. I was told that the militants had been en route to attack military personnel when they met the patrol. In another version I was also told that the militants had been meeting in a house when the patrol broke in during a raid. And then I was told that the militants were not militants at all but a group of *mistrys*, masons, knocking down an interior wall of a house that was believed to be a place where militants met regularly. The bang of their hammers was said to have been confused with gunfire.

During the summer, in July 1990, the Armed Forces (Jammu and Kashmir) Special Ordinance had been introduced. It provided 'extraordinary powers of shoot to kill, search, and arrest without warrant' to the army, police and paramilitary without the risk of prosecution within Jammu and Kashmir.

From the little I understand of gunfire I believe I heard several different calibres of gun being used on that occasion, each producing a different report, as in fire and return of fire. It is not consistent for that kind of military street patrol on foot to have used several different calibres of weapon, unless a pistol was used in addition to rifle fire. The use of pistols by the officers who carry them is unusual during a gunfight in the open.

The nights brought different images: the face of one of the *jawans* sitting in the road, pulling at his flak jacket and fatigues, the dark mark on his chest as he pulled his vest away, his expression of surprise that it was only bruising. And how one of the dead men's shoes fell off, and how I wondered why no one put it back on as his body was dragged out of the alley. How very young he looked, as did the *jawan* sitting in the road, the faces of boys in fear and death. And the bulled shine on the major's boots as he got down from the jeep. There was a remembered roaring sound that came back too, something that I thought was just another part of the noise of the firing. Since then I have learned to recognise it as the roar of my own breath, and that of those around me when the level of fear is high. There was no sense of excitement attached, no elation at having not been killed, no awe at the ability of a bullet to stop all that has gone before. I would lie in the dark, terrified that, if I could get back to sleep, I would wake up in the same place still, and that this was going to happen over and over, a constant stream of bodies being dragged away, leaking life onto tarmac.

When I found Shabir's house a few days later, across the other side of the lake from Boulevard Road, I did not tell him how I found his address, and he did not ask. One of his first questions was an enquiry as to whether my mother was in good health, and keeping warm. Once I had assured him that she was both warm and well he asked if she knew that I was in Srinagar. I told him that she did not and this troubled him.

We talked about other things.

It was a year and a half since I had been trying to persuade him to take us trekking. Everything had changed.

Now whole sections of the city seemed to be on fire, and the Valley was a militarised zone, effectively cut off from the rest of the country. Two new Indian governors had been appointed during that time and their policy had been to stamp down hard on the militants. The majority of the Pandits, the Kashmiri Hindu community, had left in the wake of attacks on their people in the first few months of the insurgency. By late March 1990 almost all the Pandit areas of the city were empty, many of their wooden houses in the Old City burned out. In May the traditional leader of the Kashmiri Muslims, the Mirwaiz, had been assassinated in his home, and violence during his funeral procession had led to further attacks and rage against the government.

Shabir was angry with Mufti Mohammed Sayeed, the Union Home Minister, the father of kidnapped Rubaiya.

'He should not have done that, he dealt with the JKLF himself, face to face, I am told,' he said.

'Why not, wouldn't you have done the same if it had been your daughter?' I asked him.

'Of course but I am not a minister in the government. See the message it sent out? The Mufti showed those boys that they could get what they wanted by waving guns around.' Shabir poked about inside two *kangris*, pushing the glowing coals towards their outer edges. He passed one of them to me.

'Did you make up excuses not to take us trekking last spring because you didn't think it was safe any more?' I asked him.

'Yes.' His expression fell as he looked around the cold room. 'All that is good here . . . everything beautiful is broken now,' he replied.

Chapter Three

ONE GOD

MOHAMMAD DAR SPENT much of the early years of the insurgency watching clouds as he went in search of ways to make up for the huge loss of business.

Tourism in the Valley ended overnight as the conflict began. The houseboats emptied and so Kashmiri salesmen rolled their carpets and shawls into bundles wrapped around in white sheets, and they went on the road, state to state, country to country, looking for new markets for their artisan wares.

'I have spent most of these twenty years on aeroplanes; truly I am just a travelling salesman,' Mohammad says of himself.

By the time I met the Dars their business was recovering, and they already had several shops in the malls of Delhi's five-star hotels.

Mohammad, his father and brothers, brought people from the Valley to work with them in the shops, but Mohammad also made a point of employing non-Kashmiris as well, or, to be more precise, Hindus.

'We have a little Kashmir here in my shop,' he said once. 'See, all of us working together, no problems, *Inshallah*,' and he smiled.

He left the second half unsaid, that his shop was as

Kashmir used to be, before the flight of the Pandits, the Kashmiri Hindus, before what some refer to as the diaspora that tore apart the fabric of the Valley. The Pandits left their homes, the wealthier ones to live in their second homes in the capital, or out of the country altogether. The majority exchanged family houses, land and businesses for squalid surroundings in refugee camps around the Kashmiri summer capital of Jammu, Delhi and beyond. Even after nearly two decades many of them are still living in makeshift tented slum conditions. Some critics say that the various Indian governments since 1990 have actively kept the Pandits in this state of emasculation, giving them just enough aid to survive so that they are an exhibit to the outside world, proving that it is not just Muslims who have suffered in Kashmir. It has made the homeless Pandits poster itinerants for a government that can continue to claim that Kashmir's problem is integral to the secular state of India.

There was a time before of entwined celebrations and festivals, of shared Muslim and Hindu traditions. The first clear memory I have of an interwoven Eid is of *shikara* men at Dal Gate, lined up on the lake steps that mark where the Jhelum River's spill channel joins Dal Lake. The boatmen's faces imprinted themselves with their angles and planes of high-boned features stage-lit by thick, late afternoon light, the kind that burnishes the skin. Perhaps their beauty frightened me because I refused when one of them held out a box of dates to me. He then took one of the dates from the box and offered again. I refused a second time. I was young enough for it not to matter, but old enough to feel my face burning.

The *shikaris* were marking the beginning of Bakra Eid, or

Baed Eid as it is often called in Kashmir, the Festival of Sacrifice or Big Eid. This is the end of the period of Hajj when the pilgrims descend from their day of prayer on Mount Ararat, honouring Ibrahim's willingness to sacrifice his son Ishmael to Allah. In the Islamic calendar this Eid comes later than Eid ul-Fitr, the festival that marks the end of the month of fasting for Ramzan or Ramadan. Both dates are set by the moon, and so they shift year by year. Bakra or Baed Eid usually falls about seventy days after the end of Ramadan. The boatman at Dal Gate had simply been asking that I join them in their small celebration, a show of warmth and hospitality similar to that made by our houseboat owner, inviting my mother and me to his family Eid feast.

I had not wanted to go. I had witnessed the cutting of *bakra*, the Arabic word for heifer. It is the slaughter of an animal for the feast, in Kashmir usually a goat or a sheep, a symbolic sacrifice, a third of which is to be distributed to the poor so that they too can enjoy the feast. This remembered Eid was long before I knew Mohammad and his family, earlier than Shabir as well, several houseboat owners before.

The family's house was just behind the houseboat on which my mother and I were staying, on the opposite side of Dal Gate from the main Boulevard. The courtyard behind their kitchen ran down to the edge of where they had made a small garden at the back of the houseboat. End-of-season roses sagged in narrow beds beside a dustbin shaped like a rabbit. 'Use Me' was written between its ears in defiance of the paper bags and wrappers that used to blow into the garden. The detail of the garden is not something that I remember so much, but there are photographs to prompt me. However, the scene I witnessed from the roof of the houseboat needs no visual nudge.

I don't know why I was up there, but I know I usually climbed up because I was being nosey and trying to catch moments of the family's life in their courtyard. A goat was tied up in the yard, tethered to a post that it was circling until it ran out of rope. It would then reverse and unwind itself to start again. It was small and pure white, in contrast to the nicotine-stained tinge of most of the white goats. I probably knew that I should not have been watching when the houseboat owner's son came out of the kitchen accompanied by other male members of the family. I know that I ducked down so that I could not be seen as the boy bent to untie the goat. One of his relatives was telling him something, and he seemed to step back in surprise, releasing the animal to skitter around the yard. All of them then flapped around after it, the boy pole-axing himself as he tripped over the stump where the animal had been tied. His relatives seemed to be both shouting at him and laughing as well. I felt sympathetic and defensive. The boy was perhaps three or four years older than me, and his emerging adulthood impressed me.

And then the goat was caught and the laughter stopped. It took two of the men to hold the kicking animal as the boy tied its hind and front legs together, hobbling it at both ends. A rope was thrown through the lower branches of the tree in the centre of the courtyard, and threaded through the goat's back legs. A large knife was passed to the boy and another round of instructions was shouted, intermingled with calls of offering to Allah. The boy tried to approach the hanging goat, but each time he did it writhed and swung away, or managed to butt him. There was a pause and then the men disappeared, back into the kitchen.

For a few moments the boy seemed unable to move, but then he jerked forward and cut the goat down from the tree.

It fell heavily and he bent over it, as though trying to make the squirming animal rest on its side. It kicked and spun in the dust, struggling to stand, only to fall each time it had managed to right itself on its hobbled legs. I might have imagined this but I thought the boy was crying. He kept wiping his sleeve across his face. I know I was, somehow in relief that it seemed to be over, that the task had been abandoned.

But the men came back, filing from the kitchen again, this time with the boy's father, our houseboat owner. He was carrying a silver bowl, the size of a pudding basin. He was not as excitable as his relations. He did not shout orders to his son but ducked down beside the boy, bending his head so that he could speak perhaps without the others hearing. As he lifted his head away the goat crumpled, dropping neatly onto its hobbled knees, the blood on its fleece startling. The knife was in the boy's hand, and his father's hand was wrapped around his.

The older man slipped the silver bowl under the slaughtered animal's throat. He got up, signalling to one of his relatives that the carcass should be hung from the tree again. The blood would drain, and then the flesh would be divided and given away as Eid charity to those who could not afford to buy meat.

I did not tell my mother what I had seen. I would not have known what to say. I had seen animals being slaughtered. I was growing up in the English countryside at a time when we were less squeamish about witnessing the transition from paddock to plate, when it was normal to witness death, be it a stillborn calf, or a turkey having its neck wrung in December. The animal deaths that I had witnessed over the years had sometimes been both ugly and sad, but I had never experienced the shock and anger that I felt in seeing the boy being made to slaughter the white goat for Eid. When we were then invited to join this same family for their Eid feast I just told my mother that I did not want to go. As I gave no explanation she pointed out that it was rude not to go as we were visitors there, and it was kind of our houseboat owner to have asked us.

While my mother put on a very bright blue and tightly fitted ensemble, made for her by one of the floating tailors, I wore a sour expression and trailed as far behind her as I could. In our disunity we crossed the duckboards from the houseboat to the garden, and on into the owner's courtyard.

It was an autumn Baed Eid, and though the days were still hot in the sun, shade and the nights were cool. The houseboat owner's veranda was full of people, a rolling sea of shawls being adjusted and re-thrown over shoulders, *shatoosh* and *pashmina*, the lightest dowry-wealth weaves of the women of Kashmir made heavier with months of hand embroidery, so fine that it is hard to distinguish the right side of a shawl from the reverse. The gathered crowd spilled down the veranda steps into the garden.

Our host was a kind man, less thrusting than some of his houseboat-owning lakeside compatriots, a popular host to that evening's mix of colour and creed. Sikhs, Christians, Hindus and Muslims stood together, chatting and laughing, making the large gestures and expressions of parties. They talked of their children, of schools, politics and the weather, all ordinary things that bore adolescents who are studiedly trying to appear grown-up. I looked about for the houseboat owner's son, though when I saw him I could think of nothing to say and so scuttled back to where my mother was amusing an audience with stories of her wild childhood among the Hollywood Raj of Beverly Hills.

We ate in the formal room of the house, white sheets spread over the carpets, bolsters at our backs covered in the same. Something had been spelled out on the floor in the middle of the room in marigold flowers. It was *Eid Mubarak*, Happy Eid, in Urdu. At each of our places was a roll of paper tied around with silk thread. We were shown where to sit and followed the lead of our host as he unwound the thread from his small scroll. Each piece of paper had a different *Sura* from the Qur'an, beautifully written out by hand. There was no distinction. We all had one. It did not seem odd to me that the one at my place was written in English. I suppose I assumed that they all were.

Our host started to read and the chatter stopped. There was a sweet silence as each person read, not one that felt forced or imposed in any way. People did not seem to fidget or cough, but perhaps that is just how I remember it now. I know I was increasingly self-conscious as the readings came closer to me, and that when it was my turn I think I mumbled through most of it, probably without making any sense of the poetry. My own embarrassment was then replaced by embarrassment for my mother because she seemed to be reading her verse with much more flourish than I thought necessary. People smiled and nodded as she finished. Of course I assumed that they were indulging her, kindness to the outsiders, the foreigners in their midst, but perhaps it was really me they were indulging, nodding to my mother in understanding of my flush-faced petulance. She certainly seemed to be having a very good time while I rehearsed how I was going to turn down dish after dish of goat, and more goat – the only way I could think of communing with the boy who had been forced to cut the throat of the small white kid in the courtyard as I had looked on.

Once the *Suras* had all been read a plate of dates was passed around to mark the start of the feast, special dates for Eid, like the ones I had refused at Dal Gate as the *shikara* man held them out to me. This time I took one and then worried what to do with the stone in my mouth, spitting it out so that no one would notice. My neighbour laughed at my efforts. I blushed again, caught up in that painful time that is so blind to kindness, so constantly self-conscious. I took an immediate dislike to the man on principle. He had laughed at me, and so I was slow to realise that he was trying to explain that the thing in the middle of the date was not a stone but an almond, that these were special stuffed dates for Eid. It would not have struck me as at all strange then that part of the Eid feast was being explained to me by a man who had been introduced simply as Pandit*ji*. That was just a name to me, one that this man next to me shared with the first Prime Minister of independent India, Pandit Jawaharlal Nehru, *ji* added to the end as an honorific, a form of respect for an elder. I did not really understand that his name marked him as a Kashmiri Hindu, a Pandit. He told me that he worked at Burn Hall School. Again it seemed ordinary information. Yet here was a Hindu teacher from a Catholic missionary school that, at the time I was sharing Eid dinner with Pandit*ji*, had among its students the future dynastic leader of the main secular-leaning political party of Kashmir, the National Conference, and also the dynastic leader-in-waiting of the Kashmiri Muslims of the Valley, the role that came with the title of Mirwaiz, Chief Preacher, the boy whose father was to be assassinated in the first months of the insurgency.

Pandit*ji* advised me to keep the *Sura* that I had read. He told me it was a particularly beautiful one. It was only then that I saw that his was written in Urdu, as against the one I had in carefully spaced English.

The servants of the Merciful are they that walk softly on the earth; and when the foolish speak unto them, they answer, Peace!

I did as Pandit*ji* suggested. I kept the *Sura* without realising that it would be a memento of a time that was dying.

I fell asleep at some point, curled back onto a white bolster amid the warmth of food, and other bodies, my belly tight with *roghanjosh*, fiery red with chillies; *gustaba*, huge meatballs cooked in soft curd; *tabak-maaz*, rib meat fried until it turned to crackling. I had only taken *dum aloo* to start with, fried potatoes steeped in a gravy of curd, flavoured with cardamom, caraway seeds and coriander. Pandit*ji* asked me if I was a vegetarian and I told him that I was not but that I did not eat goat. Without laughing he told me that the *roghanjosh*, *gustaba* and *tabak-maaz* were all made from lamb, and that though we were celebrating Muslim Eid the piquancy of *roghanjosh* came from the Pandit cooking tradition, such was the mix. I listened without taking it in, and ate a lot of all of them, my fingers sticky and stained yellow by the saffron in the long-grained Kashmiri rice.

Nita Gigoo's family own a small orchard and a grove on the road from Srinagar to Pampore, the place where the saffron of the Valley is grown. It turns the fields purple in autumn, as the crocuses have for over 2,000 years, weighing the air with their particular scent that some compare to a light chloroform, others to drying grass and hay. Nita described it as being like a drug, and that during the saffron harvest of crocus stigmas just breathing the air used to make her want to sleep. Mohammad Dar's father Sobra used to take the brothers to see the saffron fields when they were boys, the spread of purple across the fields another shared marking point of the Valley's year.

Nita Gigoo's family grew some cherries on their land, but it was mainly walnuts, the finest kind, *Kagzi*, the name implying that the shell is as thin as paper. The two big nut crops of Kashmir are walnuts and almonds, and it is the thinness of their shells that makes them even more desirable.

It has been one of the sadder jokes since 1989 that the boys of the Valley were criticised by some for not being very good fighters, that, like their sought-after walnuts and almonds, they were paper-thin militants. It is not a joke shared among Pandits.

'We used to share everything with our neighbours in the village. Mothers who gave birth at the same time would take in another woman's baby if the woman was sick and could not feed.' Nita had been born the year that the Jammu and Kashmir Liberation Front first formed on the Pakistan side of the divided state in 1965, in what the Pakistanis call Azad Kashmir, Free Kashmir, and the Indians call Pakistan-occupied Kashmir. The JKLF was the same separatist group that stirred the first phase of the militancy, and it had been behind the kidnapping of the young doctor, Rubaiya Sayeed, in December 1989. It was also the group that, in spite of its initial claims of wanting Kashmir for both Kashmiri Muslims and Pandits, levelled the first real threats against the Pandit communities in the Valley.

I first met Nita Gigoo when she was thirty. She had been living in a Pandit refugee camp on the outskirts of Delhi for nearly four years with most of her family. Like the young intern, Rubaiya Sayeed, Nita had also been studying to be a doctor when her family left Srinagar in March 1990. There had been another two years of her study to go, though she told me that, even before the conflict began, there had been tension between her mother and father as her mother thought she should marry rather than complete her studies. She said that the expense of her studies had been weighing on the family.

'I do not think the women told the men this thing. I am not sure,' Nita said of the shared wet-nursing. 'But you know what this means?'

I must have nodded because she did not answer the question then, and I made the assumption that she meant that there was the possibility that a baby who had been breastfed by a Pandit woman could have grown into a man who wanted to drive the Pandits out of their homes and lives in the Valley. There were worse possible scenarios as well.

In the first few months of the insurgency the figure of murdered Pandits given by the Indo-European Kashmir Forum was 1,500, though the Indian Government claims that the figure was a fraction of that.

What is apparent from records is that 300,000 Kashmiri Pandits were 'displaced' from the Valley, about a fifth of the population. Two members of Nita's family died. Her uncle was hit in crossfire in the centre of the city, near the Kashmir Talkies at the Palladium Cinema on Lal Chowk, in January 1990. It happened just a few days after a press release had been sent to various Urdu newspapers by one of the main militant groups, the Hizb-ul-Mujahideen. It demanded that all the 'non-Muslims' pack up and leave the Valley. The group later denied the wording, claiming that it had been a typo, and should have read '*gair-kashmiri*', non-Kashmiris, rather than the word '*gair-muslim*', non-Muslim, that appeared on the original press release.

Nita believed that her family would have left sooner but that her uncle lived for a month after being wounded, and that they could not move him. The other death was her uncle's youngest son. He was twelve when he was hit on his bicycle by what Nita described as a 'military convoy'. The boy was dragged for some distance on the bumper of a truck. She said that witnesses told the family that none of the vehicles stopped, even though people were screaming at them about the boy. He died of spinal injuries and infection, but still the Gigoos did not leave for another month.

Neither death was directly to do with the militants. This makes Nita's family an exception.

'We went on talking to our neighbours, our Muslim friends, and they said that they would protect us and take care of us. We trusted them even when we heard stories from other places that neighbours were turning against neighbours, and that terrible things were happening in some villages. There were even stories that militants were marrying Pandit girls by force, under the gun, making them convert, and treating them as less than dogs.'

It is one of the fear rumours that many Pandits tell, from refugee camp to camp, though I could not find anyone who could name a name, or give a village where it had actually happened.

But beneath the frightened hum of rumour Pandits were being murdered: strangled with steel wires, hung, impaled, branded, their organs gouged out while they were still alive, their bodies dismembered once they were dead. There were stories of terrible 'death dances' being performed around the bodies of murdered Pandits. These bred further fear, which was the intention of those who spread them, sources often traceable to the cadres of one of the separatist or pro-Pakistan militant groups.

Nita was very clear that, in the case of her family, it was not the stories they heard that made them leave, or even the death of her uncle and his son, her cousin. It was the creeping and loudening sense that their community had been marked as the enemy.

'We have always had times when things were bad. When there was trouble we would all stay in the house for some time. And those times would go past and we could all come back out onto the streets, and it was fine again for some time.'

Her hands flew as she spoke, the skin cracked, chapped, bleeding in places from the constant round of scrubbing clothes in the cold and over-chlorinated water from the camp pumps.

'While we had to be stuck in the house we would massage everything with *badam ka tel* [almond oil]: hair, head, face, hands, feet. It was nice. We did not mind.'

Nita had the sweet, round face of many of the Valley women. She wore a *salwar kameez* faded by endless washing, and her skin had the thin grey patina of dirt that pervades every thread and pore of the people who live in these conditions. She was from a family that had once owned more than many of the others in the refugee camp at Sultanpuri, but this made no difference to her situation when I met her.

It was Nita's mother who had made the final decision that they should leave. Nita said that to most people her father had seemed to be as he had always been, perhaps a little more nervous, but then everyone was. But at night he would moan, rambling in his sleep about the mosques, his hands over his ears to keep away the calls from the minarets.

'Do you remember what they were saying?' I asked her.

She seemed unsure, and could not remember the actual words. I did not prompt her with some of the calls I had read or heard about, cries for *jihad* against non-Muslims, and worse, some that had been refuted, some not.

Nita said that her family had been terrified, that the Pandits were being called infidels, and that they must leave, that only those who prayed to Allah would be allowed to stay in the Valley. I asked her why this was more frightening than what had happened with the deaths in her close family, and the stories they were hearing of what was being done to other Pandits.

'It was all the time, all day and all night at times, from loudspeakers in the mosques, the ones for *azaan* [the call to prayer].'

Nita said that her family's house was in the very heart of the Old City, in the Habba Kadal, Habba Bridge district, one of the three main Pandit areas of the city. Their house was close to Shah-i-Hamdan mosque, the oldest in the Valley, named after the Mir, or Emir, who came from Persia to Kashmir to preach. His mosque had been built in 1395 in the quiet place where he had gone to pray each day.

'They added many more loudspeakers at all the mosques,' she said. 'It became so loud we could not hear in the house when the noise was on.'

It was during this period that her father began to moan in his sleep. When her mother heard that another round of military trucks was being sent so that the Pandits could pack up their things and leave their homes she asked her eldest daughter, Nita, to help her gather together what they thought they would need for perhaps just a few weeks. They had been warned that they could bring only what they could carry themselves. Extra bags and packages would simply not be put onto the trucks. And they all thought they would be back by spring, at the latest.

'By the time our walnut and cherry trees were in flower;

that was the very longest we thought we would have to be away from our homes,' Nita said. 'How could we believe that it would be more than this?' She looked around her at the sagging lines of grey laundry hung between tents. 'But we do not have that kind of fear here. This is one good thing.'

She took me to see where her family was living.

'We have been told that neighbours and friends have watched over the trees,' she said as we edged through a narrow canvas corridor between two tents.

We took off our shoes and Nita lined them up outside the tent flap before we went in.

Her mother was curled in a corner at the back of their tent, nestled into a womb of blankets, the family's possessions pushed away against the sides. Nita's mother did not want to meet me, or to talk.

'So many people come to talk to us and nothing happens,' she said to Nita, staring past me.

I did not blame her and ducked out of the tent to wait.

'It is better than when we first came to this place,' Nita said as she pushed the tent flap to one side, following me out. 'Then we were all in a *barat ghar* [a large hall], all families together. See, I will show you.' She unhooked an old umbrella that was hanging from the tent pole at the entrance and drew a thin rectangle in the carefully swept earth in front of their tent. 'This is how much space there was for each family, no matter how many persons it comprised.'

The rectangle in the dust was the size of a narrow carpet, the kind that runs from the doors of many homes in Kashmir. On checking camp records I found that most families were allocated spaces that were roughly two feet by five feet when they arrived at the *barat ghars*. The standard size of cells on death row in America is eight feet by ten feet, per person.

For the Pandit women this way of living was both demeaning and humiliating. In Kashmir homes have always been fairly clearly divided, the women living almost separately from the men, whether it was a Muslim or a Hindu household – another shared habit. In what they hoped was temporary exile the Pandits understood that space was cramped, that families had to crush together, but as Nita said, 'For some of the older people, our women, they wanted to be dead more than to have to wash and so on in the same place as the men. A woman who is not known to me too well said to my mother that it was worse than to be made to walk around all the time without clothes.'

Nita did not laugh at the idea but bent her head in the shared humiliation.

'For us the small amount of space was not so bad as for some: just mummy-daddy, brother and me,' she added, looking at the narrow rectangle in the dirt.

When the Gigoos first came to Delhi Nita's brother Krishna was twenty-three. He had just finished a course in business and management at the University of Srinagar. The government kept its promise to the Pandits in exile and reserved a quota of jobs and higher education places for them.

A government job was the one thing that almost everyone aspired to before the Indian economy was deregulated in the early 1990s by the then Finance Minister, and future Prime Minister, Manmohan Singh. This opened the floodgates to foreign investment and multinational companies, and it signalled the re-emergence of India as an economic power. Until then a government job was the most desirable goal, bringing with it a lifetime of working security, decades of ensured backhanders and bribes, and all the perks of bureaucratic posturing that are as real as the towering manila-folder kingdoms from which the government looks down upon the people.

Even with this promised quota of positions, Nita's parents still had to pay a large 'registration fee' for their son to be able to apply for a job, and several more 'fees' while his application for interview was processed. Nita's family were one of the few in the camp who had managed to bring enough money from Kashmir to be able to pay for such 'contingencies' as these. Her father had been working in the Lakes and Waterways Department in Srinagar when the family had felt there was no other option but to leave. He knew how much money they would need if they were to make any progress away from their homes; he understood bureaucracy.

Nita told me that there were Pandits in the camps who had been given government jobs from the quota without having to pay 'registration' fees, but that was perhaps because the quota had to be filled, and some people simply did not have the money to pay what was asked or inferred.

'If my father had not paid the money it is not to say that Krishna would not have secured his job, but my father paid when the issue was made clear, and then he paid more. But my brother has this job so it is good for him now.'

Her brother's job came with government accommodation, just a basic apartment in a large anonymous block.

'With a small place for cooking in an outside kitchen that he shares with others, but he has his own bathroom.' Nita lingered on the bathroom, describing it in detail.

Though the accommodation was only for one person it would still have provided more space than the tent in which Nita and her parents were living.

'The government will not allow for this. It is just for Krishna,' she explained. 'And if we all move from this place and start to have a real home here then how will we go back to our home in Kashmir?'

Pandit families who leave the camps also lose their right to compensation money from the government.

Nita was still not married when I met her, though her status was no longer as contentious as it had been before the family left the Valley in 1990.

'It has not been a time for these things,' she said. 'People are afraid to marry outside our community. And also afraid of having marriages within the same camp in case it causes problems when children are growing.' She paused. 'We are not like the Muslims, we do not believe it is a healthy thing to marry such a close relative. For them it is normal, I know, but not for us.'

She looked at the people around us, watching them, her expression one of surprise.

I had been told by women in other camps that child marriage was being practised again because, within these enforced tight communities, the matter of family honour had become intensified. The result was that some people were marrying their daughters to boys of families that they knew long before the sexual minefield of puberty had even begun.

'Marriages were a very happy time before,' Nita said, bending her head lower over the table between us. 'All the festivals were shared, so many of them. So many gods, so many festivals.'

And then it was decided by a militant minority that there could be only one god for the Valley.

'This we all miss very much. Our neighbours I miss very much.' She looked again at the other people around us. 'I had very many Muslims friends, girls I was at school and college together with.'

I had managed to persuade Nita to leave the camp for a few hours. We were eating *dosas* in a market nearby. Though she was older than me it was like taking a child out from school as she looked around constantly, ducking her head in embarrassment if she felt someone was looking at her. And they were. Nita was pretty, pale-skinned, light-eyed, a profoundly desired combination in the Indian context. She said that they did not leave the camp that often, except in groups with other women to go to the market, and to the temples nearby for some of the main festivals, though they had a temple within the camp as well.

Nita had never eaten a *dosa* before, the rice pancakes of the south that are so thin they allow light to come through. She liked the fresh coconut *chutni*, and the wet lentil and vegetable *sambar* that went with them. She wanted to know how people ate them. I tried to show her the way I had been taught, either rolling and dipping the *dosa* in the *chutni* and *sambar*, or filling it, flipping it over, and quickly whipping it from metal tray to mouth before the soggy mix broke through the thin fried rice pancake. I failed and it went down my chin, my front, and into my lap. Nita laughed. It was an enchanting sound.

Another thirteen years on from when I spent that time with Nita the Pandits are still in the camps around Jammu, Delhi and other cities. Some have moved into more permanent homes, though the majority cannot afford to do this. Still they hold onto the idea that maybe one day they will be able to return to the homes they left behind.

A new generation has grown up in exile, the bitterness of this being that they are exiles within their own country. Though it has been instilled into them that they are Kashmiri Pandits they have no real sense of it. They have never been to Kashmir, they do not know the silence of snow, the lakes and orchards, the narrow, cluttered streets where their parents' sense of community was learned, or the temples that have long been locked and sealed. They have grown up listening to their parents' stories and looking at old photographs of a place they do not know. They live in the shadow of a world remembered, their parents' sense of rupture tugging at them all the time.

On a more recent visit to one of the camps in Jammu a woman who had been a child when she left, who had married and raised children in the camp, said, 'We have been told so many times by politicians and leaders that it is safe for us to go back now, that we should return to our homes and hearths, but what do they know of how we live? They are all living behind big high fences with so many people guarding them. We would only go back if the people of Kashmir, the people who were our neighbours, came out onto the streets and marched for us, waving banners telling us that they want us to return, that it is safe, that Kashmiri Pandits will be welcomed back and protected in the homes that they have been away from for so long.'

'How could this happen?' Ibrahim, Mohammad's third brother, asked as he rubbed a hand through his full beard, his generous mouth tight below a stubble moustache, clipped back in the prescribed orthodox way.

He was sitting on the back of one of his family's houseboats, his feet pulled up onto the cushions, eyeing his mobile phone as the scenery behind began to emerge from winter. It was an early first day of spring, so warm in the February sun after the long freezing months that everyone looked surprised, as though someone had pinched their bottom in a crowd and run away. The date was a month short of being eighteen years since Nita Gigoo and her family had left the Valley in March 1990.

Ibrahim turned and looked across the lake. A pair of black and white kingfishers was in flight, low to the water. We both watched as they passed the veranda steps.

'Do they really think that we would go out onto the streets now and march?' he asked again. 'And be smashed by the police and army, arrested, questioned and whatever else? Like all the times before when the people came out onto the streets.' He leaned over the low railing of carved cedar that ran around the balcony, the petals of a wooden lotus flower disappearing into his beard.

He called out to Maqbool, a man who has been working for Ibrahim and Mohammad's family for most of his life, since he was a boy. Maqbool has looked after the houseboats and their guests through the lush times and the bad. He has watched over me every time I have been here since I have known the Dars, his gappy smile and streaked grey beard one of the constants beside the view from the houseboat across Nagin, the five calls to prayer that seem magnified by the still surface of the lake, and the flight of kingfishers just above the water, so low that the brush of air from their wings sends out ripples.

Ibrahim turned back from the quiet scene. 'It is they who will have to show some courage, as we have for these past however many years. Some of them will have to come back, slowly, slowly, return to their homes, start their lives again, make their businesses. This will be hard. But it has been hard for us. This you know.'

'Do you think they would be welcomed back?' I asked.

Ibrahim shrugged, not nonchalantly, but as though perhaps this was not a question he wanted to answer.

It was half past three on Friday afternoon. The lake swelled the call to prayer from the mosque across the water. Ibrahim called to Maqbool again.

'I have to go now, I am late.' He pulled up the sides of his soft black leather socks, issuing orders to Maqbool about removing a particularly large blue plastic bag that was floating past the back of the boat.

I turned away as I always have to when I see one of these grown-up, great-bearded men in their leather socks that are really just zip-up, over-sized baby bootees that snuggle their feet. They make me smile every time, but they are wholly practical, the chamois leather keeping feet always warm in a place where everyone takes off their shoes as they enter a home, a houseboat or a mosque. For Ibrahim, as it was Friday, his shoes would be coming off five times at the entrance to the mosque.

Later, during that same spring last year, as the Valley unfolded in the warmth, I went to Amherst in Massachusetts. Beyond the cement-box uniformity of one of the college campuses, Pandit friends who had been able to leave both the Valley and India asked me to their Dutch colonial house on the side of a hill. Evening air through the open windows brought in the scent of the woodlands beyond.

'See, it is as though I am still at home,' the hostess said, hugging me to her. 'Now, let me smell you in case you have Kashmir on you still.'

A childhood friend of theirs from Srinagar came for dinner, the academic brother of a poet, one whose poems of loss and dislocation are easy to find, and loved by the Kashmiri diaspora, wherever they are.

As the evening came in through the open windows we were

cocooned in a circle of light and soft, rich, Pandit food. On the wall was a photograph of our hostess's grandmother on the elegant portico steps of the family house on Residency Road, a picture taken before things turned. She was a small woman, barefoot, and wrapped around in a simple sari, her great-granddaughter's suitcase on the steps beside her, the old woman's face wistful – the departure of someone she loved, the closing of an era in her eyes. At the table beneath her we chattered about where the best macaroons in Srinagar were to be bought; the bakeries of the city were another hangover from the last maharajah, Hari Singh, a man with a serious enough sweet tooth to send his pastry chef to Calcutta to train in millefeuille, choux pastry and macaroons. Our host held forth on the subject and we laughed together: two Kashmiri Pandits, a Kashmiri Muslim and an English Christian. Each of us had left our shoes at the front door, quietly lined up side by side.

It is a custom that has been carried beyond the Valley by those who have scattered as refugees and émigrés, however far they have gone. Nita Gigoo left her cheap plastic shoes in the dust outside the tent flap in the Pandit refugee camp in Delhi. Ibrahim put his shoes neatly on the running board of the houseboat veranda before stepping down in his baby bootees. It is only thousands of miles from the Valley, in the hoar frost of Massachusetts' late spring, that a mixture of faiths put their shoes side by side in the way that was once the unchallenged custom of Kashmir.

Chapter Four

ISLAMISATION – A PHOTOGRAPH

PHOTOGRAPH ALBUMS HAVE become the recent history books of the Valley. They are on every houseboat, buried among piles of sun-faded copies of *National Geographic Magazine*, curious nature guides and jettisoned pulp fiction. Between copies of *Valley of the Dolls* and *A Text Book of Algae* the pages of these albums have become the visual testament to 'the time before the trouble', when the houseboats were full, the lakes bustling, the mountains busy with trekkers, fishing and sightseeing trips.

The Dar family have been houseboatmen for five or six generations, maybe more. Even they are not sure quite how many it is. The albums on their boats chart how politics, fashion and world travel have marked Kashmir.

One of the oldest pictures is of Abdul Dar, the grandfather of Mohammad and his brothers, as a young man, in the mid-1930s, his hands tight by his sides in a baggy-fitting tweed suit, a brace of birds in one hand, a gun balanced over the other shoulder, the butt apparently nestling in the large pocket of his even larger suit. Beside him stand his clients, two tall Englishmen, one stooping and gaunt in plus-fours, the other in a carefully fitted version of the tweed suit that sits so capaciously on Abdul. The Englishmen are perhaps in their thirties, though it is harder to tell age in that meticulously groomed era. A girl stands slightly away from the men, a young woman, her neat pale hair under a tidy hat, her equally neat figure in a hunting ensemble of fitted tweed skirt and jacket, giving her a look that is mostly elegant, though also hearty. The group seems at ease in each other's company. On the back it explains why: 'the excellent Abdul, *shikari* [hunter], angler, *khidmatgar* [steward] and factotum, with Me, John, and Sarah'. 'Me' was Charles, an officer in the Indian Army who had been based in India for many years. It seems that the photograph came with a letter dated 8 November 1932.

> To Abdul Dar
> Our Butler on Board
>
> My dear Abdul
>
> Our stay in Kashmir has been made most agreeable while on board 'The Monarch' and also while fortunate enough to be under canvas in the incomparable further reaches of Kashmirs [*sic*] lovely lateral valleys. This is due largely to your keen effort to make my mother, my sister, her husband, and myself [*sic*] comfortable and happy at all times.
>
> We are now finishing our second season on The Monarch and sometime soon shall come again to enjoy once more 'The Vale'. When we come I trust it will be again to your boat wherever you may be.

These letters and photographs portray an era of time slowed down, when 'a season' meant anything stretching from two to seven months. In the case of Charles, his mother, sister Sarah and her husband John, that second season was almost seven months, from April to November 1932. The letter, or 'chit' as it was called, was written as a recommendation to future guests from the houseboat on the day of departure. The photograph is stamped on the back with 'Mahatta & Sons, Srinagar (Kashmir)', the photographic shop on the Bund in Srinagar, where everyone who was anyone had their pictures developed, their portraits taken, and their stationery printed while they were 'seasoning' in 'The Vale'. It is a time that is so often caricatured now, the English tainted as overbearing and boorish, the Kashmiris as grovelling hand-wringers being exploited by the *sahibs*. But to read the letters closely, while making allowance for a formal use of language that can mistakenly be read as being stiff and bombastic, is to witness a very real relationship.

> Perhaps the strongest thing I can express is my regret that you cannot be with us 'down country' and even on to our home in America; but it would be no kindness to remove any Kashmiri from their happy Vale, and so you must wisely stay 'in bliss'. Never again will we meet another Abdul, unless it is our good luck and fortune to return.

So wrote the Woodcock family, Margaret, Henry and their mother Alice, of Brooklyn, New York, after their seven-month season in 1931 with the Dars.

In another century I passed one of these letters to Mohammad as we sat in the same way as generations of guests and houseboatmen have done, engulfed by *pherans*, our legs drawn up inside for warmth, looking out over Nagin

Lake from the back of a houseboat, the one I have stayed on each time I have been to Kashmir since first meeting Mohammad in 1997. I have always been the only guest staying on the boat.

'Isn't this quite rude?' I asked.

Mohammad peered at the letter I was reading. 'This writing is too odd, you will have to read it to me.'

'Memsahib and I saw Lahore on our return . . .' The tone was set. I bridled. Even though the letter was full of warm thanks it was also full of demands.

> . . . please send a brief account of the places we saw after coming to stay on The Monarch. The account should be set out as follows:-
>
> Wednesday – 31st July – Lunched at The Monarch. Afternoon went to Takhet Sulaiman in Dandies [pony traps].
>
> Thursday – 1st August – By car to Verinag and thence to Achbal Gardens. Back to the Monarch in the evening . . .
>
> Please send account as shown above. Please also send your grandfather Sobana's certificates, particularly for the years 1884–1886 . . . please get all these things written and sent by your Munshi [accountant and scribe].

Takhet Sulaiman, Takht-i Sulaiman or Solomon's Throne, is better known by most as Shankaracharya Hill, rising above Srinagar town, and topped by an important Hindu temple dedicated to Shiva, the main Hindu god of the Valley. The Achabal Gardens are another of the Mughal gardens, about forty miles from Srinagar, laid out on a hillside in the early seventeenth century, probably around 1620. This one was the pleasure garden of the Empress Nur Jehan, the favoured wife of the Mughal Emperor Jahangir, and a woman said to be the real driving force of that empire in the face of her husband's debilitating alcoholism.

I passed the letter back.

'See,' said Mohammad, pointing to a note in the margin in a different hand.

'*3 copies of certificate sent by R.Post 17.9.40.*'

'No problem, these things were sent.' He waved the floating grocery man away from the houseboat steps. 'Is there anything you need? Can I send him away?'

The floating grocer turned his *shikara* back out into the lake.

'It just seems rude to demand all that information,' I said.

'Why?' Mohammad asked. 'He is showing interest. He is happy with all the things my grandfather was doing for him and his wife. My grandfather would be glad to oblige in these requests.' He paused. 'We cannot make judgement now on these things. It is very long time back. It was not so difficult at that time.'

Mohammad dropped into the ease of a simpler past, I into the apologist norm of the contemporary English in India.

He stretched up one of his arms. 'This is paining me, what can I do?'

We went through some exercises to relax his rotator cuff while the floating grocer moved across the lake, his *shikara* heavy with unsold and out-of-date goods.

During my most recent return to Kashmir I found more albums. They were newer ones with those self-sealing pages that become sticky with fingerprints. Under the bubbling plastic were pictures of Mohammad and his brothers in the 1970s and 1980s, particularly of Imran, Mohammad's second brother. Like his brothers Imran now has a thick beard, and his head is always covered with his prayer cap. In winter he wears *salwar kameez* of fine wool with a *pheran* or coat, in summer cool, plain white cotton. Like his brothers he is married, he has five children, and he lives within the family compound above the houseboats, beyond a garden that looks over Nagin Lake. Like his brothers he prays five times a day. He has fulfilled the greatest goal for all Muslims, the Hajj, several times, as have his brothers, Mohammad having been more than the others, nine times to date.

In most of the photographs Imran is laughing. He does not stand stiffly beside his clients with the formal posture of his grandfather, Abdul. In one he is leaning on the shoulder of a pretty girl. She is smiling, clad in a woman's embroidered turquoise *pheran* over flared jeans, a thick bandeau holding back that big hair of the early 1980s. Imran is wearing jeans and a wide smile, his hair just above shoulder length, a pair of RayBan sunglasses pushed back to keep his thick fringe out of his eyes. He is clean-shaven. In the group pictures on treks, the ones taken by clients of the men who have been looking after them, Imran stands centrally as the boss, and the only one in Western clothes. His cooks and camp helpers are all in *salwar kameez*, or weathered versions of the baggy tweeds worn by Imran's grandfather.

There is one of a picnic scene on a fishing trip, cane rods resting on rocks during lunch. Imran's men sit away from the main group, crouched around a tree, their backs against the trunk, a samovar beside them. They are drinking from *khassu*, cups without handles. Imran is in the middle of his fishing group, spread out in the sun. Some of them are lying on the grass, a couple sitting in the shade of rocks. Imran is happily stretched out in a particularly natty pair of checked trousers. Propped on one elbow, he is turning towards the camera with an expression that makes it hard to imagine that the photographer is not a woman. The girl with the big hair and the bandeau is not in the shot, though others of her party make up the rest of the picnic group. A line of bottles sits in the shade of a wicker basket.

There was only Maqbool on the houseboat to ask. I held the picture out to him. He was standing in a patch of warm sunshine looking in slight disapproval at the vase of roses that I had just bought. The floating flower man of Nagin was paddling away. Mr Marvellous is the number one flower-seller of the lakes; his real name has faded somewhere across three generations of flower-sellers, and the name Mr Marvellous is painted instead on the sides of their flower-filled *shikaras* in a flurry of swirls and petals. Maqbool knew that I paid a huge amount for the roses. It was the first day of spring but still too early for Mr Marvellous's own garden to be in bloom. He had bought roses and gerbia from elsewhere. He had overpaid to buy them in, so I overpaid him too. It seemed fair, but still Maqbool was not happy about it. I was looking to distract him from the flower folly.

'Are *khassu* still used?' I asked him, pointing to the cups that Imran's men are holding in the picture.

Maqbool took the photograph.

'Such very old pictures,' he said. 'Nobody uses them now.' He paused. 'Maybe sometimes out in the villages but not so often. Only people who know of the villages can know about these now.' He looked back at the roses.

I knew Maqbool well enough to guess that he was working out how much I paid per rose, to add to his indignation.

'Are those beer bottles?' I asked.

He peered at the photograph again. 'Of course.'

'So, they are all drinking beer?'

'And why not?'

'Imran as well?'

'At that time yes. Why should you ask this thing?'

'I just know that none of them drinks beer now.'

'This is correct.' Maqbool flipped the pages of the album. 'See, here is Sobra, father to Mohammad and Imran.' He passed the album back.

It is a picture of a clean-shaven man in profile, his double-barrelled shotgun raised. He wears a well-cut tweed jacket, a crisp buttoned shirt showing just the right amount at the cuff. It is a stylish image.

'He was one of the finest for hunting. Very few people could come equal to Sobra, one of Kashmir's best duck-*shikaris* [hunters]. Foreigners liked very much to go for *shikar* [hunting] with him.'

I would not have recognised Sobra Dar from the picture. When his sons first introduced me to him in Kashmir, in the late 1990s, he was in his late sixties and struggling with depression, his face sunk into a full grey beard, his body into his *pheran*. The first time I stayed with the Dars it had been one of the worst years of the insurgency, during the course of several taut months between a short war fought on the Line of Control, mainly around the border town of Kargil, and the October 1999 coup and counter-coup in Pakistan that brought General Pervez Musharraf to power. Mohammad had asked me to go up to their house whenever I could, to talk to his father about the old times, when, as a young man, he had named his houseboat group after the regiment he admired so much, whose officers he had looked after many times during their leave from the Gurkhas, when they came to the lakes. It had been a time when those boats were full every season, mostly with 'Britishers'.

I asked Sobra about camping and fishing trips to places where Mohammad had told me his father loved to take his guests, and his family too. For a moment his head would lift as he began a story, his face opening a little, and Mohammad and his brothers used to settle around him in relief that their father was speaking again. But then his voice would fade and his chin would drop back down, his attention span only long enough for one story.

To look now at the picture Maqbool pointed to in the album was to see a different and unrecognisable man.

'When did they start to grow their beards?' I asked.

'In 1989.' There was no pause before his reply.

'When the trouble began?'

He nodded.

'And before that it was the time of beer and picnics?' I looked back down at the album.

'Yes, but this is not to say they were not religious before this time,' Maqbool added. 'They were praying, and doing all these things nicely.' He looked away for a moment. 'But it was not so much like this, not always always in the mosque.'

Maqbool has a flowing beard too, white except for two darker streaks.

'See, I am like Mr Christmas,' he says when I show him the pictures I take of him.

He is still happy to have his picture taken, though Mohammad and his family do not like it now. There are times when they do not mind, on particular occasions with certain people, but there is no question of photographing the women of the family, except when they are very young, and only then up to the age of six or seven. When I first met the family the younger girls would run about the garden bare-headed. They still run about, but their heads are covered now, as early as six and seven.

After looking at the albums I walked up to the house to find Ibrahim, Mohammad's third brother, the only man of the family in residence. His youngest daughter and a gaggle of her cousins were running around the snow-burned lawns of the garden, their heads covered and their arms waving. The beds on either side were just beginning to flower and the poplars at the end of the garden, planted by Sobra and his four sons to mark the births of children and grandchildren, were hung about with catkins as they came into pale bud. Above, the steep roof of the house shaded the front veranda and the rooms where the men meet to talk of business, the Qur'an and life. The hub of the house, the kitchen, and winter rooms, are at the back, tucked away, as are the women, their lives moving around these pivotal points of the family home.

The children stopped me halfway up the lawn.

'*As-Salaamu Alaikum*, you are Joosteen Urdee,' said little Safoora, Ibrahim's daughter. 'Show me your hair.'

I bent my head obediently.

'It is like Barbie,' she said, stroking it and then giving it a good tug. 'Why is it not covered?' she said, her fingers winding into dolly locks.

If I had been outside their garden, even just crossing the meadow from the lake to their gate, it would have been covered.

At her age, if I had lived a Kashmiri childhood through the 1970s, my head would not have been covered with the conscious rigour of this girl in this time. She readjusts her *hijab* constantly, tugging it forward so that she can then slide it back to frame her face before it reaches her hairline. At her age I could have played in the gardens that spread out around the city with Muslim, Pandit and Sikh friends, all of us ignorant of the gathering storm.

And during that lost time when we could still have been running around freely, the militant group that later kidnapped the young doctor, Rubaiya Sayeed, had formed in Pakistan-controlled Kashmir in 1965, but under its earlier banner of the National Liberation Front, a separatist movement inspired by Vietnam's struggle against US control, and Algeria's against colonial France.

The group called for Kashmir for the Kashmiris, free of India, free of Pakistan, an independent state. As it first cried out for support from the people of Kashmir it believed that it was calling to everyone, beyond religious and cultural distinctions; across the mixed languages of the state; a rallying cry to Muslims of all traditions and sects, to Pandits, Buddhists, Sikhs, to the farmers of the Valley, the Bakkarwal, Gujjar and Chopan herding tribes and people of the hills.

To an outsider there was a sad irony to the state boundary of independence that the separatists called for. It had been stitched together under an imperial system that their ethos claimed to despise. This was a patchwork nation-state, the largest in India, that was awarded in 1846 to the ruler Gulab Singh for about £100,000 by the British in gratitude for his services to Victoria Regina. Gulab Singh was a leader from the predominantly Hindu Dogra people, the main clan of the Jammu region, and he had earned the gratitude of the British by remaining neutral at an important juncture during the Anglo-Sikh wars. So began the rule of a Hindu Dogra maharajah and his heirs over this heterogeneous mix of quid pro quo lands.

Just as the papier-mâché makers of the Valley use brushes with only a few hairs to paint the finest lines on their pieces, so too is the region demographically as delicately divided. No one party or group can speak universally for the people of the

Valley, let alone the collective peoples of the state of Jammu and Kashmir.

Early in the insurgency Pakistan actively supported the separatist group that had renamed itself the Jammu and Kashmir Liberation Front. But once it became increasingly clear that the group intended to maintain its call for independence from both India and Pakistan, the latter changed its war-by-proxy policy. Pakistan wanted to control the separatist movements within the Valley. It switched strategic, logistical and training support to the pro-Pakistan Islamic militant groups, most particularly Hizb-ul-Mujahideen, the Army of Holy Warriors, even though it was a group without much of a following in Kashmir during the initial stage of the insurgency. It was this group that had issued the press release in January 1990 demanding that 'non-Muslims' leave the Valley, so adding to the harsh pressure already bearing down on the Pandit community. The group may have claimed, after the event, that it was a typo, and that it should have read 'all non-Kashmiris', but this does not sit very easily beside Hizb-ul-Mujahideen's aim of Kashmir for Pakistan, and Kashmir for Muslims. Their extreme Islamist agenda was and is very clear.

But to label the Muslims of the Valley, and the rest of Kashmir, as a united 'Muslim Brotherhood' is to push a generalisation into the chamber of a gun, and to lump together cultural groupings that happen to share their belief in Islam is to do the same.

Even though little Safoora, with her very clear views on hair and its covering, released me I had missed Ibrahim. He was already on his way to the mosque by the time I reached the house.

It was just before 6.30 p.m. as I shut the garden door behind me and walked back down the meadow that separates the houses from the lake edge and the houseboat moorings. A little while earlier the meadow had been a cricket pitch, full of boys and young men, a few in whites, the batsman and wicket-keeper in *pherans* and skullcaps, their faces already half hidden by young beards. On the return walk the pitch was empty, the players hurrying away to the mosque. Two of them were still at the gate to the meadow, one of them pulling a *pheran* on over his whites, his bat and the stumps under one arm, the other pulling a *kaffiyah* up and over his skullcap. The checkered scarves are a newer import to Kashmir, an Arabic head-covering worn now for many reasons, from simple protection against the sun, to showing political solidarity with militant groups in the Middle East.

From the top of the meadow the calls to prayer came from every direction, and at all angles across the lake, from the Shi'a mosque to the left side of the local bazaar, and from the two Sunni ones towards the right and rear side. Silence followed.

Up until 1990 the evening call to prayer was accompanied by bells ringing from Shiva temples around the city. As the *azaan* finished the bells would continue for *aarti*, evening prayer. The sounds wound together.

Children born in Kashmir since 1989 have not heard that song of symbiosis. Just as the young Pandits in the refugee camps have only their parents' memories to portray the homes they felt forced to leave, so too do young Kashmir Valley Muslims have only stories and old photograph albums as proof of how it used to be before they were born.

'Are you a Muslim?' little Safoora had asked me as she tugged my uncovered hair in the garden.

I had told her that I was not.

'Why not?' she asked.

'It's all one God.' I shrugged.

She stood in front of me, one hand on her hip, the other raised, pointing. She was examining me with a look of singular determination. 'You should be Muslim.' And she wagged her finger in my face.

Walking back through the meadow, surrounded by the call to prayer, it was difficult not to wonder how Safoora might have replied if I had told her that I was a Hindu.

'Did you have Pandit friends before?' I asked Maqbool later, back on the houseboat.

'Not so many, they were not coming to our *mohalla* [neighbourhood] so much, not to our schools. But some I was knowing, they have gone now though....' His sentence trailed off.

He was agitated. The houseboat next door, another owned by the Dars, was going to be unseasonably full, with four couples flying in from Gujarat for a few days. Farouk was the man about that boat, the equivalent of Maqbool, but he had been doing the job for only a couple of years in comparison to Maqbool's long experience. He was not sure that Farouk would get everything right. It worried him.

'They make so much mess, these Indians. All they do is eat fried *dhal* all the time, and sit in front of TV. They cannot even notice when they drop it.' He was watching Farouk on the next-door veranda washing down the flower-carved woodwork. 'They will make much work. When you are staying I don't have to clean the boat so much. When Indians staying I have to clean the whole boat every day, maybe sometimes two times.'

'But there's only one of me,' I said.

He ignored the point. 'When last people staying here they asked many, many times why you are just sitting here all the time, just staring out at lake.'

A couple had come for one day a few weeks before. They were from Delhi. During that single day they had done it all: driven to the Mughal gardens around the Srinagar, taken the city tour, visited Hazratbal mosque, shopped in Lal Chowk and along Polo View, and then shopped again at the Dars' big new carpet, shawl and everything else showroom near Nishat Bagh, the Garden of Gladness, laid out by one of the Emperor Jahangir's prime ministers. Ibrahim had laughed when he told me about the new showroom, and said that he hoped it too would be a place of gladness.

The couple from Delhi rushed around, packing the whole Kashmir experience into one day and two nights. Each time they came back to the boat they would look across to where I was sitting, still on the veranda nuzzled into a nest of blankets. We smiled and talked about the beauty of the lake. They came to sit outside for a while, for ten minutes, calling for blankets, cushions and hot *chai.* Within a few minutes the wife shivered, smiled and encouraged her husband to go back inside. The buzz of the television started in the sitting room as the veranda windows slid shut.

Nothing direct is ever said, unless it is a small thing – Maqbool's complaint about having to sweep up dropped fried *dhal* twice a day when Indians come to stay. They are grateful for the business. Without the domestic tourists who have come in dribs and drabs over the past twenty years many of the houseboat owners would have had no business at all. And they go on coming, in spite of being seen by so many Kashmiris as the occupying nation. India has a love affair with the Valley and, at a visceral level, both sides accept this, the occupier and the occupied. If India brings in vital lifeblood in the form of domestic tourism Kashmiris continue to play gracious host, as is their nature.

'Of course we are pleased that they have still been coming,' another houseboat owner told me, one of the many Dar cousins. 'But you know these are not really the same kind of domestic tourists who used to come to stay. Before they would like to see the view, to maybe go for a fishing trip; sometimes they would just come to spend days in peace on the lake. Now it is different, perhaps one day only, maybe two, they make a lot of noise and want many things all the time. This is okay, but these people are doing well, they have a lot of money now, and all they are really interested in is getting things for a very cheap price. My boys on the boat have so little in contrast to these people, and the boys run around for them all the time and then these people will maybe give them only a very little tip, or maybe nothing at all.'

Caricatures are so easily created, and these then become the received version, repeated enough times to become accepted knowledge. In private many houseboat owners and their workers portray the Indian guests as loud, rude, heavy-drinking idol-worshippers who do not understand the meaning of silence and prayer, who come to Kashmir and crash around as though they own it. But then many Kashmiris, even the educated, believe unwaveringly that the attacks on America in September 2001 were a Jewish conspiracy, that all the Jews who worked at the World Trade Centre had been warned to stay at home on September 11. And many Indians and foreigners, even the educated, believe that all Muslims with long beards are somehow linked to terrorist acts perpetrated in the name of Islam. Caricature and urban myth are usually best left alone by the outsider. To argue with the absurd is not a good role for the guest, or interloper.

From 1989, when the Dar brothers, their father Sobra, and his brothers too, began to grow their beards long, they also began to take the handicrafts of the Valley to markets beyond the conflict in Kashmir.

Mohammad likes to tell the story of how it began.

'I must write this down some day, you must help me,' he said. 'I must tell people how this all started from nothing, from just going to Delhi with a few small, small pieces when the fighting started and the tourists stopped coming. It would be good for people to read it and to know how this thing is possible, to go from nothing to all this.'

The spread of the Dar empire in this generation goes beyond their shops in Delhi and beside Nishat Bagh, the Garden of Gladness. They are building new homes on the plot of land bought by Sobra. What was once a small house on a plot of land above the lake is now a compound, with two houses and another in the process of being built. It is only a short walk from the simple boat where the four brothers were born, but it is a long social distance.

'We have to build these,' Mohammad said as he showed me around the house-in-progress, greeting the workmen who were fixing cedar panelling in all the rooms. 'My sons have been to school in England, they have got used to having their own rooms. What can I do?' He shrugged and smiled.

'You know how many bathrooms there are going to be in that new house?' Maqbool asked when he knew that I had been given a tour. 'Nine, imagine! Such a lot of money.'

Several of the brothers' sons have been sent to study in England at a Qur'anic-based school near Manchester. It has been a very expensive exercise for the family but Mohammad was clear that he wanted his sons to attend this particular school. By the time his eldest and second sons, Asif and Omar, reached secondary school age the education system in Kashmir had been badly fragmented by the insurgency. Every time there was a strike or crackdown the schools were closed down, or the teachers did not turn up.

The school journey in the mornings was once one of the enchanting sights of the lakes: scrubbed children paddled in small *shikaras*, laughing or squabbling, sometimes splashing each other with their paddles as their parents shouted from the bank, telling them to stop, to hurry to school. Once the insurgency began there was little joy in the commute to school, the children unsure of whether they would find their school open or anyone there to teach them. Schools were closed for weeks at a time when the fighting was bad. Many children just stopped going.

'How can you study when you are full of fear?' one of Mohammad's younger cousins asked. 'Your brain packs up, the only thing in it is fear, that is the only thought that is coming.'

We were sitting on the back of the boat, his English exercise book open in front of him. Arshad was twenty-four by this time and trying to catch up on what he had missed during those lost school years. He pointed up to the house beyond the meadow and the garden. 'We were all living together at that time, and my father used to say to me in the night that it was late and that I should sleep. He used to send me up to where I was sleeping with my other cousins at the top of the house and he thought I was going for sleep, but I would just lie there late into the night, sometimes all of the night, and I would get no sleep.'

Arshad is a first cousin to Mohammad and his brothers. He is the son of Mohammad's father's younger brother.

'My school was just beyond there.' Arshad pointed to the other side of the lake, to a blackened shell of a building that used to be the Nagin Club, a sailing and water-sports club frequented by the British. It had been burned out early on during the insurgency.

'There was a military camp there for a long time,' he said.

One of the paramilitary groups, the Central Reserve Police Force, had a camp there for many years.

'You know it was often being bombed by militants and things? Well, sometimes these things happened when we were going or coming from school, sometimes while we were in the school.' He flipped open his mobile phone to answer a call. At the end of a brief conversation he snapped the phone closed and continued. 'Many of my friends stopped coming to school at this time.' He examined the phone in his hand. 'I did too.' His foot drummed on the floor of the boat. 'When will I have my childhood now, all that time that has just been taken away from me, from all of us who have been growing up in this time?'

He was wearing jeans, a jersey and a baseball cap instead of a prayer cap.

'I was born Muslim, it came through my father, but as yet I do not really practise. Not fully, maybe some little bits, and praying, but I have not really studied, not as yet.' He answered another call, greeting the caller with '*As-Salaamu Alaikum.*' Then he cut them off, announcing that he was in a meeting.

'I see very religious people around me, some of them very rich, and even with so much money it is as though they don't really care about it.' He paused. 'I don't mean that they don't care as in it is not of any importance, but more they feel that it is not theirs, just passing through their hands, so not for spending on so much of just things, maybe more for giving away, for helping others. To them all money is Allah's. And I see them and how they are with themselves and I would like very much to be like this.' He leaned down over the edge of the veranda watching a woman paddling past, crouched over the front of her *shikara*, bright pink *salwar* leggings under her *pheran*, a matching scarf around her head. 'Yes, I would like very much to be like this, but I will have to do a lot, a lot of study first, like my cousins have done.' He lifted his head and flicked his chin towards the houses above the meadow, Mohammad, Imran, Ibrahim and Yusuf's homes.

In another world, away from the lakes, Mohammad and I had met up, in London. It was during a bad year in Kashmir, 1998. There were large numbers of 'foreign' insurgents from training camps in Pakistan and Afghanistan crossing into Kashmir, many of their incursions made under cover of cross-border shelling by the Pakistan army. Pakistan continued to maintain a stance of denial that it was involved with what it termed 'the freedom struggle of the Kashmiris'. However, the Pakistan government of Nawaz Sharif, and his predecessor, Benazir Bhutto, consistently remained blindly partisan in their use of the term 'freedom struggle'.

For Pakistan 'freedom for Kashmir' meant becoming part of Pakistan. For Kashmiri separatists it meant total freedom and autonomy.

The militant groups being backed by Pakistan were not only on the attack against the Indian security forces, they were also in conflict with the home-grown separatist movements that very clearly did not want Kashmir to be part of Pakistan. The Valley was dogged by a level of violence that had many internecine layers: one national army fighting another by proxy, the latter using a steady drip of imported militants to bleed India's defence resources; conflict within the Valley between one militant group and another; savage crackdowns by the various Indian security forces when militants hit their targets. People were living in a constant miasma of nervous energy, from day to day, between curfews, crackdowns, searches and constant disruptions to all forms of business and daily life. The hospitals were full far beyond their capacity. Schools were closed more than they were open.

Mohammad had come to London to sell carpets, and to visit his eldest son at his new school. He chose a curious place to meet, but it seemed to be one of the few places with a location that he was sure about. He said that he had been several times because some of his customers stayed there, and it was convenient for his meeting later in the day with the carpet buyer at Harrods. He knew that it was a place frequented by wealthy Arabs, mainly from Dubai and Saudi. Some of them were his customers. He did not seem aware of the fact that the hotel was also a spot notorious for getting its clientele laid. For the boy who had been born on a boat in what had been a poorer part of town, his presence there was an announcement that he had made it.

We drank tea from tiny cups in a lobby area, where a woman with slightly green hair played a homogeneous medley of Andrew Lloyd Webber hits on a white piano, as a seamless stream of hookers, hair and hems high, clickety-clicked across the marble to meet their clients. Mohammad complimented the waiter on the small squares of Dundee cake and madeleines that had been brought for us. He ate them with gusto as the tarts wandered past, carefully turning away if any of the girls even veered in our direction.

'I have had so many blessings, and there has been much hard work, but this thing has allowed me to send my son to school in England. He is getting the very best education now,' he said, rolling up the wide sleeve of his white *kameez* tunic to stop it from drooping into his tiny teacup.

'Things are terrible in Kashmir now, very bad, and I have had this opportunity to send my son to this school. Really, it is a wonderful place. I am very, very happy that my son is there, and I hope all my sons will have the good chance to go. They learn how to do things very nicely, not just the education, but all the things. How to be with the parents, with the brothers and sisters, how to behave with their wives.' Mohammad bent over the tea cakes as a Thai girl with a propped-up cleavage teetered past.

The school where his eldest son was studying, and where Mohammad has since sent his other two sons, and his nephews, is close to the United Kingdom headquarters of Tablighi Jamaat. The school is run under the auspices of Tablighi.

Throughout the late nineteenth and early twentieth centuries Hindu nationalism gathered force as India sought ways to arm itself in its fight for independence. One of the manifestations of this nationalism was a reformist movement, both ascetic and militant in nature, the Arya Samaj. Among many aims the movement sought to draw back to Hinduism various groups that had converted to Islam as a way of escaping their low-caste status. In response to this an influential *maulvi*, or Muslim priest, of a reformist school of Islam, the Deoband school of North India, started a movement in Mewat in South Haryana, near Delhi, to defend the Islamic status of those whom the Arya Samaj were trying to re-convert. *Tabligh* means to deliver a message, or to educate, *Jamaat*, *Jamat* or *Jamiat*, a gathering of Muslim elders or clerics.

This movement, Tablighi Jamaat, intended to draw away from politics and to act as a support to those making the transition from rural to urban living, and on the grander scale from national to international life, while remaining within the boundaries of their religion. It has grown and spread far beyond South Asia to Africa, America and Europe. It is looked on by some as being perhaps the most approachable face of modernising Islam, with its broad spread of charitable and educational organisations. Others regard it as being a carefully promoted cover for various militant operations around the world. Some countries now have Tablighi Jamaat on their anti-terrorism list, while others welcome it on the basis of its charitable work and its modernity – there is even a rap group in America, boys with beards saying it their way at the same time as embracing their membership of Tablighi.

The organisation's European headquarters is based in the English town of Dewsbury in West Yorkshire. The mosque there is one of the largest to have been built in Europe since the nineteenth century. The school where Mohammad sent his sons and nephews is about an hour's drive from the mosque and very far from the persistent school closures and accompanying fear of a generation of children in the Valley.

As that latent fear became nascent through the late 1980s Tablighi Jamaat called for an international gathering of its members in Kashmir in 1988. Over 1,000 leading members of the organisation came to Srinagar from their centres all over the world. They met at Eid Ghar, the prayer field for Eid. Thousands of Kashmiris came to pray with them, and to listen to their discourses on how to live a good Muslim life. Tablighi members encouraged people to pray, to do good work, not to waste money on lavish weddings but to keep them simple, and within the bounds of what they could afford.

In a time of unrest, and in the face of a doubtful future, growing numbers of people were drawn to the way of life Tablighi Jamaat was preaching and promoting. It seemed to offer a safety blanket, an emotional support and structure, when an old way of life seemed to be collapsing.

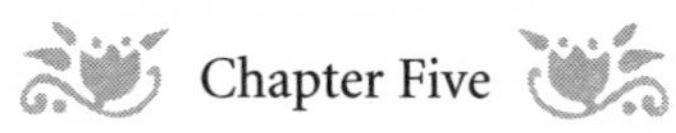

Chapter Five

MARTYRDOM

'MY SON HAS DONE a very good thing,' said Sobra Dar. 'When first he sent his elder boy, Asif, to the school many people were not so sure about this thing. They could not understand why he was sending the boy all the way to England for Islamic education. But it was best thing.' He looked down at his feet. 'What can I do about these? Look at this problem.'

Sobra is called Hajji Papa by all those in the circle of his family and friends. He has been to Mecca more times now than he can remember, and his most recent trip for Umrah, the pilgrimage outside the dates of Hajj, was the cause of the foot problem. We were sitting in one of the Dars' showrooms in Delhi, halfway along a marble corridor in the shopping mall of one of the new generation of big shiny city hotels. Hajji Papa had emerged from his long depression of several years earlier, when the worst period of the insurgency seemed to have passed.

He stretched his legs to get a better perspective on the problem. His bare feet were swollen, the skin pulled tight, the veins pushed to the surface. A Japanese tourist, her very small shoes matching her bag, her shirt and her skirt, stopped at the entrance of the shop. She paused, taking in Hajji Papa, his long beard, prayer cap and white *salwar kameez*. She looked at his assistants, two other Kashmiris, long-term employees of the Dar family, similarly bearded and dressed. And then she looked at me, her expression one of surprise and confusion.

'Come, come into my shop, see some carpets, some shawls, we have many, many lovely things,' Hajji Papa said with a smile, the line a reflex, bubbling out with the same ease as breath.

Above the sofa where he sat was a framed and greatly enlarged cutting from the *New York Times* dated Sunday, 2 April 1995:

> Halfway through her 12-day official visit to South Asia, Mrs. Clinton's good will tour has been animated with an air of high moral purpose. She has visited families, schools, a worker's union, government officials, and even one of Mother Teresa's orphanages.
>
> The stream of photo-op, shopping stops and short hops aboard the Boeing 707 that serves as Air Force One and a Half has also produced its share of low comedy, as a planeload of White House aides and reporters joined Mrs. Clinton and her daughter, Chelsea, on her journey into what the First Lady herself calls 'Hillaryland'. What follows is a strictly selective collection of impressions from along the way.
>
> March 29. After a day crowded with a speech on women's rights, a lunch with the Indian Prime Minister (Narasimha Rao) and an evening reception at the American Embassy in New Delhi, Mrs. Clinton undertakes a midnight economic development mission: she buys several chain-stitched rugs at the National Cottage Emporium in the Sheraton Hotel. The Kashmiri

> proprietor, Mohammad Dar (a salesman straight from Central Casting) coins a new title worthy of a major Memsahib: 'Her Ladyship'. Mrs. Clinton's Deputy Chief of Staff, Melanne Verveer, becomes 'Her Deputy Ladyship'....

Hajji Papa tried to direct the Japanese woman's attention to the article above his head, but she raised a hand and backed out of the shop.

On other walls there are similarly framed articles and letters, several of them from the Clinton family, both husband and wife. Bill Clinton shopped with the Dars on his swansong Indian tour in 2000. Even as Hajji Papa and I were sitting in the National Cottage Emporium in New Delhi Hillary Clinton was back on tour again, this time battling it out with Barack Obama in the US primaries. The Dar family were taking Mrs Clinton's progress very personally. They were not sure about Mr Barack, as Hajji Papa referred to Mrs Clinton's rival. As the coverage of the primaries ratcheted up many Indians were confused by Barack Obama and thought that he was probably a Muslim. Their confusion was not helped by the fact that quite a lot of the news made it seem that the fight for the US presidency was just between Hillary and Barack. That they were in the same party did not seem to have registered with some people, but Hajji Papa was very clear on the protagonists of the US electoral process.

'Terrible news.' He shook his head, reflecting on Mrs Clinton's bad start in the polls against her main Democratic opponent.

I looked at his feet. 'You flew back a week ago, this swelling should be going down by now.'

'I know, I know and I have been taking all advice from the

doctor, walking, putting them up, all these things. What else can I do?'

We discussed massaging his feet and ankles with various essential oils mixed with evening primrose oil while the Japanese woman retreated from another Kashmiri rug shop on the other side of the marble corridor.

'What can I say to people like this?' Hajji Papa wrapped one hand around his hennaed beard, its earthy red colour another badge of his visits to Mecca. 'That I do not hide grenades in my beard, or have guns rolled into my carpets?' He shrugged. 'I should have offered some *kahwa chai*, Japanese people like to drink tea.'

As sales patter is a second language, so *kahwa chai* is the water of life for Kashmiri salesmen. Green tea combines with cardamom, cinnamon, shaved almonds and sometimes saffron to create a delicate, clean-tasting tea, easy to drink in great volume, as indeed Kashmiris do. And as with almost all cultural specialities many also eschew them. Most of the Dars like to drink sweet, thick *masala chai*, spiced and much boiled milky tea, while their guests and potential customers praise the fragrant *kahwa* and wonder how to avoid spending too much money.

Hajji Papa sighed some more about his presidential hopes for Mrs Clinton and then returned to the subject of his grandsons' education.

'How would it have been if they had stayed? Imagine, those boys would have been trying to study at the time when things were terrible, all the schools closed, and those Pakistanis were trying to find ways to make our young people join the fight, even though we were already at that time so tired of it.'

While Bill had been buying chain-stitch and silk carpets from the Dars in 2000 Pakistan had been pushing hard on the war-by-agency for Kashmir, trying to get as many 'foreign' militants into the Valley as possible, to fight and to recruit local people to the cause.

'You know these Pakistanis, what can you say about these people? You know where they were having the camps, where they are training all these boys for militancy?'

Hajji Papa was talking of the training camps, particularly the ones in Pakistan-controlled Kashmir.

'These people are not properly educated. You know what they like to do the best? They have these pigeons and they make them fly up and peck, peck, up in the air. What is this called?' He made beaks with his index fingers and thumbs, one hand attacking the other.

'Pigeon-fighting?'

'Yes, this thing, and they like to play cards all the time, drinking, drinking and playing cards.' His hands became cards, slapping down, one on top of the other. 'It is a well-known game they like to play, though I am not remembering its name at the moment.'

He paused to offer me *kahwa chai*. We both settled for *masala chai* instead.

'The other thing they like most of all is those, what is the word, the things up in the sky?' he asked again.

'Kites?'

'Yes, yes, this is all they like to do, pigeons, cards, drinking and kites.'

'Some would say that was a rather good mix of things.'

Hajji Papa looked at me closely. 'Sometimes this English humour is not so comfortable.' He called for *masala chai* to be made. 'Really, they are very ignorant people. These things I am coming to know over time.'

How might the smooth-tongued Pakistani intellectuals I

had met respond to Hajji Papa's perceptions, and indeed to his adopted way of following Islam? Some of them use variations on a theme of Hajji Papa's portrayal when describing those they regard as being '*mullah*ised', caught up with strict doctrines or literal interpretations of Islam: 'The blind leading the dumb' as a colleague from Karachi labelled them. And while the kites and pigeons might be flying and fighting in both poor rural and city areas of the country, performances of *The Vagina Monologues* were being given standing ovations in Islamabad and Karachi.

In Srinagar *shikara* journeys through the canal system of the city pass among old *mohallas* (neighbourhoods) of timber-framed houses, their upper storeys left open for drying hay, vegetables, fruit and clothes. Often the houses have a thin wooden frame attached to the roof, a high perch for pigeons – fighting pigeons. On the wooden footbridges and causeways that zigzag over the water and thick riverine mud, whenever there is a little wind there are boys and adolescents flying kites, throwing the fragile paper diamonds up into the air, grabbing the string from each other to see who can make them fly the highest, and dance the most. Few girls are to be seen out kite-flying.

Hajji Papa swept aside any possible comparisons and focused instead on the approaching election across the border in Pakistan. He felt as strongly about this as he did about Mrs Clinton's bumpy progress on the other side of the world.

'These mullah types that everyone is so afraid of, these ones that have control in small, small areas. But why, there is no reason to follow them? This is for ignorant people, just the ones with their pigeons and cards. Maybe they get bored of flying their kites, maybe they are looking for something different, and someone is saying to them: "Go and fight a war in Kashmir." So they come and cause all these problems. But they do not have so much of support, really this thing I know. Maybe it is interesting to some people for a while, but it will not last, you will see. Then they will stop trying to make our boys join them, then slowly, slowly some of this problem will begin to change.' Hajji Papa tried to move his swollen toes. 'How many drops is it that I put in of those oils for the massage? he asked. 'You will have to tell me again.'

When Hajji Papa's grandson, Asif, first went to school in England Pakistan was on another recruitment drive in the Valley. At the government level India and Pakistan seemed to be making overtures towards negotiation. In February 1999 the Prime Minister of India at that time, Atal Bihari Vajpayee, took the first bus journey across the border to Lahore since 1947. But even as he boarded the bus Pakistan was in the process of mounting an aggressive push across the Line of Control, one that ran through the winter of 1998 and into early spring 1999.

Within the Valley foreign *jihadis* were recruiting hard. Their methods were sometimes obvious, and at other times devastating in their manipulative cruelty. When it came to talking to the media the spokesmen for the various Pakistan-backed groups often boasted of the fact that the Valley continued to offer them unlimited potential for sourcing *jihadis*.

They carried on using their established method of sweeping up angry young men and boys from villages, towns and city areas that were regularly targeted for crackdowns by the Indian security forces. But the militants were becoming sharper in their techniques, often moving faster than the security forces and intelligence, constantly adapting their methods, learning all the time from those who trained them, and who brought new insurgent methods to the training camps from other Islamic nations and states including Afghanistan, Egypt, Sudan and Chechnya.

For an increasing number of Kashmiris at that time a decade of conflict was already too much. The generation of idealistic young separatists had become battle-scarred and prison-battered older men, if they had managed to survive. Some of the more extreme separatist groups were beginning to move towards negotiation with the Indian Government, beyond the barrel of a gun. While earlier support and allegiance to the *jihadis* started to wane the recruiters began to play increasingly on the by-products of conflict – unemployment and the emotional instability of a generation that had been growing up through the fighting.

The traditional breeding grounds of insurgency, university campuses, had mostly been alienated by the extremism of the foreign and Islamist *jihadi* groups. The recruiters turned to other places where the young went to meet in their efforts to forget for a while what they were having to live through. They posted lookouts and trained them to wait for the right moment of approach.

On a cold November afternoon in 1999 I was sitting above one of the main intersections in the busiest part of Srinagar, Lal Chowk, Red Square, so named during a period of intense flirtation with Moscow and with the notion that communism could be the key to autonomy for Kashmir. Just down the street was a check-post and brick-built bunker in front of what had once been the city's most glamorous cinema. All Srinagar's cinemas had been forced by militants to close in the early days of the insurgency. The groups claimed that all films, and most particularly jiggy-jiggy, wet sari Bollywood ones, were un-Islamic. Sandbags, camouflage netting and barbed wire blocked what had once been the art deco entrance to the Kashmir Talkies at the Palladium Cinema. Above the bunker the green mosaic entrance pillars and now jagged façade were only that: blank window frames beneath a gapping space. The Palladium Cinema had been firebombed in 1990 by the Jammu and Kashmir Liberation Front.

This had been a volatile section of the city since the beginning of the insurgency, the buildings pock-marked by gun battles. From inside the check-post guns pushed through the protecting grilles, covering off most angles of approach. Almost directly opposite the gun barrels a group of teenagers huddled together outside a shop that was quite openly selling tapes and videotapes, even though this too had been declared un-Islamic at the same time as the Palladium had been forced to board up its entrance.

I was just enjoying the company of a friend in one of the old coffee houses. He was a local, a veteran chronicler of the conflict. I was not paying the huddle of teenage boys much attention.

'Watch,' he said, pointing through the wooden casement of the upper storey where we were sitting to where the youngsters stood bunched together. 'Just watch.'

Some of the group were chatting, some laughing. I watched.

'Now look there.' My friend nodded to another shop, a few doors down from the cassette and video shop. 'See him?' He pointed to a man leaning on the counter, talking to the people in the shop.

He was clean-shaven, his hair short. He wore jeans under his *pheran*.

'See his boots?' my friend asked.

They looked new, standard military issue.

As in so many other places, cheap and broken shoes are

one of the common signs of hardship in Kashmir. But in the Valley poor men and boys can get good boots in two ways: by joining the militants or the security forces. There was not much of the latter in 1999.

'Look now,' my friend said.

Some of the boys from the huddle were peeling away. Just three of them were left, and two of those were arguing with the third, a slight, unkempt boy. He was shoved by one of the others, hard against the cassette and video shop front. Someone inside the shop shouted and waved the boys away. The pair went one way, the slight boy in the opposite direction, his shoulders and head hunched into the neck of his *pheran*, his gait that slow shuffle of teenage despondency.

As the lone boy walked away the man in the jeans and good boots left the shop where he had been waiting. He seemed to be speaking to other people as he passed them on the street, exchanging greetings. As he got closer to the boy, he asked him something. The boy turned and answered, waiting for the man to catch up with him. They disappeared in the direction of Amira Kadal, the bridge that leads out of Lal Chowk.

I looked back at the check-post. There was no movement from inside.

'I've been watching him for a few days, and those boys too.'

My friend used the low wooden benches of the coffee house as his office. He was there every day.

'Those three left at the end, that *tamasha* [drama] has been going on for a few days. Those two bullies pick on the little guy and get money from him. The little one thinks he can buy his way into the gang. None of them has any money but the little one has managed to give the others a few rupees when they have picked on him before. Who the hell knows where he has been getting the money. He probably stole it, and probably from his parents.' He fiddled with the small metal beaker of coffee in front of him. 'You see that then sets him up, makes him an easy target. He's already committed a crime, from the point of view of his own conscience. See how it happens? And then today he did not have anything to give them and so they shove him around, make him the odd one out again, and that guy watched the whole thing play out.'

On the street below two paramilitary soldiers came out from behind the bunker and stopped a man in the street. Three other soldiers appeared from somewhere near the bunker and stopped some other men as well. The detained men were pushed up against the wall, rifle butts in their backs, arms up, hands flat against the bricks.

'The crime of suspicious *pheran*-wearing,' my friend said as the men were searched. 'These street military guys, they are always picking up the wrong people. See how obvious these ones are? Look, they've got everything, beards, prayer caps, they look desperate, they're wearing *pherans*.'

The men against the wall were all that he said. Also they wore cheap, broken plastic shoes beneath the dirty hems of their *salwar*.

'And that one, what about him?' He waved in the direction that the slight boy and his new friend had taken. 'No beard, no prayer cap, no look of desperation.'

'He was wearing a *pheran*?'

'That's the only thing, so they don't stick out from the crowd, but they aren't in the crowd either. You sit here for long enough and watch them, they are really smart. They also know that they don't have as many friends here as they had a few years back, so they keep moving, they keep changing the way they do things all the time.'

'So what's the point of recruiting so hard still if the fight is going out of people here?'

He looked down to where the three men were splayed against the wall, to where people were walking past, hardly deviating, making just enough space between themselves and the search to be out of the range of a rifle swing.

'They'll let them go now,' he said.

And they did, the soldiers nudging the men away from the wall and waving them on with their rifle butts.

'That boy, he'll go to a camp somewhere maybe, over in Azad [Pakistan-controlled Kashmir]. He will be trained, come back here, get involved in some attacks on the security forces, get killed in an encounter, be paraded about by the cops or army or whoever it is who catch him, and they will make a big noise about how dangerous he was, another terrorist cleaned from the Valley. His family will say he is a martyr because that is what everyone will tell them to say.' He smiled sadly at the place where the huddle of boys had been outside the cassette and video shop. 'In Pakistan they tell them they will be martyrs, in Delhi they call them terrorists. Here they are just boys like that, someone you were at school with, played cricket or football with once.'

It can be said of any hero or murderer that they were just a boy, a son, a husband, a brother, a father, that circumstance gave them a gun and put blood on their hands, or a medal on their chest. The Valley is full of martyrs' graveyards. Throughout the conflict the Indian security forces have been instructed to demolish signs at any of these graveyards that glorified the men buried there, just as the Dogra ruling establishment tried to minimise the glorification of one of the Valley's very first heroes.

Abdul Qadir was a local Kashmiri butler in the service of a European. He was an early separatist firebrand. In July 1931 he made a speech that called on the people to fight against their oppressors, and to massacre those Hindus who stood between them and freedom. His arrest resulted in the prison being mobbed. The police fired into the crowd and twenty-one people were killed. They became the first martyrs to the separatist cause. Since the beginning of the insurgency, fifty-eight years later, 13 July, the day of Abdul Qadir's speech and arrest, has been marked as Martyrs' Day, and the *kabar-i-shaheed*, the martyrs' graveyards, became places where people went both to pay homage to the martyrs and in defiance of the security forces.

'I will take any steps, any means I have, to keep my sons from being around people who might be telling them that to be a martyr is a good thing,' Mohammad had said to me in London over those tiny teacups as the prostitutes walked on by.

'The most terrible thing is that when the situation is as bad as this the idea of martyrdom seems glamorous to boys who think there is nothing better to look forward to than whatever it is they are being sold about paradise. They see no jobs, no way of earning a living; to them their lives already seem to be over because there is nothing to look forward to. And then they are offered the gun, and a salary to go with it,' my friend had said as we had watched the slight boy and the man in the good boots walk away in November 1999.

In a different kind of coffee shop, nine years later, another local journalist gave his view.

'It has not been about martyrdom for a very long time now, not since the earliest days of the fighting. From a few years in they did not even have to mention martyrdom as an incentive when they were trying to get people to join the militancy. They did not have to. They had thousands upon thousands to chose from who were just sitting around with no jobs, no sense of any future.'

There are no signs of crossfire at this coffee shop, Café Arabica. It is on Maulana Azad Road, opposite what used to be the polo ground, but is now a series of cricket pitches and a football field in spring, summer and autumn, a soggy mix of fallen leaves, mud, frost and snow in winter. There is a police headquarters just up the road, the usual barricades, razor-wire tunnels, and brick bunker lookouts around the compound wall. But it is out of sight of the coffee shop in this wealthier part of the city.

They sell cappuccinos and Diet Coke in Café Arabica, and cakes with wild rainbow-coloured frosting. To have ordered a Diet Coke in the old coffee house, above Lal Chowk, in 1999 would have been tantamount to supporting 'the occupation' of the Valley by Indian security forces. Even though India was still clinging to the remnants of an import control system that had kept the likes of Coca-Cola and McDonalds at bay for several decades, to ask for foreign things in Kashmir was almost the same as siding with the enemy. Now the partisan passion for all things Kashmiri, from *kahwa chai* to papier-mâché boxes, has eased as the situation improves; commodity jingoism and economic hardship usually travel in each other's company. Even to drink coffee, regarded as an unnecessary stimulant under some of the stricter codes of Islam, was rebellious ten years ago. Now to ask for a cappuccino in Café Arabica, listening to the Beatles belting out 'Love Me Do', seems normal. Ten years ago just the volume of the song could have elicited some kind of backlash. Now people smile at the familiarity of the tune, the same smile given as coffee is ordered.

For most people coming in from the outside it would just seem to be a slightly average sub-continental coffee shop, limited still to one kind of milk, and only white sugar. To the better off of the city it represents the change of the past few years, somewhere they can meet that has an atmosphere and design that belong to another world than the one that they have been surviving in for twenty years.

The doorman has been the same old man for a few years now. He wears a green semi-military uniform, the epaulettes sliding off his narrow shoulders, the sleeves too long. He always runs to get the door when he sees me. We greet each other in both Kashmiri and English. 'Good day to you,' he says in the language of the photographs and chit letters in the Dars' photograph albums.

As I walked towards the café to meet the journalist the old doorman saw me through the window. He ignored a young man who was making his way out of the café, his mobile phone pinched to his ear as he lit a cigarette. The phone is a sign of change too. The network providers were also kept out until a few years ago because of the huge advantage that mobile phones would potentially have given to the militants. When the first provider was allowed in the vetting process for mobile phone applications was thorough and lengthy.

The young man stopped just outside the door of the café, tall in tight jeans, and one of those skinny jerseys that did not flatter an early growth pot-belly. His shoes were grass-green faux crocodile skin, the toes long and slightly curled up to match heavily gelled hair that was scooped up extravagantly above his clean-shaven face. He was talking right into the phone, shouting a little. The networks are still not very good, the connection dropping regularly.

A shepherd was passing, the dust and mud on his *pheran*

matching the fleeces of his flock. They followed him down the pavement, dividing around the young man on the phone, re-forming on the other side. The young man continued to shout into his phone, the sheep went on their way, and the old doorman ran to greet me.

I had to wait. The journalist was going to be late. The climate of violence has changed, but it still continues. He was finishing his story on a recent attack.

Even in this very modern addition to the city, root patterns remained unchanged beyond the music and the froth on the coffee. Only men served behind the counter, and only men were being served. A couple followed me in, but sat as far from the crowd as they could manage. Women and girls rarely come in together, occasionally a mother and daughter, or a family group, but most of the female customers are foreigners, employees of the International Committee of the Red Cross keeping a check on the 'political' prisoners in Srinagar's Central Jail, members of other NGOs (non-governmental organisations, non-profit) and working groups researching the damage of two decades of conflict.

Twenty years ago, when I last came with my mother, we walked wherever we wanted; we wore shorts and T-shirts in the spring sun, and no one noticed. Ten years on from then, in the late nineties, I could not go to most parts of the city, and I had to be escorted to the ones where I was allowed. Now I can go to most places in the city alone, though when Maqbool hears the rattle of the door on the houseboat, when he knows I am going out, he comes to check that I am suitably dressed. He knows that I will not risk anything, that I have worn the *burqa* during the times when some of the militant groups were targeting women who did not subsume themselves under a collective black covering. Still he checks, to make sure that I am wearing a *pheran*, that my body is shapelessly concealed, my head as well. It remains a patriarchal society, a pattern of behaviour traced into the culture. Almost everyone is courteous to foreign women, though our relevance is only fully recognised with the presence of a husband; otherwise we are tolerated mostly as an anomaly, a curiosity.

Even with the generation that managed to leave the Valley during the worst years of the insurgency, who have lived and studied in the UK or America, and have returned now in the hope of being part of the post-conflict era, even with them there is this same ingrained behaviour towards women. We are nodded to, acknowledged, a role-play that conforms to acceptable behaviour.

One of the men behind the counter in the café called out that my order was ready. He nodded and passed the tray, smiling over my shoulder.

When the journalist came he was still caught in the detail of his story.

'Of course things are better, but still this stuff is going on. We are all so tired of it, you can't imagine how tired. It is a malaise that all the young people have – it is in all of us to some extent or other. What can the government have expected? They gave us all that education, lots of degrees on pieces of paper, but nothing to back it up, no experience to find jobs, no jobs to find. Why were they surprised when young people joined the militancy? It wasn't about being martyrs, it was about earning bucks.'

He talked fast. He too never looked at me, but always over one shoulder, or around the room as he made the speech he perhaps feels he has to give to every foreigner.

'I am luckier than so many of these kids though. I was born

before it started. I am old enough to have memories of what it was like before, to have a sense of how we used to be inculcated into me. That at least gives you a core to hold onto.'

On Martyrs' Day each July it is mostly women who gather at the graveyards. Many of them have no graves over which to mourn. These are the mothers, wives and sisters of 'the disappeared'. They cannot grieve fully because they do not know what has happened to those they want to be allowed to mourn. In almost all cases the security forces picked up their men during crackdowns or house searches. Some of those taken were involved in the militancy; some were taken because of mistaken identity; some because a quota of arrests had to be met in order for a police or paramilitary officer to achieve promotion, or a financial bonus. Many of these women are referred to as half-widows. They have lost their men but there have been no bodies over which to grieve. They have no status. They cannot remarry or receive the government compensation given to women whose husbands have keen killed in the conflict.

A small, tired woman with heavy circles under her eyes runs the association that represents these people.

Parveena Ahanger is a local woman from a poor *mohalla*, the laundry neighbourhood of Batmaloo. She was a wife and mother who had never moved far from her home until her son Javed was taken in 1990 during a house search. In defiance of her cultural conditioning Parveena did not bend and break when her son was taken. She knew that her sixteen-year-old boy was innocent and that it was a case of mistaken identity. Once she had dragged herself down every avenue of enquiry, alienating herself from many around her in the process, she started the Association of Parents of Disappeared Persons (APDP) with other campaigners in 1994. They have little funding or heavyweight support, but Parveena, and those who have joined her, help others face their situation of loss.

Each year Parveena marks Martyrs' Day. She too has faced her own persecution several times over. On Martyrs' Day in 2001 Parveena, and the other founders and members of the Association of the Parents of Disappeared Persons, tried to raise a monument to 'the disappeared' in Srinagar. Their ceremony of mourning was disbanded by the paramilitary forces. By the following day the monument had been demolished and removed.

'I have no room for more anger,' Parveena said in the early days of her leadership of the APDP. She ran it from her home then, just one room in a damp grey house in the laundry quarter.

'Where could I put it?' she asked. 'I am all filled up with it.'

At the time the APDP had been in existence for only five years but already Parveena's whole psyche was frail and fragmenting, and her husband's family were raging at her for being so public. For an illiterate and barely educated woman Parveena was crashing through many cultural protocols. She was making enemies even as she brought comfort to fellow sufferers who had found themselves floundering in the same situation, unsure of where to turn.

In desperation some of these people put their trust, and money that they had begged and borrowed, into the hands of *mukhbirs* (police informers). These parasitic middlemen always promise to find the whereabouts of 'disappeared' family members, charging high prices up front, and then dangling only bitter hope and red herrings in exchange, or simply disappearing as soon as they have the money.

It is just one of the many ugly little businesses that have grown out of the insurgency.

There are so many martyrs' graveyards, and so many who cannot be mourned in full because they cannot be found, but martyrdom has come to mean something else to some of those watching as the conflict has moved from stage to stage.

Since that first time on the Boulevard when I stumbled into crossfire there have been many martyrs: straggle-limbed and lifeless on roadsides; in the aftermath of explosions; bouncing loosely in the back of military lorries, their thumbs bound behind their backs with wire; lined up for photo-opportunities to advertise the latest counter-insurgency success of the army or paramilitary. Yet the real martyrs of Kashmir are the living ones, those who continue to suffer the torment that this conflict has brought.

Is a Muslim man being dragged along the cold tarmac of the Boulevard beside Dal Lake any more of a martyr than a young soldier who, dogged by fear and inexperience, shoots himself rather than have to continue doing a job that he does not have the belly for, be he Muslim, Sikh, Hindu or Buddhist? Martyrdom does not require death.

Mohammad Dar has educated his sons in a place that he believes keeps them far enough from the conflict and the 'call of the cause', or 'Martydom Inc' as the journalist in Café Arabica dubbed the recruiting methods of the militants (a riff on '*Jihadi* Inc', the term used by some for the production line from militant training camps in Pakistan and Pakistan-controlled Kashmir). It is often hard to understand martyrdom when it is a name in a graveyard among so many other names, but when seen in the suffering and self-sacrifice of the living it has a brutalising clarity.

Room 19 in the psychiatry clinic of the out-patients

department at the Shri Maharajah Hari Singh Hospital is a place of living martyrs. It is at the end of a wide corridor on the ground floor of the city's main hospital. Every corridor in the hospital has the same human traffic, barging into each other, heads down in the urgency of their need. If you stop for a moment you are pushed from all sides, shoved out of the way of the flow. Outside various doors inert bodies lie on old gurneys. The air is thick with the clash of disinfectant and human waste. The latter is everywhere, in all its forms.

Room 19 is where Dr Arshad Hussain holds his follow-up clinic for those on prescription medicines. He prescribes for over 300 different kinds of depression.

I go to see him to research the state of psychiatric treatment in the Valley. When I am there the crowd outside Room 19 is always pressing against the door, pushing appointment notes into the chink that opens now and then. Inside Dr Hussain sits at a desk with his registrar, junior and graduate assistants. There are five or more patients at the desk at any one time, their family members pushing from behind, the next layer of patients already in the room, pushing as well, trying to get one of the doctors' attention. It is a crowd of fathers and husbands bringing in their wives or children, or mothers and wives supporting their husbands and children. And there are children too, trying to lead their stumbling mother or father through the crush, trying to stop them being pushed too much by the others in the mass.

Sitting in the corner of the room on a recent visit, the smell of urine came through the window on warm spring air. Below the window a bed with a broken leg was separated from the rest of the room by a wooden partition, like a stable. The graduate doctor, a woman, her head uncovered, her clothes western, led one of the patients to the bed. An old man shuffled behind her, helped by his daughter, who talked to the doctor constantly, giving a stream of information about her father's symptoms. Both of them helped the old man up onto the lopsided bed. He wanted to get down. He needed to take off his socks and shoes, the outer heels on both worn down to nothing. As his daughter tried to help him he pushed her away. Both women waited for him to finish. His movements were slow but precise. He lined up the shoes under the bed and laid one dirty sock on top of the other. For a moment he stared at a discarded syringe lying under a leaking radiator. The doctor interrupted his gaze with her hand, waving him back onto the bed. She asked questions as she tested his reflexes, and his range of movement, pushing his thin legs in their striped pyjamas into his chest, and scratching the sole of his foot with a car key from her pocket. All his responses seemed slow, but within the range of normal. The doctor and the man's daughter helped him up and then left him as they pushed their way back through the crowd to the desk. The old man bent to retrieve his socks, and shoes in the fragment of privacy, or dignity.

A woman barged through the door as the man taking chits opened it a chink. She must have been beautiful once, with perfect symmetry in her features, but an internal imbalance had twisted her face into a staring mask. We smiled at each other, and she came at me, grabbing my rucksack, tipping things out of it, pulling out my wallet and phone and pushing both into the pocket of her *pheran*. She wound her hands into my hair and pulled, jumping up and down as she did so, saying in Kashmiri, 'This is mine, this is mine.'

The junior doctor turned and smiled. 'Sorry for this,' he said in English.

I forced a smile as the woman yanked, though she did not resist when I reclaimed my wallet and phone from her pockets. As long as she could keep her hands tight in my hair she seemed biddable. When it became obvious that she had no intention of letting go the female doctor and the door-keeper had to come and untangle her. She shouted at them, in crude, spitting anger. Then, as quickly as she had started, she forgot. Letting go of my hair she turned her focus on the junior doctor, shoving a plastic bag at him that she had twisted around her arm.

They all have plastic bags, the patients or their keepers, old bags, the shop advertisements on them worn away by constant use. They are carried wearily from doctor to doctor, from chemist to hospital pharmacy, every prescription, X-ray, MRI, scan and note kept and bundled together in these bags that they carry, these records of deterioration.

The woman's focus faded again, she swung around and fixed back onto me.

'She will trouble you some more,' the junior doctor said with a shrug.

The doorkeeper, the doctor and I smiled in a triangle as the woman came at me again, and I pulled my hair back under a scarf.

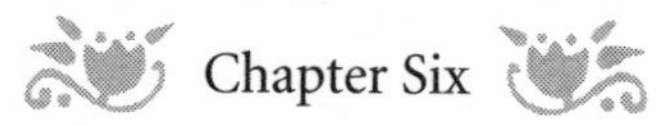

Chapter Six

ANOTHER MARTYRDOM

Zubeeda has a gentle face. Even when her features are framed by the hard black lines of a *hijab* her pale olive skin and pink cheeks soften the outline. She is still girlish.

She is married to Yusuf, the youngest of the Dar brothers. When I first met her, thirteen years ago, she was the newest and youngest bride to come into the family home. It meant that she was both indulged and criticised the most. When her second child was born, a son, the criticism diminished. Her first baby had been a girl.

'I would like to have maybe one more daughter too,' she whispered once, standing at the edge of the kitchen in the old house, just far enough away from her senior sisters-in-law not to be heard. She giggled in the nervous way of someone confessing something to a stranger.

'They all have daughters. Why are you being secretive about it?' I asked her.

Zubeeda put one hand on my arm and the fingers of her other hand across her lips, to silence me. We looked into the gaggle of women in the kitchen, mothers with their daughters, all of them fussing over their sons and brothers – their men.

Among ordinary Kashmiris the world of women starts with the family they are born into, and then becomes the family that they marry into. Female friendship is confined within the family structure, except when the girls are younger, and if they have the chance to go to school and make friends there. The conflict has brutalised women but they do not turn to each other in their pain. They turn inwards, into silence, and away from the calls for their men to pick up the gun; from the sounds of rifle butts against their door demanding entry; from the cry of a neighbour telling them that their boy has gone; from the extremist throwing acid in their face for not wearing the veil; from the rapist between their legs, demanding entry. Almost every time they have turned back into their homes, closed the door, and tried to carry on until they cannot take any more. Then the sad journey is made to Room 19 at the Shri Maharajah Hari Singh Hospital.

The women of Kashmir are not like other women. They do not come together, seeking to share their pain with other women. They turn away.

There was a story told during the early years of the insurgency, during the hardest stamp-down by the Indian security forces. A local journalist said that he had been with some soldiers, just talking. The soldiers had not realised that he was a journalist. The subject of reported rapes by the security forces came up. The journalist claimed that one of the soldiers said that he did not understand why people were surprised by the rapes, that it was obvious; after all, Kashmiri women were so beautiful, it would be too much of a waste not to. As this story circulated it became more elaborate. I heard it several times, with increasingly graphic embellishments of what the soldier claimed to have done to some women during his tour of duty in Kashmir.

*

On the night of Friday, 22 February 1991 a unit of the Indian Army's Rajputana Rifles surrounded a mountain village in the Kupwara region of the Valley. More than 800 soldiers rounded up the men of Kunan Poshpura. This was the standard procedure during a crackdown. The men of the village, or the local area, were ordered to assemble for identification. They were held while houses were searched for weapons and explosives. On this occasion the soldiers then ransacked each house they searched, and they raped indiscriminately. Kunan Poshpura is a small village. Many of its women were victims, their ages ranging from fifteen to eighty-five. News of the crackdown and rapes spread. The army threw a security cordon around the village, but not before the story had reached far enough to make it into the international press.

At first the Government of India and the army denied the reports, maintaining the line that had been in use since the beginning of the insurgency: that all reported abuses of human rights in Kashmir by the security forces were either rumours or lies. This line became unsustainable as evidence mounted. The government had to respond.

A fact-finding group was sent. It was reported that the group spent just half an hour in Kunan Poshpura. A 300-page report was produced from the visit that concluded that all the women in the village had lied.

Two years after the mass rape the village was divided: many of the women had been deserted by their husbands and families; young girls could not find husbands, regardless of whether they had been raped or not; one seventy-year-old woman had been thrown out by her son for bringing ill fortune on her family because of her rape. Young girls told visitors that they were taunted by the men of the village: 'Did you enjoy it, do you want some more?' It appeared that the men of Kunan Poshpura seemed united in their condemnation of the women for having brought this brutality to their village.

Seventeen years later Kunan Poshpura is still referred to as the raped village.

It was a *mukhbir*, a police informer, who told me about what had happened in Kunan Poshpura, the day after it happened. He did not even tell me directly but just that I should try to go to the village. It was an unusual piece of information. As a foreigner it was very hard to get to most parts of the Valley unless travelling with the military or paramilitary.

There was a bus that went to the nearest large town in the district, or I could take a jeep and driver, but it would be harder to get through the check-posts. On a bus I could get into more trouble. I did not have local ID. As a foreigner, and a journalist, I needed permission and an escort, both of which were rarely granted, but on a bus it was also easier to get through unnoticed.

I went to the bus station wearing a *pheran*, with my head covered. I did not wear a *burqa*. I did not try to disguise myself, and I did not expect to get further than the outskirts of Srinagar.

It was bitterly cold and dank in the aftermath of a snowfall that had turned to sleet during the early morning. The passengers on the bus bent over their *kangris*, most of them men returning from buying and selling at markets around the city. Village women have never travelled too much around the Valley, and since the beginning of the insurgency it has been even less. Yet there was a small group of them towards the back of the bus with some of their children. I went to sit with them. They too were in *pherans*, their heads covered. Even though it was a time when women were being targeted for not wearing the full *burqa*, these were village women who did not know that women in the city were being targeted by militant groups. They had come to the main hospital, the Shri Maharajah Hari Singh, as they needed to see good doctors. One of the children had lost a finger in an accident; one of the women had burned her arm badly when her *kangri* had broken, and the burn had become infected. They had agreed to make the journey together, accompanied by two male relations who were sitting further up the bus.

The road from the city was marked out by long lines of poplar trees, and by patrolling soldiers, their boots heavy with mud, their camouflage fatigues puffed out by flak jackets. Some stood by the roadside, some alone in the middle of blank paddy fields. In more exposed areas they were in pairs, back-to-back, covering themselves from both directions at road junctions. One lone soldier waved down the bus, walking along the side and peering at us through the windows. The village women stared back. The soldier got on and braced himself in the entrance, facing into the bus, his boot jamming the door open, his rifle off his shoulder, watching us as he directed the driver to move on. He did not raise his gun but held the barrel towards the floor. I slid lower into my seat. The woman beside me passed her child onto my lap. We had not even spoken but she just put her small son on my knee, his dark curls blocking the soldier's view of me. Nobody spoke as we drove on.

The soldier was simply shortening his march back to base, or to the collection point for his patrol. It is a common thing, riding the bus, or hitching with a passing car, but only something that the more confident ones are prepared to do, the ones who have been in their posting for a while, who know how to play the local people, those they know to be unarmed.

Many of the faces in fatigues on the roadsides and in the fields would not have dared. They were just boys pushed into the garb of men, nervous fingers on triggers all the time, safety catches off, their breath shallow in their upper chest, sweating in the cold for long patrol hours, waiting to be attacked by an enemy that knows how to emerge from the landscape as though from mist, and how to melt back into it as silently. So many of the deaths in Kashmir have not been the result of planned attack, or at a given command, but because of the terrified jabbing of a shaking finger on a trigger made slippery with the sweat of fear.

The soldier on our bus hit the side of the driver's seat with his rifle butt at a curve in the road. He knew exactly where the next check-post was, and that he needed to be walking when he reached it. As he jumped off he slammed the metal door and hit that too. The driver turned and spat into the stairwell where the soldier had been standing as he clunked the great gearstick and we moved away.

At the first of the check-posts the bus was made to stop in front of the barrier. Soldiers walked the length of the vehicle outside, their rifles raised. One of the women near me lurched at the window as a soldier approached. As she retched, her vomit splattering down the outside of the bus, two more soldiers ran at her, one waving her back into the bus with his gun barrel. She could not move, the involuntary lurching pinning her to the edge of the window. One of the soldiers was shouting at her. She continued to vomit. An officer called the soldiers off, shouting to them in Hindi to take care, his order delivered to a subordinate, the language an adult would use to a child: '*Dyan se!*' (Be careful!). The soldiers stopped and lowered their guns. The woman's back continued to heave as they were called off. The boy on my knee began to cry, and his mother stroked his head, but did not take him away. We both talked to him, and so to each other, our heads bent together over the sun-bleached ends of her son's dark curly hair.

The bus was pulled over at each check-post but only the driver was called off until we reached the check-post at the junction to Kupwara, the name of both the district and the main town. We were moving into an area marked by the security forces as being high risk due to local sympathy for the militants. All the men were ordered to get off the bus and to stand along the length of it. One by one they were made to lift their *pherans* and to turn around slowly, arms stretched wide to keep their *pherans* above their heads. Two of the children on the bus pressed their faces against the window to watch what was happening. A mother pulled them away, leaving their circles of breath on the window to fade as the men on the other side placed their hands against the glass and spread their legs to be searched. In the seat in front the woman with the burned arm fiddled with her dressing, rubbing at the dark iodine staining around the edges. Someone else was clicking their fingernails. We waited.

When the men were allowed back onto the bus the driver was sent back to where we were sitting to get our ID cards. They were collected. He did not ask me for my passport and I did not hand it over. He came back a few minutes later and passed the small pile of them to the woman whose son I was holding. We continued to Kupwara.

I was told later that an order had been issued straight after the crackdown at Kunan Poshpura. Until further notice local women were not to be stopped or challenged.

From the depot in Kupwara it seemed too easy. The woman who had passed her boy to me took him back as we pulled in. I had told her that I was trying to get to Kunan Poshpura. As the women from the bus were met by other children and women she pointed to a couple of taxi jeeps at the edge of the muddy square. I could pay a small fare and pack in with other locals to get to the village. She took the chocolate that I offered, turning it over as though she already knew that there was money pushed into the wrapper, a way of thanking her for the risk she had taken. She held my hand as we said goodbye, only letting go as I began to walk away.

From the road the village looked as any other that sits among the rises and ridges above the Valley, timber-framed houses with simple, strutted verandas and balconies ribbon-spread along the road, and then thinning out into the hills, many of their wooden tiled roofs replaced by corrugated iron. Thin, angled sun had turned them to silver below a line of mist that clung to the mountain above. An innocent would have been charmed. The place was still, the distance between the travelling jeep and the road offering up the image of a pretty place hugging at the knees of the mountains above, the snowline mixing with cloud just above the village.

Once again we were stopped by a group of soldiers, though this time it was a makeshift check-post, several empty petrol barrels rolled across the narrow, pitted bitumen, creating a slalom for any vehicles. Usually taxi jeeps were jammed, often about fourteen bodies piled around and on top of each other, creating a coarse, fuggy intimacy, but it was only the driver and three passengers, a man and his wife beside me, the couple old enough to be my parents. The soldiers made the driver get out and show his ID. Ducking again, I pulled my shawl forward, lifting the end to cover everything but my eyes, the way so many women did, particularly unmarried women, especially now under the constant crude scrutiny of hungry-eyed men with unlimited powers of stop and search. The soldiers did not ask us to get down from the jeep, nor even to see the old man's ID. Their only demand was that we stop beyond the petrol barrels and walk from there into the village. Our driver had to come with us if he wanted to try for any return passengers to Kupwara. The soldiers wanted to count people in and out, on foot; not an official cordon yet, but it was close.

My fellow passengers did not challenge me, speak to me, or even acknowledge me as we walked away from the vehicle. Nor did they seem to mind that I walked close to them as we made our way along the road. They had not even looked closely enough to realise that I was an outsider, unusual in a place where every detail is sucked in during a long, slow perusal.

They had every reason neither to notice nor to care.

A small figure wrapped in a blanket was waiting for them at a *chai* stall on the edge of the village, loud checks of red and purple in defiance of the silent grey atmosphere. He was the couple's grandson. It did not require explanation to realise that this boy's mother had been one of the victims of the night of 22 February. From their brief exchange it seemed that the boy had rung his grandparents in Kupwara, somehow managing to make the call before the lines had been cut during the long night of the crackdown.

It was the boy who wanted to know who I was, the first to ask directly since I had climbed onto the bus at the depot in Srinagar. I have never since felt as stupid and inappropriate as then, standing in the street of Kunan Poshpura wondering what to say to the parents and son of a village woman who had just become another collateral statistic. All I could do was greet them and move off, incongruous and out of place.

As the little family group walked away the boy turned to look back at me. I turned as well, back towards where the jeep had stopped, to see if the driver was still there so that I could call out to him and begin the return journey.

Low, wet cloud veiled part of the village. Like snow it seemed to mask sound. I did not dare call out and turned again to watch the little group in the road ahead. The old man beckoned me above his grandson's head. I followed as they made their way into the village. There were still no questions, no words at all.

It was too soon for a response: from the army, from the victims, even from their families. Everything seemed to be in the slow motion of collision. There seemed to be no afternoon and evening calls to prayer from the small mosque at one end of the main street. If villagers were going to prayer they moved noiselessly through the streets beyond closed doors.

In cold, smoky kitchens there were no questions to be asked. Hands were held, faces touched during long silences. Men seemed absent, the sound of crying usually that of a female relative, not the victim, but someone still able to make sound. Cold stones were settling into the cores of those silent women, sealing off the soft part of them that it would no longer be possible to reach. Some of them were curled up, shivering, regardless of how many blankets had been laid over them to try to smother what had happened. Some squatted on their haunches, rocking back and forth. Most of those I met had not even washed since the attacks, the salty shock of their abuse still smeared on bruised skin and torn clothes.

*

More than eleven years later, towards the end of October 2002, I sat with some of the women of the Dar family: Mohammad's wife Fadia, his next brother Imran's wife Kudji, and Zubeeda, Yusuf's wife. It was before the beginning of Ramadan, a beautiful autumn afternoon, the day dividing into wedges of light that made even mounded rubbish in the streets behind the house seem somehow elegant. But the women of the house were not going to go out into the day. They had settled into the kitchen for a long afternoon of *chai*, snacks and chatter. They had called me in to join them on the raised platform in the kitchen where they always congregated. There were still nine days until Ramadan but they were stocking up. All the wives were heavier than the year before, when I had last seen them, enough to show in their hands and faces in spite of the coveralls of loose *salwar kameez* and *pherans*.

Their world has shrunk. The long afternoons spent on the kitchen platform mark two things: a way of pretending that all is well, that things are normal, even though the to and fro of their lives is almost entirely confined to the family compound.

Kahwa chai was made for me, brewed the way they knew I liked to drink it: the almonds ground to make the green tea cloudy, and without saffron, the expensive, slightly musty taste I do not like. It was poured from a beautiful little silver samovar into a delicate teacup while they drank sweet milky tea in mugs, hands reaching out for each plate of food as it came. The first was of small hard rounds of bread speckled with sesame seeds that were broken up into their *chai*, the liquid sucked in noisily before the soggy bread was slurped down as well. Then there were biscuits, heaped high, and twirled with thin pink icing, or dotted with almonds and cashews. They were dunked into another round of *chai*, as was the honey cake that came at the same time, a thick layer of crushed almonds, coated with honey and baked onto crumbling pastry. Crumbs scattered down *pherans* and onto the carpeted floor of the platform where we sat. The wives were teasing each other about their weight as they reached for more, another plate of chocolate brownies, their favourite, also studded with nuts, thick, dark and moist in the centre.

One of Imran and Kudji's daughters, Saqeena, began to be teased too. She got up and left, clutching her mug and a brownie, eighteen and self-conscious. Her younger sister looked across at me. Sabeena was sixteen then, and about to be engaged to her cousin, one of Mohammad's sons. They had grown up together in the same house, though Omar, Mohammad's son, was then away in England, at the school near Manchester. The other women were laughing as they teased and ate to escape. They waved Sabeena and me off to retrieve Saqeena from her sulk.

'She just wants to be alone, doesn't she?' I asked Sabeena as we climbed up to where the sisters slept.

'Alone, why would she want that?' Sabeena said. 'It is better for her to be with us, then she will not be sad. Alone she will be sad.' She stopped and turned to me. 'You know about Omar, how we are to be married?' she asked.

I did.

She smiled and took my hand. 'This is most exciting, no? Don't you think it is good?' She called up the stairs. 'Saqeena! Come!'

'Will you marry soon? I thought you wanted to study?' These were the overly obvious outsider's questions to the girl layered in the expectations of tradition, old and new, the *burqa* and honey cake.

Sabeena looked up the staircase to see if her sister was on her way down, and then she took hold of the banister, pulling herself in and out. She waited until she was sure that her sister was not coming.

'You know I like to study.' She let go of the banister, dropping down onto a stair just above me. She started to pick flakes of pink varnish from her fingernails. 'I would like to be a lawyer.'

'I know.'

'You have to understand this is not something that can happen here.' She looked up. 'You do understand this thing?'

I nodded.

'When I have said about these things to my father—' She stopped as a door above slammed and her sister came down to join us, heavy-footed, tugging at her *hijab*.

She flopped down onto the stair beside Sabeena.

'Are you talking about me?' Saqeena asked.

'No, about me.' Sabeena poked her. 'How my eyes are pretty.' She pulled her own *hijab* a little further back. 'Look, look now, who has better eyes, Saqeena or me?' She opened her dark chocolate eyes wide and pouted.

Her sister laughed but looked up as well, wide-eyed.

It became an argument, gentle, teasing. They would not accept a tie. I had to choose one. Sabeena kept looking at me to check that I was not going to refer back to our conversation. Saqeena seemed bored by the lack of a result and wandered away to find her youngest cousin, Mohammad and Fadia's baby, a new boy for all the girls to play with. We were alone again on the stairs. Sabeena waited until she heard the door to the kitchen close, several rooms away.

'You must not say any of these things. It is not like with you here in Kashmir. If you are a girl and you want to do something that is different people do not understand.' She began to whisper as the door in the hall below us opened and closed.

Her father Imran greeted us from the foot of the stairs. 'Why here, why sitting here?' he asked.

'We are talking of study,' she replied.

I looked at her, surprised, and then at her father. He was smiling.

'See my daughter, see how good she is in study. You know she is helping to teach other younger girls in studies of the Qur'an at the school we have for girls nearby.' He waved me down the stairs. 'Come, come and drink a cup of tea with me.'

We both got up.

'What is it that I am allowed to study now?' Sabeena asked her father as he turned towards the door next to the kitchen, to where the men gathered to eat, separate from the gathering of women.

As he opened the door he looked back. 'Kitchen,' he said. 'This is a good subject for study now.' He smiled at his daughter.

Sabeena looked back at me and shrugged. Imran was watching us.

'What else is safe for our girls to study at this time?' he asked.

He did not wait for a reply as he closed the door quietly to the room beside the kitchen.

There is no single casualty of war, no one noun that sums up all that has been lost, but education is one of the first to go, and more specifically in most cases, female education. At the time of Indian independence in 1947 there was little choice of higher education for women in Kashmir. If they wanted to learn more there was only the choice of male colleges. Few applied, and almost all of them were 'outsiders', the daughters of bureaucrats and businessmen working in the Valley. It would have been unthinkable for a traditional Kashimiri girl, either Muslim or Pandit, to apply. It was not felt to be respectable. And then in 1950 a woman, Mahmuda Ahmad Ali Shah, a Kashmiri Muslim, became the first female head of a women's college in Srinagar. It was a cultural revolution of its kind, a wild, exultant manifestation of progress in a time of hope. The first girls into the college had barely studied the history of their homeland and suddenly they found themselves performing plays about their own history, written by their professors in English, with songs in Urdu and Kashmiri. At the same time they were rehearsing the plays of the literary Bengali giant, Rabindranath Tagore, translated into English and Kashmiri, of Bernard Shaw in English, of Molière translated into Urdu. Many of the students became the first generation of Kashmiri Muslim literates in their families. They carried the banner on to become the first Kashmiri women to enter professional life as lawyers, doctors, teachers, hoteliers, journalists, policewomen. Across more than twenty years the landscape of possibility for women stretched wide.

At the Government College for Women on Maulana Azad Road in Srinagar, progress and integration felt one and the same. The girls wore their identical uniforms of a beige *kurta* tunic, white *salwar* and white *dupatta* shawl with pride. The Muslim girls enjoyed wearing saris and winding flowers into their hair for the Tagore characters in plays, and all of them acted the male roles, teasing each other as they slipped into Western costume to play the greats of Shakespeare and Bernard Shaw.

The pace of change was so rapid that there was not even

time for an organised feminist movement to form. Within less than a generation the women of Kashmir seemed to have come out of *purdah* and into every field, from higher education to the high court. Girls whose older sisters had simply had no choice but to stop at secondary school level suddenly found themselves in the campus environment, free to move around without a male relative, and allowed to march beside their male peer group in the uniform of the cadet corps of the state. They were being exposed to visiting speakers such as the Welsh socialist and father of the National Health, Aneurin Bevan, Nobel economist in waiting, Amartya Sen, and poetic champion of social injustice, Stephen Spender. The pace of change was such that those living through it, their possibilities expanding all the time, never imagined any other way of being. Why would it change? A place once thought of by the rest of the country as being an educationally backward state was producing students from non-fee-paying government colleges who could compete with the best that the country had to offer, even against those from the most elite male schools and colleges.

As the Central Government of India continued to invest heavily in education in the state, hoping to nurture Kashmiri loyalty, the college girls of Srinagar produced better and better results. The Valley was held up as a great success story of female emancipation and education in independent, post-colonial India.

And then in late 1989, as the wall came down in Berlin, leaflets were thrown over the walls of all the schools and colleges in Srinagar. More than anywhere else they were hurled over the walls of the Government College for Women on Maulana Azad Road. The leaflets were very clear in their message. In order to avoid 'unnecessary harassment' Muslim students had to wear the full *burqa*, and Hindu girls the *bindi*, the forehead mark, even though it was traditionally only for married women, the symbol of the wedding vows taken.

For the first time in Kashmir the *burqa* and the *bindi* became weapons of communal division in the hands of the militants.

The girls at the college said they would ignore the threat, even when a rumour buzzed around the campus that a man had been posted outside the college gates with a big stick to beat any girls who did not follow the diktats of the leaflets. Many of the staff were proud of the girls and their defiance.

It was a defiance that would be forced to fade. During the winter break the threats of the leaflets came not with a stick, but at the end of a gun. When the college reopened in March 1990 almost all the Pandit students had gone, many of the teachers too. The campus was draped in black, every girl covered from crown to toe.

As the city's tailors bent over unending lengths of slippery synthetic black polyester, forced on them for the mass-making of *burqas*, sometimes at gunpoint, schools and colleges were burned to the ground. Lovingly collected libraries and carefully built laboratories, school and college auditoria were firebombed.

A few, a very few, girls wore the new uniform with conviction. Those who did became zealous, parroting the language of the leaflets, and the loudspeakers at the mosques. They did not stay much longer at their schools or colleges, institutions that they claimed were representative of Indian hegemony in the Valley, the same institutions that had been teaching them the freedoms of education and expression they were unlikely to experience again. Their teachers and principals tried to talk to them, but the feverish pitch of the time did not allow for reasoned argument or dialogue.

Some of them left to join Dukhtaran-e-Millat, the Daughters of Faith, sometimes translated as Daughters of the Nation or of the Community. This was a group that had first hit the headlines when its leader, Asiya Andrabi, led a rally in Srinagar in 1987 against the 'pornography of film posters', defacing the familiar hand-painted posters of full-lipped, -hipped and -breasted actresses in wind-whipped saris. This veiled group became the vociferous supporters and messengers of some of the militant groups, easy donkeys beneath their *burqas*, able to gun-run, deliver packages to addresses, and letter bombs to offices that were Indian owned or funded.

Andrabi is still the leader of Dukhtaran-e-Millat. She speaks well, and she gives powerful copy for reporters, her speeches made potent by their delivery from behind the veil. She offers *kahwa chai*, tea, coffee and pastries to journalists who have been led, sometimes blindfolded, through winding streets, double-backing in echoing dead-ends to add to the confusion, in order to reach another secret press conference location. Andrabi presents herself elegantly, in fluent English from behind the *burqa*, her easy delivery and diminutive height often lulling the gathered journalists into believing that she really cannot be as hardline as previously reported. Her agenda clearly champions Osama bin Laden, al-Qa'eda, the Taliban, the 'success of the attacks at the heart of corrupt America' on September 11 2001. She has poured hatred on the Pandits of the Valley, and she has been accused of throwing acid into the faces of her fellow Kashmiri women, quite literally.

'I don't believe in *Kashmiriyat*. I don't believe in nationalism. I believe there are just two nations – Muslims and non-Muslims,' she claimed in an interview after having lain low because of her espousal of acid-throwing. There was a series of warrants out for her arrest.

She had reason to stay out of the media limelight as well. Since the beginning of the insurgency, and the arrival of the Daughters of the Faith onto the conflict landscape, Andrabi has remained constant in her extremism. Her cadres had been attacking women who were not covered from the earliest stage of the insurgency. When other militant groups did the same she was public in her support and applause for their action.

Yet Andrabi had been a college girl herself, her results in biochemistry, bacteriology and diet therapy the highest in her class. She wanted to continue her studies and to become a scientist, but even though her father was himself a doctor it was made clear to Andrabi that she would not be allowed to continue her education. Once she understood this limitation the eighteen-year-old shut herself away and began reading about Islamic female revolutionaries. In 1981, still a teenager, Andrabi formed Dukhtaran-e-Millat and she began to preach to other women the ways of *jihad*. She demanded that her father marry her to a *mujahid*, a *jihadi*, and she only met her husband, a well-known member of a militant group, on their wedding day. She encouraged, even pushed, her husband into marrying again, and again, these other wives being widows of *jihadis* killed in the Valley.

'I would be more than glad to share my house with other wives of Qasim [her husband],' she has told journalists, while explaining how far she is prepared to go in order to stop the 'dehumanising act of dowry'.

She abhors the tradition that demands even the poorest family of a bride produce goods and money for a potential bridegroom and his relatives. One of her ways of boycotting dowry has been to force poor women to marry *mujahideen* fighters, in much the same way as she pushed her husband into taking more wives. Many Kashmiri women have applauded this part of Andrabi's activism and action, and it has meant that some of them have chosen to ignore her extremism and support her because of her stance against dowry.

She says that she formed the Daughters of Faith to fight for the rights given to women by Islam, but she then confuses many of those who watch her by insisting that 'women look after the kitchen and men are supposed to work' while she herself makes speeches, leads rallies, and trains her cadres to use the *burqa* as a garment of *jihad*.

Imran's daughter, Sabeena, like many who have found that they had certain sympathies with Andrabi, has also been confused by some of her apparently contradictory behaviour. But Sabeena, like her sisters and her other female cousins, has also been sheltered from much of what Andrabi and the Daughters of Faith have been doing, just as they were shielded from the reports of atrocities in villages such as Kunan Poshpura.

Sometimes, when I am with them, they will ask me to confirm rumours that they have heard. In the case of the raped village they had been given a strange, mangled version that had reached them via the *dhoban*, the laundrywoman, who had heard it from a fishwife on a stall at the Friday market who had a cousin married to someone who lived in Kupwara, where the bus had stopped on my journey to the village. The Dar girls had heard that terrible things had happened to the women there, that their heads had been chopped off and thrown into the village *nalas*, drainage channels, to be eaten by dogs. This version was even regarded by some as a better fate than rape.

In 1991 many of the women of Kunan Poshpura said they would have preferred death, and many still say the same thing today, so long after the attack on the village that the 300-page report claimed never happened. Still the girls of the village remain unmarried. It is said that there has not been a wedding in Kunan Poshpura since February 1991.

And Andrabi is insistent that she has never carried arms. She will argue at length with journalists who challenge her on the subject, even though there have been many reports of Dukhtaran-e-Millat and gun-running beneath the *burqa*.

The Dar girls challenge me about the rumours, asking about one, and then another. It puts me in the position of being either an informer, and so disloyal to the four brothers, or the reverse, misinforming and remaining loyal to the Dar men and their lengthy efforts to shield their women from the stark truths of the conflict. These are truths that often the men themselves have turned away from, closing their ears both metaphorically and physically to what has been happening beyond the walls of their house and garden beside the lake.

Sometimes I can dodge the questions, answering the girls indirectly by telling them other stories, tales of herders up in the hills who were so tired of the militant and military skirmishes and stand-offs, the fighting over their grazing pastures and along their herding routes, that they would set booby traps, deep ditches feathered with spiked bushes. They would ignore the cries of anyone who fell in and tend to their flocks, sometimes stuffing sheep or goat wool in their ears if the hollering got too loud.

The girls laugh and usually the stories are enough to distract them from the original questions, but however high the walls have been built around the house and garden, they could never be high enough.

Chapter Seven

NO WALL THAT HIGH

THE BROTHERS WERE born in a *donga* boat, one of the plain wooden ones that are moored along the canals, and beside the much larger and ornately carved houseboats. These simpler boats are just great planks of cedar stapled together. They are purely functional but they have a low, seasoned loveliness of their own.

Many of the houseboat families used to live on them before the tourist industry provided them with the means to buy land above the lakes, and to build solid houses, with brick walls, and thick floors that did not rock in the night when the wind blew.

As families prospered and moved onto dry land an increasing number of *donga* boats changed from homes to service vessels for the houseboats, floating kitchens and dormitories for the staff who looked after the guests.

The biggest tourist season in Kashmir was 1989, with the highest figures up to that date. That year, 80,000 foreign tourists were recorded as having come to the lakes. There were 1,200 registered houseboats to choose from, probably more, as a careful bribe could circumnavigate the need for official registration. Domestic tourism figures were higher still. Business was booming, and even though the message from the streets was bad and the death toll no longer random but mounting, the sheer volume of paying tourists made for a fool's paradise until the main season ended in October of that year.

By the following spring, when the colleges opened to a sea of *burqas*, and the Pandits had fled, so too had the tourists. As the economy sank so too did the *donga* boats. Most houseboat families lost their entire source of income and the upkeep of the boats was no longer something they could afford.

A well maintained *donga* or a houseboat has a life expectancy roughly the same as those who own them. In the good times it is a leisurely spread of sixty to seventy years. In the bad times both boats and men face a sharply curtailed run.

The Dars did well though, travelling far outside the Valley in order to sell their carpets and handicrafts beyond the effects of the conflict. While others watched their businesses fade to nothing the Dars kept travelling, and selling, and so they were able to keep their boats in good condition in the hope of a time when the fighting would end and the tourists return. They built a new home on the land that their father, Sobra, had bought above the lake. As the insurgency began to seep into every area of life in the Valley the Dars came together in the new house and lived as a joint family with Sobra and his brother, their children, and increasingly their grandchildren.

By the mid-1990s it was a still growing family of twenty-five, excluding the men who worked for them. Even though more than half of that number was male there were often times when there were only a couple of adult men staying in the house with all the women. The others were scattered and travelling, in Delhi, Goa, Singapore, Thailand, Dubai, London and beyond, keeping the sales going, and the *dongas*, houseboats and their families afloat.

During the same period, starting from the early 1990s, Pakistan withdrew its support from the local Kashmir-for-Kashmiris separatist groups in the Valley. It put its weight, arms supplies and training behind the pro-Pakistan militant groups instead. With the cut-off of funding, weapons and training, the separatist groups had to find funding and supplies from elsewhere. They became inland pirates, hijacking such things as the timber industry so that they could extort 'protection' money from timber merchants and their customers alike.

From the outset of the insurgency in 1989 the crackdown by the Indian security forces made no attempt to disguise itself as anything other than a campaign to wipe out all the militants, and anyone who sheltered, fed, clothed or associated with them. The man appointed to oversee the crackdown, Governor Jagmohan, saw the extinction of the militants as the only way. He held the post for a brief six months but during that time he managed to turn the people on the streets from idealistic dreamers of freedom into a united front that despised India with the intensity only possible among the mortally aggrieved and mourning. The separatist groups harnessed this hate and so made the assumption that the people would be with them wholly and unquestioningly. As their supply lines from Pakistan dried up they turned on their own people, using them as a resource, unswerving in their belief that their own people would always be behind them, that their loathing of India outstripped all else.

During the same period, particularly in 1994, the world's media focused on the ideological and territorial war in Bosnia: Serbs and Bosnians, Christians versus Muslims. It was a brutal year in Kashmir too. The attacks by militant groups on the Indian security forces reached their highest level, and the fatalities inflicted by the security forces on the militants peaked at the same time. It was also the year of the greatest number of deaths among ordinary citizens caught in the crossfire and the crackdowns, the most dangerous to date for those just walking the streets of their city, trying to lead their lives. It marked the worst point for the amount of money looted by militant groups from businesses.

It was also one that reached a low point for international coverage of Kashmir's situation.

When high summer makes the plains below unbearable and unbreathable the Valley bottom also sinks into lethargy. The months leading to the July monsoon sit torpid in the heat haze. These people of the Himalayan garden do not enjoy either the harsh cut of mid-winter or the weight of summer. During the hot months everything slows, and when there were no more tourists to look after and sell to, it was as though the whole Valley stalled, nothing doing, except for those employed by either side of the insurgency.

Sobra Dar's nephew Arshad was a boy at that time. He is a young man now, the one who was at school across the lake, near the paramilitary camp. His school was more often closed than open during the worst years of the insurgency, and his ability to study was paralysed by fear.

Arshad comes to see me often, clasping books and notes from the English classes that he goes to now.

One time when he came to see me recently he was looking for a very particular word.

'You have to help me. My teacher has asked me to ask you, what is it when someone cannot feel so strongly about a thing?' he asked.

We tried 'unmotivated', 'bored'.

'No, that's not it. Say my friends all go off to fight with the militants and when they are talking about it before going they are excited, shouting, full of anger and things, but I cannot feel these things?'

We tried again: 'pacifist', 'dispassionate', 'apolitical'.

'There is a word in Urdu for it but we cannot find a translation. Not even my teacher and he is too good. You have to find one.' Arshad turned the book around and showed me the word on the page.

I stared at its graceful curls.

'Fearful?'

'No, it is not fear. We use it a lot to do with our women. Say I have a very pretty girlfriend and lots of men are flirting with her, and I am not doing anything about it, my friends will ask me why I am like this word.'

'"Ambivalent", "unmoved"?'

'No, no, not these either,' Arshad said, flipping his mobile phone over and over in his hand.

He looked away across the lake and began to talk of a hot night, during the summer of 1994, when all the men were away from the Dars' house, except for one of the four brothers' uncles, Arshad's father, and the youngest of the brothers, Yusuf. It was late, sometime just after midnight. Every house had the windows wide open, but only those above the first floor. Any entrance that could be reached from the ground was no longer safe. This in itself was a new sorrow for a people who had worked on a system of trust and unlocked doors for most of their lives. Some who could not sleep in the heat still went up to the open top storeys of their homes, hoping to catch any movement of air among the spread of drying early summer vegetables and pickle jars. But most people were no longer prepared to risk unprotected exposure any more.

When the banging started on the Dars' front door it woke the whole household. It was a loud battering that must have woken the rest of the street as well. The two men of the house, uncle and nephew, met on one of the landings. They knew they would have to answer the door because it would be broken down if they did not. They also hoped that if they left it a little longer it would give the police time to come, that neighbours would go for help, that someone would respond.

'The noise at the door was as though the whole of the house was being knocked down. I do not remember clearly but I think my father went to open the door. He told us to stay where we were, me and my cousins, not to move from the room. I remember him saying as he went that he could not understand how they had come to get in. The gate at the back of the house was locked and the walls were high.'

At the time Arshad was sharing a room at the top of the house with Mohammad's two older sons, and with his father.

'They came in and just broke everything, and what they did not break they took away with them.' Arshad stopped for a moment, his fingers pushing in and out of the carved flowers of the veranda.'It went on and on….' The sentence drifted again. 'There were many of them. I do not know the number, maybe twelve, twenty. I could not count them. There was nothing that could tell us what they were. They had uniforms but not of a kind we recognised. We all knew the police, and all the army, and other kinds of uniforms by that time. It was a uniform, just not one that we knew, and they had black masks. They were Kashmiris, this thing we knew. I was too small to be able to understand these things, but my father knew.' He paused.

The attack carried on through the night, until dawn; every

room was ransacked, everyone beaten, even the youngest children.

'I tried to get myself under the bed but one of them pulled me out. They were shouting at all of us, all the time, just shouting and beating us. This man who had taken hold of me dragged me to the window. It was open. He screamed at me that he would throw me out of it, just throw me out if I did not tell him where more things were for them to take.

'It went on for so much time and then my father started to read from the Qur'an, and asking these men to listen. Even while they were still beating us and wrecking our home he was reading out the Qur'an. Imagine this thing?' He looked away, staring at something intently. 'Somehow I had climbed back under the bed by this time. I don't remember how it was, I don't remember when the man let go of me, the one who was screaming that he would throw me out of the window. I could hear my mother crying, all the women were crying.' He took a long, slow breath.

We sat for a while, silent beside the water until Arshad began to speak again.

'At one point they went out of the room and my father was saying that we must let them have everything, all that they asked for, that money would come back, even if they took everything we owned we could find a way to make it again, but our lives, those we could not make again even if we had *crores* and *crores* [tens of millions] of rupees.' He paused as the boat shifted, leaning out so that he could see along the length of the houseboat beyond the veranda. 'No one coming,' he said. 'They were firing their guns, all the time, in every place they went, every room of the house. At that time I did not think of this thing because I was small but my father, he was praying and reading, and saying to them to take whatever they wanted because with so much of noise, with all the shooting, he knew that someone would come, the police, army, someone would come soon.' He stopped again.

'No one came. For all the noise, the shooting, the hours and hours that passed, not one person came; not one policeman, no army, no neighbour.

'And my father just went on praying and reading. Each time they shouted to him to get more things for them, he would tell them where to find something more, another bag in a cupboard that had a little money, some small thing. You know they left the biggest thing of all, a cheque that just fell out of one bag even while they were shaking what they could find from it. They did not even look to see what it was. It was for an amount bigger than all the other money they found. I think it was the very last bag of all, when there was no other place for them to look. Every *almirah*, cupboard, that was locked had been shot open and emptied out. They did not even bother to look and see what that last piece of paper might be. And this is the thing I remember so well, they said to my father then, "You are lucky, you are free to go now."'

We sat in silence. There was nothing to say.

'Hello, hello.' There was a voice from the steps of the veranda, beyond the low gate down to the water. 'The sun is setting, the time is good to shop.' The leather and suede man's head popped up over the gate.

It had been his *shikara* against the steps that had nudged the boat. He looked at Arshad.

'*As-Salaamu Alaikum.*'

'*Wa-Alaikum As-Salaam*,' they greeted each other.

Arshad nodded curtly but he did not order the leather man away.

'I have the socks you asked me for,' said the salesman. 'You will see them now?'

I had already turned him away once that day. I looked at Arshad but again he was staring out over the lake, his phone in his hand.

'Of course, yes, the socks,' I replied.

He had brought the suede bootees I was after, the ones that the four brothers and their father wore, making their feet so small, neat and warm through the Kashmiri winter.

'Hey, Chotu,' the leather man called back down to the *shikara*.

A boy of about twelve came up the steps with a large wicker basket.

'No talk of school.' The leather man raised his hand, ready for my standard question about the rota of young cousins he had working for him. 'See the time, it is now long past school end.' He tapped his watch.

Chotu, Little One, said that school was fine when I asked, his face well hidden behind the basket he was carrying.

Arshad turned back from the lake. 'You have to go,' he said to the boy. 'Look, see how much older I am to you, and see this, still a school book. I missed too much of school. You must study now.'

As the leather man took the basket from the boy, Arshad waved him over. 'Look, still basic stuff, still learning English.'

The boy stared at him. Arshad repeated what he had said in Kashmiri, telling the leather man off as he finished.

'His English is not so good, by class six he should have completed, all his studies should be in English by this stage.' He flipped the front of his phone, his focus on the screen.

'See these, just the size you asked for.' The leather man had already managed to lay out two rows of bootees in a wide array of sizes.

'It was just size five,' I said, picking up a pair of the funny little zip-up suede sockettes.

'Yes, you have them in your hand, but you know how good they are so maybe some for your family, for your father, some of your friends?'

'I'm not sure.' I picked up a larger pair, trying to imagine my father in a pair of suede bootees, in fact anyone I knew over the age of two.

Maqbool came with tea as the leather man laid out more rows, and Chotu was sent to get another basket: cashmere jerseys, mounds of them. Arshad went through them, checking each one, separating them into two heaps on either side of him, blue on yellow on pink on fudge, the colours mounded up into messy heaps as he threw them to one side or other.

'See this side, these have problems, some buttons missing, or marks on them, do not sell these here,' he said to the leather man in Kashmiri. 'This side, these are okay to sell.' He pushed the pile at the boy who began to refold them, sliding each one carefully back into its plastic bag.

The leather man nodded without complaint and the reject pile was pushed to the back of the veranda while the bootee trade continued. Maqbool stood watching over the transaction as Arshad bargained on my behalf, bartering the leather man down far lower than I would have dared to go.

The leather man smiled over the money that was passed to him as Chotu re-packed the wicker baskets. Arshad and Maqbool seemed to approve of the final price paid. My feet were warm in brown suede bootees, and two cashmere cardigans sat neatly folded and bagged beside me. Tea was cleared as the leather man pushed away from the steps and Chotu bent over his heart-shaped paddle.

'Good time to you at school,' I called after him in mismatched Kashmiri.

The boy lifted one hand from his paddle without looking back, and the leather man laughed.

Arshad's mobile rang. He looked at the number flashing and got up to leave as he answered, one hand raised to Maqbool and me as he climbed out onto the running boards.

'He was here for some time. You do not mind?' Maqbool asked as Arshad walked away.

'Not at all.'

Maqbool watched closely as I collected up the cardigans and bootees.

'The problems have been hard for him,' he said.

'For all of you,' I replied.

He leaned back against one of the main carved struts of the veranda, his posture for settling in to chat.

'He was telling me about the attack,' I said.

'Which one?'

'The one on the family, when all the other men were away except for his father and Yusuf.'

'This was a very bad thing.' Maqbool shook his head.

'How old was he?' I asked.

'It was quite some time ago, maybe ten, fifteen years. He was a small, small boy still, small enough to hide under the bed.'

'Yes, he told me.'

'Maybe eight, nine years.'

Time and age are vague here; even when a moment in time is brutal, still the exact detail gets blurred. It took a long time to pinpoint more closely the date of the attack, the vagueness a form of escape, of remove from the events of that night. It is a common trait among so many of those brutalised during the conflict.

A report made both of us duck, Maqbool squatting low as gunfire from a few boats down rolled back across the lake again in rumbling echo off the mountains. We looked at each other, breath held. Gunfire is a difficult sound in the Valley.

It was just two shots, a double barrel, and then some shouting.

'They are killing birds,' Maqbool said, raising himself from his knees.

We both looked out over the lake. A pond heron, or paddy bird, floated some way out from the boat, its brown speckled plumage puffed, its head submerged.

Two boys, young men, about the same age as Arshad, were crouching on the roof of the houseboat three down, hidden from the birds by the boat's name board. One of them was reloading a shotgun. A third was pushing out from the houseboat in a bright orange pedalo, churning across to the dead heron. He leaned over to collect the bird and draped it on the front of the pedalo.

'Why herons, why are they shooting them?' I asked Maqbool.

He shrugged and turned away to adjust the woolly hat he was wearing over his white *topi*.

'Don't you want to scream at them, tell them not to shoot here, not now? And why herons, pigeons would be understandable, but why herons? Can't you ask them to stop?' I asked.

'They are Dar cousins, it is their boat, I cannot tell them what they cannot do.' He was still turned away, his voice distressed.

He went back into the houseboat as one of the boys stood up to take another shot. I had to follow him.

No one had gone to the Dars' house when the place was being ransacked and shot up by looting militants, and no one tells young men not to shoot protected birdlife on a lake surrounded by families shattered by two decades of gunfire. There is so little confidence now, beaten down by twenty years of conflict, that almost everyone turns away, lowers their eyes and keeps their mouth shut.

At supper that night Maqbool took up another of his talking positions, this time in the corner of the dining room, his back against the dresser, where the corner of one of its octagonally fretted shelves fits perfectly into his stiff right shoulder. He works it like a horse, digging the shelf edge further and further into his aching muscles as he talks. Across the years in this dining room we have moved around variations of the same theme: the conflict. We had to start talking, otherwise it meant that Maqbool would just stand watching as I slurped soup down my shawl, or chewed on *papads* (poppadums), the only other sound the slow creak of the dresser as he worked it into his shoulder.

Every family in the Valley has been marked. Maqbool has had his share.

He had just brought in the usual supper, soup and *papads*. We had slid into the same winter routine without anyone having to ask or tell. He presented the soup, took up his position, whipped off his bobble hat, and adjusted the *topi* underneath.

'My cousin-brother, son to my uncle, he is maybe five, ten years younger to me. That was a big problem. He was saying that he was going to the militants, and he was taking others with him, going to Pakistan for training. He was telling everyone. And my family were too much afraid, all the time fearful that the army would know and come bashing at the door, and that they would take everyone, not just my cousin-brother, but all of us men.'

He looked across and checked my bowl. 'More soup?'

'No, thank you.'

'It was getting so bad. But somehow we managed to keep him in the house, and someone would stay with him, talking all the time, talking, just talking. And slowly, slowly, maybe the anger he had came out in all of the talking, and he became more calm. Slowly, slowly he found that he was not so full of anger and that it would not be a good idea to go with the militants.'

'Was there any particular thing that changed his mind?' I asked.

Maqbool thought for a moment; his mobile buzzed in his pocket, he answered, shouting into the phone a bit in his excited way, and then he put on his woollen hat again. 'I have to go and help in the kitchen. I will be coming back in small, small time.'

In some families it can almost seem an inherited gene, the hurt, frustration and anger passed from one generation to the next, but it is more collective in nature. Maqbool is in his fifties now. His generation were the first to take up arms when the insurgency began, the separatist dream their fuel. Their children inherited the damage of those early years, the fighting, crackdowns, intimidation, curfews, their fathers, brothers and cousins taken during searches, many never to return. The anger was passed on with no economic buffer to soften it. There were no new jobs for the next generation to go into. Militancy was the main employer through the 1990s. The Jammu and Kashmir Police recruited from the local people too, but it was not a job that most wanted, almost to be part of the great booted occupying force as it was seen – unpatriotic to many, un-Kashmiri.

Maqbool's sons are still teenagers but they have inherited the collective damage. They have known only the conflict during their lives. They have no reason to believe that things really will get better and so they respond with anger, or lethargy, and often a combination of the two.

'Why should we study, why should we bother to try and find any work? What future is there for us?' they ask, the fuel of teenage angst adding sharp edges to their anger.

'This is one of those failures of understanding,' the local journalist friend had said as we sat in the old coffee house, looking out over Lal Chowk in November 1999.

It was when we had just witnessed the enlisting of a boy, the one across the road from where we were sitting, who had been picked on by two other boys, and who had then been befriended by a recruiter.

'So many people, so much of the foreign press, have come up with this theory that all these boys are going off because they have a burning desire to be Allah's warriors, to fight *jihad*, to get their seventy-two virgins. That, what you just saw, that is the main reason, all the confusing stuff of being that age combined with a sense that there is no future for them, so why not pick up the gun and get it done with if there is nothing to look forward to?' he had said. 'And the seventy-two virgins, the houris, you have to be messed up already if they are what makes you do it. They're supposed to be twenty-seven metres high, transparent, hairless; it somehow makes them sound like terrifying, intact, inflatable dolls, no? It doesn't even say how many there are in the Qur'an, or whether they are male or female, and they are not promised just to martyrs but to all Muslims. It's only some of the crazier commentators who go on about the wonderful sex they're all going to have. I think I'd want my money back if I'd been sold that idea and had a bullet coming for me, or was about to set off some device strapped to my chest.'

We sat and talked for a long time, though I did not know enough of Hadith (the sayings and traditions of the life of Muhammad), or the Qur'anic commentaries to be able to argue the lure of the houris. Whatever the rational arguments, in a time of fear and insecurity, I could see that the pure, ever virginal, voluptuous breasts that were promised by some of the commentators and recruiters would be potent to boys and young men struggling to get from day to day in a place that seemed to them to be without hope, or any kind of future other than the depressing round in which they felt themselves to be trapped.

I have watched across the years as those boys and barely men have been recruited, from the streets, markets, mosques and even from cafés, the recruiters changing and adapting their methods all the time.

When Café Arabica on Maulana Azad opened in 2002 it became a sanctuary for many, a sign that things were improving because the owner-managers, a Pandit hotelier family, had been forced to shut up their big hotel, the Broadway, in 1990. They reopened the hotel in 1999, and the café then followed three years later. It is one of the few places in the city where people feel they can go, drink coffee, eat cake and pastries and just forget for a while. The owners' greatest fear was that it would be firebombed, that militants would see it as a manifestation of all that they hated: influences from outside the Valley, a place where men and women socialised equally, and where music played. But enough locals from the wealthier sections of the city, people from respected families, and men who had been sympathetic to the militants' cause over the years, became regulars, providing the café with a security of its own. Though for all its modernity, the protection of its regulars, and its proximity to a large police base, the café was not beyond the reach of the recruiters.

In the later stages of the insurgency the militants added a new method of attack to their repertoire, what the security forces call 'the one-off agent'. They tapped the ennui, frustration and confusion of the next generation of teenage boys. This was not new, but the social sector they targeted was the educated and more privileged, those who gathered at Café Arabica.

An army officer explained the method when I asked him why some of these boys from relatively privileged backgrounds were being hauled in for questioning and arrest.

'The militant recruiters are clever. It is so much harder for us to track down someone who just makes one hit. They have their smarter agents now, clean-shaven, good English speakers, quite neatly dressed. They stake out places like the café and Lal Chowk during the busy shopping times in the evening and on Saturdays. They watch groups of friends and then focus on one boy and girl who are maybe flirting a little. If the boy and girl start to spend time together, they will keep watching, waiting until something happens, the girl upsetting the boy, or breaking up with him. This is the time when they approach the boy. They'll chit-chat, be sympathetic, and offer him a few thousand bucks [rupees] just to fling a grenade into a paramilitary post or bunker somewhere in the city. It's pretty hard for us to catch them, and those who turn down the offer are too frightened to tell the police about it in case of reprisal, or in case the police decide to take them in for questioning.'

I asked whether there might be other reasons why they would not tell, that perhaps they admired the militants and sympathised with them.

The officer thought for a while before replying.

'We realise that this is the case, and so we have to find ways of making the young see that this cycle of violence will only bring more, that violence breeds violence. We have to make them understand that the cycle has to be broken.'

I asked how this idea sat with the cycle of violence perpetuated by the security forces in the Valley across the arc of the conflict.

'Each period of a conflict requires different procedure. We learn and we adapt. As the militancy changed tactics, so did we, and now that another time of change is here we have to work with the people as extensively as we can.'

And how could the single-act-agent method be addressed?

The officer looked down. 'My own son was angry about these kinds of emotional issues when he was at that age, all those difficulties of trying to grow up. How can we know how even our own child would be if someone offers them an outlet of violence when they feel hurt, shamed, humiliated, especially if this thing happened in front of their friends? How well would we have done ourselves?' He looked at me and apologised. 'Of course not you, I am sorry, this was not meant in that way.'

It was a kind human gesture in a place where so often they are left out.

'This is not about belief, about Allah, or a set of religious principles that a teenage boy holds up above all else. This is the simple harnessing of a resource for violence. It is not a courageous act. This is how I see it: how we can stop them, by making it clear to them that there is nothing brave in this, nothing to inspire others, and that Kashmir will not be able to change if this is how they act.'

Would the army be in favour of a movement of truth and reconciliation, I asked him, sometime in the future, after enough time had passed?

'As they did in South Africa?' he asked.

'Yes.'

'It is the most human way. Things done on all sides can sit in people's hearts for a long time, years, even a generation, and it can trigger violence again. There has been progress here, you have seen how much has changed in the past few years, that things are getting better, but how does that saying go: "There is many a slip twixt cup and lip"? I am not sure that people here will be strong enough for truth and reconciliation for many years to come. A lot of courage is needed to speak the truth, and to face it. I think that it will take quite some time for people to have that courage here, don't you think?'

In the dining room on the houseboat I sat in front of half a bowl of cold soup, waiting for the sound of Maqbool. His 'small, small time' in the kitchen had become a bigger time, but he did come back, singing as he came, a plate of blackened *papad* in his hand. He padded about the dining room and the small galley kitchen next door, in mild dudgeon that I had not finished the soup, and had let it get cold. As he pottered about I asked him again if there had been any one particular thing that had made his cousin change his mind about joining the militants in the early years of the insurgency. He put a fresh bowl of soup in front of me and returned to his scratching post, woolly hat back on.

'I was thinking on this while I was outside, and for some time I could not remember, but then I did. It was my father, a story my father told to him. Some time back, many years it was, in the time of Zia-ul-Haq [the military dictator of Pakistan from 1977 to 1988], a cousin of our family came to see us from Azad side (Pakistan-controlled Kashmir). There was a short amount of time when they allowed that, I cannot remember in what year, but that was when he came. And he was staying with us in our house, and spending time again with his family here, and there was much celebrating. We were so happy to see him. I had not known him and he was from my mother's side, but my father was knowing him as well, and they were close for some time, but they had not seen each other for so many years, not since the invasion [the Pathan invasion of Kashmir in 1947 that led to the division of Kashmir between Pakistan and India]. And we were taking him around the city and all the places to show him things. He enjoyed it very much but he also seemed most confused by one thing. And he kept saying to my father, "Why is it that you do not have guns here, how can you move about without a gun? In my village now if I do not have a gun I am not a man, I cannot go out of my house without a gun. You have no guns here, you have paradise."

'It was this story that my father was telling again to my cousin-brother, and saying to him, "You see, we have been destroying our paradise, every gun that is picked up, every bullet fired, is killing our paradise."'

'What happened to the cousin who came from Azad?' I asked.

'He had to go back, he was being followed by the CID [the Crime Investigation Department] more and more and so he went back.'

'Do you know what happened to him after that?'

Maqbool shrugged. 'It was what, more than thirty years ago. He must be dead by this time.'

'And your younger cousin-brother who wanted to be a militant, what about him?'

'He has a small tea shop now. He found a wife, things were coming okay, okay with him. There were some more problems, we had to keep him in the house for some time longer, but slowly, slowly it was all coming right. He has sons now, his tea shop is good.'

Maqbool took the soup bowl away, and padded back out into the cold night.

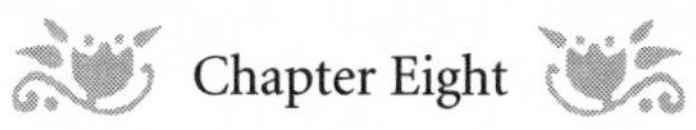

Chapter Eight

THE SINS OF THE FATHER, AND THE SON

OF COURSE MOHAMMAD decided to send his children to study outside the Valley. Almost everyone who could afford to get their children away from the state for schooling did so. Some were too afraid, having been warned off by the militants, and so their children went through years of chequered schooling, unsure each day if their schools would be open, their teachers there, whether militants might attack the girls, or the security forces harangue the boys.

Some children did not make it out of the Valley for education abroad even if places had been found in schools, and the fees met. They fell down on the visa application. The high commissions and embassies in Delhi were flooded with visa applications from Kashmir. It presented them with a constant moral and security dilemma as to how to assist and support the human tragedy of what was happening in the Valley, while being sensitive to the security requirements of their host country, India.

After September 11 2001 security became a larger issue again with the spotlight turning on male students from Islamic countries travelling to study at orthodox schools around the world. Indoctrination was not confined to the often-quoted and also misquoted *madrasah* schools of Pakistan, Afghanistan and Kashmir. Wherever there were people parading as teachers, but fuelled by a mission for *jihad*, there was indoctrination, whether it was in an apparently innocuous suburb of London or Manchester, or in a remote corner of Azad (Pakistan-controlled Kashmir). In many cases the schools were just traditional ones, following a *madrasah* practice of a syllabus split between *hifz*, the study and memorisation of the Qur'an, and *'alim*, a broader term encompassing all study that will lead the student towards being a scholar within his community.

As these schools are gathering places for boys and young men pursuing an Islamic-based education, they present themselves as easy targets for *jihadi* recruiters. In some cases the recruiting is from the inside, a student or teacher who is already part of a *jihadi* group and so uses the school as a place to encourage others to join. And there are other schools that are openly run under the auspices of militant groups and organisations. They are very obviously training camps rather than school campuses, with a token nod towards what is broadly recognised as an educational syllabus. The *madrasah* system, particularly in Pakistan, is a vital one for many rural parts of the country. It is the only education on offer, especially so in such unruly areas as the Federally Administered Tribal Areas, the North-West Frontier Province, and Pakistan-controlled Kashmir, where so many government schools are either ghost schools that exist only in a file in some regional office, or if they are real where teaching staff fail to turn up.

Of course Mohammad wanted to get his children away from Kashmir once the family had been attacked in their home. As he, and most of the other men of the family, had been away travelling at the time of the attack there were overwhelming feelings of guilt that they had not been there to protect their wives and children. It spurred Mohammad and his brothers into a campaign to get their children out of the state. The school near Manchester offered places, and both of Mohammad's elder sons were granted visas without trouble. Arshad, Mohammad's first cousin, his uncle's son, was given a place as well.

'My cousin-uncle made me too nervous before the visa interview,' said Arshad. 'It was badly hot in Delhi, June time, something like this, and in the car on the way to the High Commission I was sweating too much, my whole *kurta* was soaked through. And my uncle was saying to me all the time about how I should say things to them when they asked me this question, and that question. It was making me more and more nervous. I was trying to remember what he was saying, but it was also things that I would not have said by myself.

'By the time we got to the High Commission I was just all sweat, nervous and confused. The room that I was taken into the air-conditioning was strong and so I was shivering then, and I think now that even though I was nervous maybe it seemed to them that I was scared too because perhaps I was trying to hide something.' Arshad smiled. 'It is quite funny now in its way, but then it was just bad.'

He looked away for a moment. He was sitting with me on the back of the boat again, another slow end to the day, wound around in conversation.

'The man who came to make the interview was not so bad at all. In many ways he was kind and tried to help me not to be nervous, asking the questions slowly, and saying them again if he thought that perhaps I had not really understood.

But I know some of the time when I was giving answers I was confused because I would start by saying what I thought, and then I would remember my uncle and try and think of what it was that he had been telling me to say, so I would stop and then say something different, and then repeat myself and then do that thing when you say something that is the opposite of what you just said. What is that word?' he asked.

'Contradicting?'

'Yes, this one – so I was making contradictions. Is this how to say it?'

'Yes, perfect.'

'Good. I was making contradictions.' He liked the word, and said it again slowly, pushing each of the four parts out from behind his front teeth.

He smiled, his face bright as he looked up for confirmation of his pronunciation, and then he began to work again at his lower lip.

'This man, he asked me one thing I did not have any thought about how to answer it in the right way. I do not remember the words of how he put it but it was like, "What will you do when you are not at the school during your time in England?" and I did not know what to say. I sat there shivering. I do not remember this thing exactly but when the visa was turned down it was told to my uncle that I had seemed too worried, that I had been gripping the chair that I was sitting on very hard, as if maybe I was telling them lies.'

'What did you say about what you would do in England when you were not at the school?' I asked.

Arshad shrugged. 'I don't remember so clearly but I know I did not have any idea what to say. I think maybe I talked about spending time with my cousins who were already at the school, but I do know that I said I hoped I would meet new people, and in whatever way it was that I put this it caused a problem.'

'In what way?' I asked.

'The interview man, when he told me that he would not be granting the visa, said that he did not feel confident that I would not meet someone in England and maybe fall in love and want to be married there.' Arshad shrugged again and looked down. 'I wanted to ask him why he thought this thing, but I was still too nervous.'

It was as though the interviewer at the British High Commission had seen into Arshad's heart. Of course he would not have known of the attack on the family, or how very much Arshad's father, uncle and cousins had hoped that he would be able to go to England for his education, but he had seen this young man's vulnerability, his wide-open heart that was looking to escape from the place that was so full of pain for him.

'So that was it for my visa for schooling,' Arshad finished.

If any recruiters for the militancy had thought that the Dars' growing orthodoxy meant that they were good potential targets they would have been wrong. If any of the younger generation had ever flirted, even if only in thought, with the idea of fighting beside their fellow Kashmiris for the freedom of their nation-state, the idea had been killed by the militant raid on their family home in 1994. Though the Dar men and boys did not offer fertile ground for the recruiters there were plenty of others, particularly during the first decade of the insurgency. To fight still seemed heroic to many, and the belief persisted that freedom for Kashmir could be won from India. Often the recruiters did not even have to ask. It was not until later, as the attrition of fighting wore down the people, that the militants began to abduct boys from villages and local schools for the training camps.

During the first few years of easy recruitment to the insurgency, up until the mid-1990s, boys would just stick their hands in the air at the end of a meeting outside a mosque, or after a speech at one of the militant group's safe houses. They had not necessarily planned to volunteer, or even thought about it. They just saw their friends sticking up their hands to volunteer, and so they did the same.

They found themselves in small groups, despatched to village bus stations, taking long bumpy journeys to *jihad* that did not match the heroic challenges made by the recruiters and leaders. Instead boys hopscotched through their valley on local transport, trying to get to some point where they had been told to meet a man with a code name. Some of them were stopped along the way at military and paramilitary check-posts, or during house and village raids when the security forces had been tipped off by a *mukhbir*, an informer. Some of these boys were so badly beaten and tortured during interrogations that they were either incapable of living a normal life afterwards, or, if they were able to heal, their hatred of the security forces, and therefore India, propelled them straight across the border and into the training camps.

A militant told me about how sick he had been during the bus journey. He had kept getting off the buses to rest, sometimes just lying by the side of the road and falling asleep, exhausted by travel nausea. He would wake up thirsty and hungry and wander off to find food, stuffing himself full of whatever he could from roadside vendors, their hot fried snacks filling him up for the next leg, and the next round of sickness. It took him such a long time to get to the meeting point that he had to wait there for another week until someone came to meet him, and by the time he got to the end of the next leg of the journey he had been so dehydrated and weak from vomiting that, when he had finally reached the camp, they almost sent him back. One of the camp cooks made him drink warm rice water for two days and he had recovered. A year later he was commanding a cell of fighters based on the edge of the town where he had grown up in the Valley. His motion sickness continued but he learned not to eat when travelling. He chews raw ginger to counteract the sickness, a habit I adopted from him in that strange, casual way you learn survival techniques from strangers.

Others got to the camps travelling in groups led by those who had recruited them, often trekking for several weeks to avoid detection, away from the areas with the heaviest military presence. The various militant groups had set up route systems of safe houses up in the hills, in villages and outlying farms, places where they could rest and eat along the way to the Line of Control. Often they waited several miles away from the imposed border, sometimes in safe houses, but more usually roughly camped out, their leaders making sure that they did not get settled in, moving them on every few hours. For most of the boys this was the first test, and though few of them had led particularly comfortable lives, living rough in the hills was a hard beginning.

'We had two leaders taking us across. We were a bigger group than usual, sixteen we were. We split up many times. One group was captured by the Indian Army. Only the leader had a weapon and the others were killed or taken away for interrogation and such,' a *mukhbir*, an informer, told me. He had been trained by the militants and then captured by the army when he came back into the Valley to fight. Because he was willing, educated and wanted to live he had changed allegiance. His training with the militants had been in one of the largest camps in Azad (Pakistan-controlled Kashmir) in the late 1990s and there was a lot of information that he had been able to give to his new employers, the security forces. He agreed to speak to me because I had asked him three times across three years. When I went to see him for the third time, in 2003, he seemed to find the long pursuit amusing.

'You must think I have very interesting things to say.' He laughed.

He still wanted to drive to another place, away from his village, even though he and his family had been moved and given new identities.

After an hour we stopped at a *chai* shop in Baramulla, a place well known for both its militancy and the huge army presence of one of the largest camps in the Valley.

The town, once a growing trading post, its success marked by the streets of wealthy wooden merchant houses, never recovered from Partition. It had been on the old main road to Srinagar, when the most direct route into the Valley ran via Lahore and Rawalpindi, both now in Pakistan. First it lost its trading post status when the routing into the Valley from India had to change dramatically. Then it was heavily ransacked by the Pathan invaders of October 1947. They had stormed the Valley with the aim of securing it for Pakistan, while the Dogra (Hindu) maharajah, Hari Singh, prevaricated about joining India or Pakistan, in the hope of negotiating autonomy for his majority Muslim, but Hindu-ruled state of Jammu and Kashmir. Baramulla is one of the longest standing municipal victims of the Valley's unrest. It was an appropriate place to meet, in a *chai* stall, next to a butcher's shop, the front of which was hung about with spread-eagled, bloodless sheep's carcasses.

'Those of us who came from here were teased all the time by the other militants, and not in a nice way, not for fun, but bullying,' he said as the *chai-wallah* clattered metal cups behind us, insulating our conversation with his noise.

By the time the *mukhbir* was being trained Kashmiris were outnumbered by foreigners in the camps. The majority were Afghans and Pakistanis from the South Punjab, with a few Arabs, Chechens and other foreigners, mostly of Pakistani origin, though born or raised abroad. Many of the camp leaders, commanders and specialist trainers were seasoned *mujahideen* fighters who had fought against the Russians in the Soviet-Afghan war that ended as the insurgency began in Kashmir.

'Most of the time there was a big problem with language. In some ways you could say that the camps were well run, that the training was good. When I was first there it seemed to me that the whole thing was being organised by the Pakistan Army, and that all the commanders were also officers from the army. The others who came at the same time as me thought this same thing. In many ways we were impressed. And then, after just a few days, it became clear to us all that two things made it possible to do well in the camp: the first was that you could speak as many languages as possible, and so be a translator for others; and the second one was that you could only get far if you were not Kashmiri.'

The first method of succeeding in the camp was easy to grasp, the second confused me. The *mukhbir* did not want to elaborate. He pushed past the subject and talked instead about what it was like when he came back to his family after being captured by the army.

'In my heart I hoped that they would be happy that I was returning to my home and it was very difficult because, though they were glad that I had come, they were also very frightened. My father and brothers had been taken in for questioning many times since I had gone over to the camp, and one of my brothers had been beaten very badly. He is just an ordinary man. He used to help my father with his work of delivering milk in our *mohalla* [neighbourhood]. He did not have anything to do with the militancy. My family were very afraid that the army would come to take them all if they found out that I had returned.

'They did not understand when I told them that I was working with the security forces now. It was very hard for them. My name and everything else had been changed and they had to move as well, for their protection. We were given a new house, and work was found for my brothers, but it was not possible to find something for my father. He was old by this time, too old for the work that was there. He would sit around and he and my mother seemed sad all of the time, except when one of my brothers got married and his wife came to live with us in the house.'

By the time we were talking in the *chai* shop his father was already dead, and his mother was frail, though he said that her grandchildren, his brother's children, were giving her great joy.

He had not married.

Towards the end of our conversation he returned to the subject of the camp and the treatment of the Valley Kashmiris.

'It seemed they did not like us, I mean all the other people in the camp who were not from the Valley. Even those of Azad (Pakistan-controlled Kashmir) were not good to us. We stayed together in the camp, and many times we would have to help each other because one of us did not find it possible to understand what one of the commanders was teaching us. Some of the training was good. They worked us hard all the time to make us stronger, but I have spent some time with the army since that time and all the training that is given with weapons is very clear and good. In the camp there was one big problem that we were not allowed to make waste with ammunition so we were often doing training without ammunition so we did not know how good we were in accuracy.' He stopped and called for more *chai*.

We waited in silence until it came. Soldiers walked past in pairs, heavily armed, patrolling the street beyond. The butcher was serving two women in full black *burqas*; another waited behind them, her face open, her skin dark and crumpled by high mountain weather that funnels through the town in its cleft at the end of the Valley, the point where it was said that Kasyapa, the old sage, persuaded the god Shiva to strike the mountains open and create a flat place, drained of water.

When the *chai* came and the owner had retreated to the crashing of his pans the *mukhbir* talked of his treatment.

'The camp was near Muzaffarabad [the capital of Pakistan-controlled Kashmir], at Bakryal. At that time there were perhaps five or six camps in that area. I was told that more came up after this time.'

I asked how many men he thought there were in the camp. He was unsure.

'I did not count,' he said. 'There were good supplies though, and always enough food, even if it did not taste good. I have heard that in other places, camps I mean, there is often not enough to eat. And we were paid at the right time. But it was different amounts. The people from the Valley were paid less, 1,000 rupees per month [about £14]. I know some of the others were being paid twice that amount, 2,000 rupees per month, and the commanders were being paid more than this again, but that is how it would be of course.

'There were times when we were out on an exercise when we would not have any food for some days, even when we were doing these in the worst of weather. They said we would need to be ready for these kind of things. But always we [the Kashmiris] would be the last to get food when we got back, and they were always saying to us that it was because we were weaker and not so good, and had to be made more tough this way. Some from these parts did not eat so much meat and if that was all there was to eat they would have nothing. It was hard for them. Some of them were too weak and became ill.' He paused and we sat in silence once more, surrounded by the sounds of the street.

When he spoke again I could not hear him properly. His voice was lower, but I did not want to lean in. Like most of the villagers of the Valley he was a man who was not comfortable in the company of women he was not related to. I missed parts of what he was saying but he was talking about how the Kashmiris, particularly the younger ones, were picked on by other men in the camp because of their prettiness, and not just picked on, but pulled out of their tents at night, returning later, some of them angry, others crying, some in cold silence. He used the expression 'donkey boy'.

Penetration in sodomy is not regarded by some as being a homosexual act in parts of North India and Pakistan. But the one who is penetrated is derided as a 'donkey boy', the one who is ridden, subjugated, humiliated.

'Not me,' the *mukbhir* said, his voice clearer again. 'Too ugly. My sisters have always said this thing. I do not mind. I was glad to be ugly,' he finished with a weak smile.

He was not an ugly man. Sisters tease their brothers about being unlovely lumps, but he was as good-looking as so many Kashmiri men are, his high cheekbones underlining the signature velvety brown eyes of the Valley, that iris colour-range that moves from chocolate through hazel and greens to blue. It gives the people an unusual beauty, particularly in the eyes of some of their darker neighbours, and so a vulnerability. The *mukhbir* was certainly not ugly but his claim to ugliness was his protection against whatever had or had not happened to him in the camp. The anger and hatred of the security forces that he claimed had spurred him to become a militant had somehow been dented during his time in the camp in Pakistan-controlled Kashmir. When he spoke of being captured by the army, and of being offered the chance to become an informer, he spoke with relief, a sense that he had been able to get away from something that was worse than working for the security forces, a concept that many of his fellow Kashmiris would regard as treasonable.

When I asked him whether he felt that he was now working for what so many of his people regarded as 'the enemy' he sat nodding, thinking, making the same rocking movement people make when sitting over the Qur'an, studying, memorising.

'I am alive now, and my family have a better house than we used to have. Much of this is not perfect, but the reason we have the things that we have is because I was educated. I had good English, Urdu and of course Kashmiri. So this thing made me useful to them, and this is why they made the offer. When this thing was said to me I was in handcuffs. Already my ankle was broken, and some ribs as well. Perhaps I am not so brave but I did not have any further room for pain. Without this offer that was made to me I would be dead at this time, or in some prison far from here in very bad conditions. I went to a government school with good teachers, before the trouble, a place that was made possible because of money from the Indian Government.' He gave another weak smile. 'If you see it this way they saved my life.'

Most of the boys and men from the Valley who have become militants were trained in camps in Pakistan-controlled Kashmir, the majority of which were or are close to the Line of Control, in the north of the region, an area that feels very remote from the political capital of Pakistan, Islamabad. Even if it is not so geographically removed it seems to be a different country.

This is a world within a world, a place with little recourse to standard justice, where the rule of tribe and patriarchy trumps that of government or god. Stories from the wild north-west, from Skardu to the Khyber Pass, seem overworked in the telling, driven by levels of testosterone and excessive gunfire that make them seem absurd, their characters heavily bearded figures, slung about with ammunition belts, their bellowing laughter mixed with attitudes that make killing appear a banal thing to them. It can seem that only brutal codes and brute strength are the language of the Federally Administered Tribal Areas, the North-West Frontier Province and the Northern Areas. The various invaders and empires have stepped carefully through these territories, allowing almost total autonomy, with varying quid pro quo arrangements.

These warrior regions became part of the new nation of West Pakistan in 1947, the title then truncated to Pakistan when East Pakistan became Bangladesh after the bloody Bangladesh war of 1971. Pakistan continued to govern the

Federally Administered Tribal Areas, the North-West Frontier Province and the Northern Areas in a remote way, leaving them to their own devices, with what seemed to be a policy of out of sight, out of mind. The Pathans of the region were easier to control if left uncontrolled. This seems to be the nature of these people, ethnically of eastern Iran, intrinsically Afghan, written of as far back as Herodotus, divided into tribes and clans that will go to war over as little as a stolen goat. Their world is geographically insulated by raw ranges and wild Himalayan weather patterns that reflect the ways of the people, the Pathans, or Pashtuns, as the same people are called in their Afghan context and geography.

This world of crags and *Pashtunwali*, a pre-Islamic tribal code of honour, has always offered itself as an ideal region into which those outside the conventional rule of law could disappear. The people regard *melmastia,* hospitality to strangers, as a core part of their code, whether that stranger be a nineteenth-century British officer of the Raj on tour, a common thief in hiding, or Osama bin Laden pursuing right of residence, incognito.

The region has also long played host to the training camps of contemporary history, whether it was for the multi-nationally backed *mujahideen* that fought the Soviet-Afghan war of 1979–1989, or the militants of the Kashmir insurgency from the late 1980s to date. The immediate geography of the camps changes, depending on which border it is that newly trained fighters need to cross. While the most recent physical one has been the Line of Control between India and Pakistan, the mental borders of Islam in the mind of the modern *jihadi* have made the location of the camps in the warrior heartland of the highest mountains in the world a powerfully symbolic thing.

The camps that I have been to had a shifting, temporary quality, but also one of military organisation. It is as though the military has mixed everything up at the local frontier bazaar, camouflage fatigues beside rough *salwar kameez*, *pakul* hats, their sides rolled in upturned muffin-fashion, next to carefully adjusted berets, variations on the theme of turbans, some Wahhabi-wrapped, echoing the style of the *jihadi* hero of the camps, Osama bin Mohammed bin Awad bin Laden.

When I talked to the men it seemed that there was little cohesion, a sense created partly by language and cultural divides, and partly due to the lack of the minute-by-minute military precision of a conventional army camp.

But within each camp there was always one powerful uniting force that transcends what can appear to be a hazy chain of command. The *mullah*, *sheikh*, *maulvi* or *maulana* of each camp, whichever title he travels under, is both the religious leader, and usually the undisputed overall leader as well. Those in this position, whatever their extraction and from wherever they took their title of master, elder, teacher or religious leader, have great power. They are zealots who give no ground in the pursuit of *jihad*. Many of them have an extensive knowledge of the Qur'an and Hadith, combined with the ability to give impassioned speeches and discourses that create a strong cohesive bond amid the disparity of the recruits. Even if they are speaking in a language that is not understood by all their audience, when they are preaching Islam and proselytising *jihad*, the power of their rhetoric is unifying in itself. Beyond this cohesion there is the simple act, five times a day, of prayer. Whether I was mid-conversation with someone in the camp, or watching training, everything stopped as every man in the camp joined in silent bowed rows after the *muezzin*'s call.

I have also been to another kind of place in one of these areas. It was referred to as a camp but it was almost entirely different to the ones just described. It was a gentle place of Islamic learning, the surrender of the religion's name central to all their practices, the teaching of Hadith and the Qur'an, and Sufi poetry. It was a place of sanctuary for young men who have lost their way and their sense of purpose in a volatile situation and time. It was more a seminary than a camp, but not in the sense of a *madrasah* because the men who were studying there were older. The teachers were passionate about trying to keep their students away from all that those other camps stood for.

One young teacher talked of their form of *jihad*, the struggle only within the heart of the individual.

There were battered and broken men in this place, internally and externally, ones who had managed to find their way from the other camps.

'How could we think of *jihad* as fighting now that we have studied in this place?' one of them said when he talked of how his understanding of *jihad* had been changed by the teachers in the seminary camp.

It is a sad thing that very few who have crossed over from the Valley to train have found their way to this refuge, 'the home of the heart' as one of the students described it to me.

During the early stages of the insurgency the recruits to the militant training camps from the Valley were of all ages, from teenagers through to men in their forties. Once the enthusiastic first flood of volunteers began to dwindle as the insurgency wore on the average age of those in the militant camps dropped.

'We were taken from our village, eight of us. They followed

us when we were coming back from school and grabbed us. We were made to lie at the bottom of a truck for a long time. We did not know where we were going but we knew they were militants. This is how we came to be in the camp,' a boy told me, his face young but already a man after all that he had been through.

Ahmed said that he was just fourteen when he was picked up with his friends on the way back from school and taken to a training camp near Muzaffarabad in Pakistan-controlled Kashmir. One of his brothers had been taken at the same time, not from the school group, but from the market place in their village. They had been in the same truck, face down on the floor under wet sacking, but unable to speak to each other. Ahmed's brother had been taken to another camp, not far from where the boy was trained.

Months later Ahmed heard that his brother had been killed in an encounter with security forces while he himself was still being trained. It seemed more likely to have been during a raid on a militant safe house that was then reported as an encounter, or a fairer-sounding fight that would then not raise the complicated question of extra-judicial killing by the Indian security forces. Ahmed heard that those who died with his brother had been killed by shots in the back of the head, though their bodies had many bullet wounds by the time they were produced by the security forces after the reported 'encounter'.

It is a sorry and familiar theme to many reports of confrontations between the militants and the security forces in the Valley. Across the conflict many killings have been restyled as 'encounters'; dead militants have been brought from where they have been executed to another location, the setting dressed to make it look as though there was a big shoot-out between the security forces and the militants, and the long dead bodies re-presented, often to the local press, with new wounds. Local journalists learned to recognise the method; the 'twice-dead' barely bled from secondary bullet wounds in bodies that had no longer been pumping blood when they had been shot again.

Ahmed had been picked up by the militants, or kidnapped, with his school friends in 2005. He had been moved from one camp to another. He was small and wiry and he said that he was being trained with explosives. He was also being badly bullied and sodomised. He had picked up a water-borne illness that had dragged on and that had made him very weak. His pay had been cut while he was ill, the sexual abuse had continued, and then he had heard a rumour that the Indian Army was offering to rehabilitate militants who surrendered to military personnel at specified army posts or camps. More importantly, part of the rehabilitation package was payment, the equivalent of a good salary by local standards, until the surrendered militants were back in work.

Ahmed left the camp he was in with two others from the Valley, both from the original group taken on their way back from school. He was sixteen when he handed himself over to an Indian Army officer at a military post near the Line of Control above Uri, just inside Indian-controlled Kashmir.

The group that surrendered to the officer was dishevelled, afraid, cold and hungry. They had walked for three days through thick snow to reach the post. One of them had broken his arm as they were leaving the training camp. They had dug their way out under the fence that surrounded the camp. They had been told by their commanders that the ring fence was mined, but they had also been told by other recruits that this was just talk to stop them from leaving. Ahmed did not use the word 'leave' when he described his departure from the training camp. He talked of running away, of his escape.

The three Kashmiri boys, or by now trained militants, who reached a military post just across the Line of Control late at night in December 2006 were barely able to walk. The one who was injured had bad frostbite in the hand of his broken arm. Ahmed, the ex-militant, as he was later introduced to me, said that as soon as they had surrendered and had given the information about the camp that they had left, they were taken to the main army base nearby. The convoy that transported them through the dawn to the base had made a mark on them. The line of military vehicles had a grandeur to it, an established power and organisation, that impressed them.

When they arrived at the base they were separated, though Ahmed said that it was explained to them that they would only be kept apart until they had each been more fully interviewed.

'I was led to a place where I could take a bath. It was very long since I had washed in this way. I spent much time doing this and no one came to tell me to be quick. In the camp often we did not have time to wash well and many times it was in very cold water, from the stream that was close by to one part of the camp. We did have to wash many times, every time for *wudu* [ritual washing before prayer], but still it did not mean that we were so clean.'

Clean overalls had been left for him to put on after the bath.

'It was warm inside after we had been walking for all those days and hungry all the time. I was told to sit and wait and that someone would come and collect me. I know there was a soldier nearby but I was not locked in. It was a nice place.'

He sat on a bed to wait but fell asleep. He was not disturbed or woken until much later in the day. He was then taken to eat before his interview.

'I was so hungry. There had been no food to eat since we left the camp. We did not take any with us. They watched all the time to see if any of us were keeping food. People were running away from the camps. We had heard this thing. We were watched a lot of the time. It was not possible to save up food to carry with us. I ate so much when I was taken to eat that first time.' He smiled in the same way as he had when describing the long bath he had been allowed to take. 'But then it was a problem because the interview was right after eating and it was in a warm room and I was so full it was a big problem not to go to sleep again.'

When I asked why he had believed the rumour about the rehabilitation programme, and why he had not been suspicious that it might just be a trap to capture militants, he shrugged.

'There was nothing that could be so bad as the camp,' he said.

Ahmed was interviewed by various different officers over a period of several days, as were the other two who had surrendered with him. They were allowed to spend time together after the first round of interviews. They were also given long rest periods between the sessions of questioning, plenty to eat, and, apart from the boy with the broken arm, the other two spent time with some of the soldiers.

'We played some cricket and football on one of the days and the whole area was cleared of the snow, all of it scraped away so that there was room to play.' Ahmed stopped for a moment and thought about it. 'That was very good, to be able to play when there was so much snow all around. They are good players, the soldiers, and strong.' He stopped again. 'We were playing these games together and then you see that these are just men the same as us, but if we had been outside of their camp it would have been their job to kill us.' He paused. 'And we had been trained in the other camp to kill them.'

A senior officer, one of the instigators of the rehabilitation programme, stood on the edge of a road that cuts along the mountains between Uri and the Line of Control. It was raining hard but The General had made his driver stop. As he got down from the front of the jeep one of his men burst out of the back to hold an umbrella over his head. The convoy escorting him backed up along the road behind. Soldiers with mounted machine guns stood in the turrets of the vehicles immediately in front and behind The General's jeep. It was a stretch of road where one of his predecessors had been killed by shellfire from the Line of Control above. The General had stopped to take a cup of tea with a *sarpanch* he recognised (a *panchayat* or council leader). The local man had waved, and so the convoy was halted. It was just a small thing but it had an enormity in the landscape that we were in. The *sarpanch* had simply raised his hand in greeting, and this senior officer had stopped a whole military convoy in response.

Both men stood in the rain under large black umbrellas, the local man, slightly stooped, his beard henna-dyed to mark his journey to Mecca for Hajj, The General clean-shaven, his posture making him seem taller than his actual height. The two men were laughing. The General has had many postings in the Valley across several decades. He knows the people well and, as a result of a long personal campaign, he has achieved a rare position for an Indian soldier in Kashmir – he is trusted by the people. This does not protect him from those who see only the uniform and not the man, and so soldiers all up and down the convoy jumped from vehicles to line the road while the *sarpanch* and The General drank a cup of tea together.

Two boys from the *sarpanch*'s village had recently surrendered at a military post near where we are on the road. They were being rehabilitated. The General was giving the old man news of the two boys.

Once tea had been drunk together, under the umbrellas, the convoy moved on, The General and the *sarpanch* waving one another goodbye as we drove away. I was sitting behind The General, bent low under the reinforced roof of the jeep so that my face hovered just behind his shoulder.

I asked him why he had been so confident that militants would respond to the rehabilitation programme, and why they would trust the Indian Army after so many years of brutality on both sides.

'After September 2001 the situation changed. Pakistan had to prove to America that it was fulfilling the request to close down the militant training camps. They had to act because they thought that either we [India] could make air strikes against the camps to prove to America that they were still there, or that the Americans would pick them up with satellite imaging. The problem was then of what was going to happen to the militants if and when camps were disbanded. Where would they go? And if the ones from the Valley were able to get back in they might become an increased internal risk. This was an important starting point for a rehabilitation programme.'

He expressed his great hope for the programme as the herald of a new era in the Valley, a time of unforced co-operation. 'When we are no more than a peace-keeping force,' he said, 'then there will no longer be a need for the counter-insurgency forces and trust can begin to be built. This will be hard and it will take a long time, but we must hope for this.'

We talked of the cycle of violence again, as we had when I had last met with him.

'There seems to be a conventional point where it is felt the cycle can be broken, the point between anger and revenge,' The General said. 'That may work if you can act at that point. But the history here is too old and long.'

The cycle that he spoke of follows a sequence: an act of violence is followed by shock, then fear, grief, anger, bitterness, the need for revenge, then retaliation with violence, and so the cycle goes around again.

'We had missed the point of anger. The cycle had been going around many times. If a father had been a militant, then it was very probable that his sons would become the same. It is a sad form of family business, no? We had to find another entry point. After all this time people are tired, and when they are very tired they just want things to end. You can only end this kind of conflict if you give the men who have been fighting something better to do, and then pay them to do it so that they can look after their families, and feel proud of themselves again.'

So often, when Mohammad has been talking to me about his children, he has emphasised how important it is that he and his brothers create a future for their children, and now their grandchildren as well.

'We have had to find ways to make them see that there is something more to this life than these troubles we have been living with,' he has said.

It is the same point that The General made. Both men are fathers.

Chapter Nine

CORRUPTION

IN A FINAL THRUST of winter at the edge of spring 2008 Ibrahim and I were walking across the meadow above the houseboat and below his family home. There was a thick frost and he was kicking at tufts of frozen grass, sending out puffs of ice ahead of us, making use of a pair of new trainers, bright white against the sage of his *pheran*, one side of which was pulled up charioteer-style, the way he likes to wear it. He was irritated by the idea of the army paying surrendered militants.

'If they are paying money in part I understand this thing, but also it is wrong. It will come out of the taxes that we pay and why should we pay these men who have caused so much pain here?' He kicked again. 'I know they need work, and to be able to pay for their families, but why should I have to pay for this?' He stopped to examine whether the frost had damaged the early cherry blossom, his fingers carefully testing fragile buds, but then he hit the branch as he turned away. 'It will just encourage more corruption, it will become another business, like all of these ones that have been wounding my valley all this time.'

Corruption has been a secondary infection digging into the wounds of the insurgency. In a culture that accepts corruption as a part of the machinery of life the insurgency has been a wonderful and all-encompassing veil that has blurred the accountability of the state. It has allowed many to get fat and rich on money allocated by the Central Government in Delhi for housing, education, basic hygiene and medical programmes, support packages for victims of the conflict – it is a bulging list. Every government and ruling body in Kashmir since the early 1980s has been tainted with corruption charges, both officially and unofficially. The charges range from the lowest levels of petty bribery through to what seems impossible, the trading of human life.

In the morning frost Ibrahim was not in the mood to be accommodating towards surrendered militants, considering his family's story and the attack of summer 1994, though his mood was more the product of a letter that he had just received from the Lakes and Waterways Development Authority, LAWDA, this in itself usually being enough to spoil anyone's day. The letter was about Ibrahim's family *donga* boat. It is one of the small stories of corruption – a parable.

Before Ibrahim's father, Sobra, bought the land above the meadow, and the house was built, the whole family used to live on the old *donga* boat that sat between two of the houseboats that the family rented out to tourists. The boys had spent their early life in the *donga*'s wooden box rooms, the sills low enough for them to be able to trail their fingers in the lake when they leaned out of the windows.

'We slept so well on the water, just that little, little movement, like in a mother's arms,' Mohammad had once said.

As the family survived and flourished through the bad years in the Valley the *donga* boat survived too, even though it became just a service boat, a place where Maqbool made *kahwa chai*, and where the boys and men who worked on the houseboats slept during the summer months because it still offered cooler night air over the lake.

It was a family talisman and Ibrahim and his brothers had always made sure that the *donga* was in good condition, well kept, and any repair work done as soon as it was needed.

The houseboat owners pay a registration fee to LAWDA for their boats. This is how the number of boats on the lakes is supposed to be controlled. There is corruption already at this first stage. The official number of houseboats allowed is 1,200, but there are more than this, and there were certainly many more than this in the high tourist seasons before the insurgency began. I have stood beside the Shankaracharya temple, on top of Takht-i Sulaiman Hill (the Throne of Solomon), above the city and the lakes, trying to count the boats. Once I got to over 1,350 and another time to over 1,400, but I was still counting. Every extra boat means that a houseboat owner has had to pay someone to overlook the fact that the houseboat allocation was already full, and then pay for an illegal registration certificate, and go on paying each year for the illegal re-registration.

Each registered boat, whether a *donga* or a larger houseboat, needs on-going maintenance work to stay afloat, and in business. Each round of maintenance work has to be cleared through both the Department of Tourism and LAWDA. First the houseboat owner has to apply to the Tourism Department for permission to carry out work on his boats. If permission is granted it is then referred on to LAWDA for further permission. These two steps involve their own extortion. It is made clear to the houseboat owner that he needs to pay someone in order to allow progress to the next stage. Meanwhile time passes and the *donga* or houseboat in need of maintenance work sinks a little lower into the lake.

Ibrahim had filled in all the forms and applied for the

correct permissions at the right times. The Department of Tourism had given permission. Ibrahim and his family are shining examples of houseboat owners, as well as being leading members of the community. The Department of Tourism had recognised this by doing Ibrahim the great honour of not asking him to pay a bribe. LAWDA was different. No, he could not do the work, and no, he did not have the right permission. He would have to wait longer.

'Unless,' Ibrahim said, 'I pay an amount of money to such and such a person who will make it all happen.' And he kicked the ground again.

His irritation stayed with him throughout the day. By mid-afternoon spring sun had softened the frost so that everything glistened in the garden. We sat out on the back veranda and drank tea. Ibrahim showed me the mound of paperwork that had already built up about the *donga* maintenance while he dunked a small round of bread into his tea, pushing it down hard into the cup.

'I will wait until the end of the week and then we will have to see,' he said, rereading the letter from LAWDA.

We both read it again, just to make sure we had not missed something, and then Ibrahim shook off the breadcrumbs that he had dropped onto the page as he read and ate.

Nothing changed during the week. The *donga* boat continued to sink. Ibrahim called LAWDA, they repeated what had been written in the letter. No work could proceed until the 'correct permission' was granted.

Ibrahim called the boat restorers. The *donga* had to be broken up as it was now too late for the maintenance work that he had applied for. His brothers and his father were in Delhi, and further afield. Ibrahim made the decision alone and asked the boat restorers to come the next day.

He stood beside the lake and watched as the boat men ripped out the metal staples that had held the long planks of the *donga* together. He walked away as they began to smash apart the floorboards and the walls of the rooms where he had slept as a boy.

We met again for tea in the afternoon. This time he came to the houseboat so that he could smoke quietly after the exigencies of his day. The *donga* was now on land, stacked on either side of the houseboat in piles of wet wood that hissed and whispered as the water seeped out of them.

'We do not pay bribes. This family, we do not do it. It makes things very hard at times.' His voice was tight, his eyes tired as he looked back from the veranda at the piles of wood and lit a cigarette, his remaining vice.

We told corruption stories, trying to outdo each other.

'There was a housing official. He was responsible for one part of the city. He was given huge amounts to build a whole set of buildings in one place, housing for people who were being moved from an area that was being cleared for a shopping mall.' Ibrahim blew a smoke ring as he warmed to his theme. 'Then it was the end of his time in the post and he was handing over to someone new. This new man comes and he is being very attentive to his work. He looks at the records of building work completed, and he goes to see some of the sites. He finds there to be no buildings, just one big nothing, not even a pile of bricks. And he seeks out the man who was in the job before him and asks him what was happening.' Ibrahim, stopped, listening.

He stubbed out his half-smoked cigarette and popped it back into the packet and into his pocket as he heard someone on the duckboards at the back of the boat.

It was Maqbool. Ibrahim dug out the packet again and relit the half cigarette.

'And the first man says to the second, "So what can I do to help you with this, what can I give you to make this easier?" And the second man did not know what to say. The first man then had an idea: "I know, you apply to the government for funds to pull down the building and you tell them that you have seen the structure and that it has been built on poor foundations, that it is unsafe and must be demolished. Then we both will have benefited." Can you believe it, this is the very thing that happened. Money was given first for a building that was not built, and then more money was given for a building to be pulled down that was never there.'

We both laughed at the joke of it, the lunacy.

'And if anyone asks them what happened to the money these people just say that the militants stole it from their department, or that they extorted it from government offices with threats against lives. No one challenges this.' Ibrahim had stopped laughing. 'And this is how it is. Nothing changes. Too many people are involved in this and we all know about it but no one is big enough and with enough power to say, "Stop this thing."'

Maqbool came out onto the veranda and passed an ashtray to Ibrahim. Both men smoked, though Maqbool would never do so in front of the man he worked for.

'The worst of this is that people like me and my family, we can deal with this. It is our choice not to pay these bribes, but we could also choose the other way, we could pay them. The people who are the most damaged by this are the poor. They cannot afford these bribes. So many houseboat owners have lost their boats over the past so many years of the problems. They were the only things they owned, their whole family livelihood, and all they could do was have them broken up and they sold the wood just for its timber value.' He shook his head and closed his eyes so that he did not have to look at the *donga* pile beside the boat.

It is the poor who are destroyed, whether it is the vegetable-seller who has to pay a bribe to the police so that he can put his cart in the same place each day, or a wife selling her wedding jewellery, her only insurance, to pay a police *mukhbir*, informer, who has promised her information that does not exist about her missing husband. The brave few who try to stand their ground are simply left to struggle alone. The poor cannot afford the luxury of taking the high moral ground. They will admire the courage of the rare individual who is trying to make a point. They might even try to help a little by giving some food to a struggling family, or by supporting a widow or a half-widow. They might watch over her children while a woman undertakes menial labour to support the family in the absence or loss of her husband, and indeed the income he brought in. But it is almost unknown for anyone to back up a poor man or woman who is trying to stand in defiance of bribery and corruption. The mechanism is entrenched. It will crush anyone who dares to confront it, alone and tiny, in the face of this gargantuan machine that ploughs over almost every bud of progress and change that dares to raise itself up out of the dirt of the conflict. Too many are invested in the status quo of the corrupt system.

While corruption is part of the Indian way, in the Valley it is a nuclear-charged version, literally, heightened by conflict, and exacerbated by the position of the fragile state as a possible nuclear trigger between Pakistan and India. The Central Government of India pours in money to soothe the constant insecurity of the place, and so the pickings are rich, the bureaucrats lining up to take the jobs and all the backhanders that come too. Even though corruption is pandemic, the government cannot always just turn away as the *crores* (tens of millions) of rupees are thrown out of an ever-open window. Sometimes the extortion or bribery is too obvious and then someone is arrested and charged. Intermittently it is someone in the position of a minister. There is no great show of surprise, little indignation, apart from the highly dramatised shock played out by the family of the accused, and the man himself. People accept it, shrug, carry on regardless. These occasional arrests do not set an example. They are neither preventative measures, nor apparently even particularly effective in stopping the culprit, once either the charges have been dropped or a small price has been paid for the graft committed.

From early in 1995, six years into the insurgency, the Indian security forces began to address the problem of not being able to use the large and growing Jammu and Kashmir Police Force for counter-insurgency operations. To use the local force would have been inflammatory as well as a risk, as many in the Jammu and Kashmir Police were thought or known to be in favour of the insurgency. Two separate groups were formed within the police to tackle counter-insurgency, both recruited mainly from among non-Muslims and non-Kashmiris. The Special Task Force and Special Operations Group were fleshed out further with former and renegade militants. It was believed that if these specialist counter-insurgency forces within the main police corps were seen to have local support they would have more success.

Most of the work of these two forces was carried out in joint operations with the Rashtriya Rifles, the National Rifles, a force raised in 1990 specifically to fight the insurgency in Kashmir. Its strength of approximately 40,000 men is considered as a paramilitary force, its job being to engage with the insurgents, freeing the main army to protect India's border with Pakistan along the Line of Control. Almost every man of the Rashtriya Rifles is on secondment from the main army. As the principal counter-insurgency force it is the one that has had the highest number of human rights abuse accusations levelled against it, and, in its joint operations with the special police groups, the highest number of corruption charges as well.

In the febrile environment of the Valley it was inevitable that the formation of local counter-insurgency forces would be a breeding ground for bribery and extortion. Behind closed doors, and in private, most Kashmiris agree that the paramilitary forces and specialist counter-insurgency groups have taken corruption to new highs. They will nod, agree and tell stories that you hope have been made up, are rumours or appalling exaggeration. But they will not go on the record.

It is very understandable why they will not. During the worst phase of the insurgency, through the 1990s and into the first years of the twenty-first century, the interrogation centres set up by the security forces destroyed many lives. It is still not a time when people can talk freely and openly of what they have witnessed or been subjected to, both at the hands of the security forces and the militants. People have spoken out over the years, and they have also, in many cases, been further brutalised for doing so.

There have been many 'incidents' since the formation of the specialist counter-insurgency groups in 1995. Most of them have not been recorded. People refer to them, they tell stories, but they also ask me not to retell them.

There was one local man who was prepared to divulge more than most. He agreed to let me write down his story and to relate it, indirectly.

He was 'under arms' as he described it, with one of the main separatist groups when I first met him, more than ten years ago. He certainly could not talk then, but I have met up with him again across the years. He is no longer with that separatist group. He was invalided out, in as far as that is possible in Kashmir. He had lost part of one foot. A bullet wound was not treated because, at the time of his injury, the counter-insurgency groups were paying very close attention to the hospitals, particularly to the Bone and Joint Hospital in Barzullah, on the road to the airport. Most people have called it the Bullet and Bomb Hospital since the insurgency began. The local man's wound became infected and then gangrenous. Part of his foot had to be removed.

When the situation in the Valley improved after the Assembly elections in the state in September and October 2002 he and I met up again. He was trying to become as mobile as he could with his half foot. His method was to walk a lot, even though the surgeon who had operated on him had warned that too much walking could cause further nerve damage.

We drove up into the hills, to Sonamarg. His mother's family were Chopans, herders, from that area and he could draw maps of the whole region with his eyes closed. It was his party trick. He liked to show people. He said it was how he had managed to survive because he was kept away from the high-risk missions on account of his value as a mapmaker.

Sonamarg – the name means meadow of gold – is the upper grassland path to the High Himalayas, on the road to Ladakh, the kingdom beyond the Zojila, the pass that separates Muslim Kashmir from Buddhist Ladakh. It has been the star of more than a thousand films. The scene is almost always a close variation on a theme: a girl stands, arms flung wide, her face to a wind that lifts both her glossy mane and whips the end of her sari about. She bursts into song about the man she loves and how his funny little smile makes her heart go bounce, bounce, boom, boom. Or rather she lip-synchs to the fabulous warbling of a famous playback singer. The lovely's love then pops up from behind a rock, much more suitably clad for the climate in mitts, scarf and bobble hat. Spreading his arms to the snowy peaks behind, he joyously sings of how all the mountains cannot contain his love, nor the blue, azure-blue, peacock-blue sky above. Together they skip and shimmy, flirt and embrace (demurely, though suggestively). And then she disappears, to emerge from behind another rock, now in fluffy wear: a cosy sweater, ear muffs, bunny boots, all ready for a sledging scene with a few hip bumps and one long lingering shot of her mouth, then his, just not of their mouths together. At the crucial moment of maximum mouth it is all change to a sultry backwater in Kerala with a whole new set of clothes, and a whole new round of dance moves.

Throughout the 1960s, 1970s and 1980s the luscious meadow was movie gold dust. Bollywood's huge audience seemed never to be able to get enough of the sparkling peaks and the fecund fields below where their favourite stars bounced and burbled around trees and from behind rocks. The domestic tourists rolled in on the back of the Bollywood dance items, rushing to honeymoon in the high altitude, also bunny-wrapped in strangely coloured furs, bundles of fluffy pink and green nylon fur, heading up to the snowy meadows where Shammi swooned around Saira, and Sunny spun Amrita in celluloid bliss. The pony and sledge men had never done so well. As pre-independence tourists the doughty Brits had liked to stride about the meadows on their own, fishing, climbing, trekking and skiing. The new generation of visitors, shivering Indians from the hot plains, queued up for the ponies to take them up to the edge of the Thajiwas Glacier, and then again for an ice ride, to be dragged by skinny sledge-pullers up and down the greying snow amid as much merriment and chirruping as in the *masala* movie versions.

Then the insurgency began and the army closed off the area as they opened a series of camps and supply stations across the meadows. The pony men and the sledge-pullers had nothing to do but be porters for the camps. During those first few years many of these men, their work gone, joined the insurgency.

The lame man wanted to climb away from the even and softly rolling grass of the meadows. He turned down offers of help, even though he would lose his balance every few steps, his jaw locked as he righted himself. Then he fell, crying out as he did. After that he was prepared to accept a strut, leaning on my shoulder as we made a slow advance towards one edge of the glacier, skirting around one of the army camps.

He seemed unworried by the proximity of the military, even when a couple of bored soldiers called out to ask what we were doing. The meadows were no longer out of bounds as they had been in the early stages of the insurgency, though tentative visitors were challenged and checked, as we had been. Soldiers had jumped into the jeep each time we had been stopped at a check-post over the fifty or so miles between Srinagar and Sonamarg. They had just been hitching lifts, as they did on the local buses, by way of a little intimidation, or vice versa.

The man replied to the soldier's questions, calling back that we were just going to take a look at the glacier. They asked where I was from, assuming that I did not speak Hindi, but that the Kashmiri did. He just told them that I was a foreigner. It was not enough for them. They wanted to know where exactly I was from, whether I was married, what I was doing in Kashmir. One asked if the man was 'poking the little chicken'. He asked them to be polite to a stranger and bent his head to his chest, trying to move away from them faster. He stumbled again, apologising to me as he did. We walked on. The soldiers continued to shout after us but the wind that funnels down off the ice of the glacier batted their questions away.

When it seemed that the terrain was becoming impossible for the man we stopped. He sat down, lifted his head, and called out to the hill above. Where there had seemed to be only hillside a turf door opened and a herder came out from a hut, its walls camouflaged to the colouring and curve of the slope. He had a little girl at his side, and a lamb apparently casually stuffed into his pocket. They came to sit with us. No introduction was made beyond a nod. The herder eased the lamb out of his pocket and continued with the task that had been interrupted, feeding the lamb from a small leather pouch, the end of it pointed and dripping warm milk. The lamb gobbled at the leather nipple, milk spilling out of the sides of its mouth and down its tiny heaving flanks. The little girl laughed, flicking the newborn's long tail while the men talked and the lamb fed.

The herder was a cousin, the lame man's mother's nephew. He had just brought his flock down to Sonamarg for the winter. It had been a difficult summer, the military moving the herders on from some of their usual high meadows, and the grazing had been poor, but not as bad as during other recent years.

The Bakarwals, Gujjars and Chopans, the herding tribes and shepherds, have witnessed much. Nomadic by nature and ethnicity, both the Bakarwals and Gujjars are of Hindu origin, of the warrior caste, *kshatriyas*, though many have converted to Islam, depending on the geography of their grazing areas. The Bakarwals are more concentrated in North India but the two tribes intermarry, their clans stretching out across the Indo-Gangetic Plain from Gujarat through to eastern Afghanistan. Chopans are the local herders and shepherds of the Kashmir Valley. They do not like to be confused with the Bakarwals and Gujjars. They are Kashmiris. The Bakarwals and Gujjars are wanderers to them, termed as scheduled tribes, living at the edges of society. The Chopans carry registration cards, showing them proudly for the title that it gives them: 'meat supplier of Government of Jammu and Kashmir'.

All these herders lead hard lives, moving their flocks into the high pastures through the summer months, constantly on the hoof during the grazing season. As they move they carry news, village to village, region to region. Before the arrival of a telephone system they were the main mountain network, disseminating news of births, deals, marriages, clan feuds and deaths. When the insurgency began, and telephone lines were cut or failed, the herders became a main news network again. The majority of the news they carried was of death.

They move through the landscape, disappearing into its shape as they go, re-emerging from behind turf doors, hillocks and rocks, performers in their own kind of dance, witnessing the news that they then carry. Throughout the conflict they have seen the corruption it has bred, the human exchanges: paramilitary operations that surprise militant groups up in the hills, the negotiations between the captors and the captives, releases granted in exchange for large amounts of money.

The shepherd-cousin knew the lame man's story. He had been the carrier of the news of his capture and release, passing it to someone who could contact his aunt in her neighbourhood of Srinagar, passing on the information about her militant son. The shepherd had not seen his cousin at the time. He had just carried the news, and he had heard about his cousin's foot from another herder. Our meeting on the hill above the army camp was the first time they had seen each other for several years.

So they sat and talked about ordinary things in their extraordinary lives. The shepherd described how their main summer pastures, up around Kargil, butting up against the Line of Control, were still tainted by the war that had been fought there in the summer of 1999, three seasons before. Cordite from months of continual shelling had contaminated the grazing land. As members of a registered union the Chopans had been able to complain to their government representative. The question had been raised in the parliament in Srinagar. Money had been promised for treating the grazing areas with sodium hydroxide, simple caustic soda, to neutralise the acidity of the soil caused by the cordite and other explosives. The money had been delivered but it had not been used to buy the caustic soda required for the high pastures.

The shepherd reported the situation to the lame man; the lamb wriggled in his lap, and his daughter was bored by the talk, now sitting at his feet, plaiting strands of her hair, then plaiting the plaits. The shepherd did not complain but nodded at the inevitability of money for caustic soda being sidelined, stolen, transformed into houses, cars, or just stashed by those who were supposed to be serving the most basic needs of the people. For the shepherd it meant that he and his family would have to cut enough fodder to feed their sheep and goats twice a day, all through the bitter months, because the animals had not put on enough meat during the summer grazing time to carry them through winter on the usual one feed a day. He just shrugged and squeezed the last of the milk into the leather nipple for the orphaned lamb. The ewe had died after giving birth to the lamb and its stillborn twin.

'Too weak,' the shepherd said, shaking his head.

The lives of both men sitting on the hillside were controlled by corruption. The lame man was alive because of illegal money changing hands, and the shepherd would have to work longer days all through the winter because promised money for pasture renewal had gone astray. The glacier above creaked mournfully as we drank *noon chai*, salt tea, that made bile rise in my throat.

It made me sick again and again as we drove back to Srinagar. The lame man stared out of the window as soldiers took advantage of our sick stops to hitch lifts. Some of them were formal and polite when they asked for a lift, others were playful or flirtatious, and some were just crude and belligerent, whacking the side of the jeep with their rifle butts, getting in without asking permission, staring hard, laughing as I vomited and then peppering me with questions as I got back to the jeep, wiping my face, and cutting another piece of raw ginger to chew.

We changed vehicle twice between the outskirts of the city and where we stopped at the edge of the lame man's *mohalla*. He hoped it would shake the tail he believed we had picked up on leaving Sonamarg.

RAW, Research and Analysis Wing, the Indian Army's

main external intelligence agency, often came to visit his family, particularly when any member had been up to the meadows to see their Chopan relatives. The lame man's mother did not even want to go any more because of the inevitable visit that would follow: the knocking at the door, usually after midnight, the rounds of questioning, sometimes polite, sometimes brutal, good cop, bad cop. She missed seeing her family very much, her son said, but she did not think that her heart was strong enough any more to withstand the knocking at the door in the night.

The lame man said that there were two things he had not been able to tell his mother when she had asked: the first that he had been trained as a *fedayeen*, a potential suicide fighter; and also about the amount of money that had been paid to the Indian paramilitary group by the militants for his release. He said that he had lied to her about the former, but the latter he had not known.

When others told stories of the exchange of money for the lives of men the sums swung wildly from just a few thousand rupees to *lakhs* (hundreds of thousands), enough for houses and cars. When questioned further the sums swung around again, no one seeming sure about how much had ever really been paid. In contrast the amount sanctioned by the government for the purchase of sodium hydroxide for treating the pastureland around Kargil in the aftermath of the Kargil war in 1999 was twenty-five *lakh* rupees (a bit over £35,000). That seemed to have gone missing in its entirety as no caustic soda was delivered to treat the grazing areas.

Whether I have been sitting with shepherds, ex-militants, soldiers, militants, village people, city people, the old or the young, the subject of corruption will come up as often as the weather. In Kashmir there is an on-going conversation about the state of the sky, the blueness of it, the depth of its grey, the brilliance of the sun, how close the stars seem, a velvet night, a saturated morning, the colours of mist, or the silence of falling snow. Corruption enters the conversation with the same regularity, as ugly to the people as their sky is beautiful, and as over-arcing in their lives.

When I came back from the journey to Sonamarg with the lame man, Maqbool was waiting at the top of the meadow, where the road ends. When I am away for a day, or sometimes more, I seek him out when I get back, wandering from the kitchen building in the meadow to the houseboat, calling out to him. But not that time – Maqbool was standing by the meadow gate, upright and agitated. It was several hours later than I had said I would be back, but time is a relative value in the Valley; hours drift, days, weeks. It made Maqbool's agitation unusual.

'Where were you?' he asked.

'You know where I was. I went to Sonamarg.'

Though this was only a few years ago there was still no mobile network in the Valley. Staying in touch when out meant queuing up at STD, long-distance dialling, booths and, in the social tradition of Kashmir, with everyone listening in on your conversation.

Maqbool came to the side of the jeep and looked into the back seat. Then he walked further down the road, peering into the dark. I looked at the taxi driver. He shrugged. Maqbool took his time to come back.

'This is not the driver from this morning.' Maqbool opened the back door of the taxi jeep and took out a bottle of water and some dried apricots I had left. He held them out to the driver, pointing at them as though to accuse him of trying to steal them. The man shrugged again.

'We changed driver,' I replied.

'How many persons is "we"?' Maqbool asked.

I had left on my own in the morning with a taxi driver, hired for the day. I had told Maqbool I was going to Sonamarg alone. He had talked to the driver and ordered him to look after me.

Maqbool now signalled that I should pay this driver and let him go. I did.

As he drove away Maqbool turned to me, the closest to anger he has ever been with me.

'You were not alone. CID has been here all day. They have been saying to me I am liar because I told them you were going to Sonamarg only with driver, and then they get report that you are on the road with driver and one other man. This is very bad for me. Now they will not believe me when they call to check for these things. They will say I am lying on their face. They will start to come now again every day to see for themselves. DIG CID was involved. It is very bad.' And he marched away down the meadow bearing the water and apricots before him.

I ran after him and he stopped and turned as he heard me thumping down the steep meadow bank behind him.

'Slow, slow, you will fall,' he said.

'I'm so sorry, Maqbool. I was stupid. I thought it was better not to say anything and that if you did not know you would not be lying if you were asked. I know that was wrong. I am sorry.'

He looked at me for a moment, more closely than usual. 'It is a very bad thing for us if something happens to you, terrible.'

I looked down at the grass, ashamed.

'Come,' he said. 'Food is spoilt but you must still have some. It is chicken.'

He had arranged a special supper. Chicken was usually just for high days and holidays. I followed him, still blushing, still ashamed. He led the way to the houseboat, holding the water and apricots aloft.

'You will speak with the DIG CID tomorrow,' he announced.

The DIG CID is the Deputy Inspector General of the Crime Investigation Department. The CID is the government body that investigates serious crime in India, from 'grievous murder to all heinous acts' as they say of themselves. They are also the main spooks within the Valley. Whenever I am there they are watching me as they watch all journalists. It is RAW, the military intelligence, that investigates the locals while the CID deals with foreigners.

They know me well enough now, to the extent that when the worst years of the insurgency were over they did not even bother to pretend any more. They became increasingly overt about tailing, checking and shadowing. By the time of the trip to Sonamarg with the lame man the CID was so used to my fairly quiet schedule that they did not take the trouble to tail me for days at a time, just ringing Maqbool instead to find out what I was doing on any given day. On that particular day they had rung the boat to check, Maqbool had told them that I was going on a sightseeing trip to Sonamarg, and that I was going with just a driver. When I was seen leaving the city with a driver and another man, the CID were on the phone to Maqbool, and then at the houseboat within an hour. It had culminated with the call from the DIG CID, and so Maqbool was agitated, but also quite excited that I should merit such close observation from one so senior in the hierarchy.

It was resolved the following day by a short visit to the DIG at his office in the CID headquarters in town. He was most courteous, seeing me within minutes of my arrival, even though I had not made an appointment. He made it seem as if the whole thing was nothing, that I need not have bothered to come and see him, and that it had all been purely for my own safety. He barely asked me who it was I had been with in Sonamarg, and he only posed the question as I was leaving, and in the manner of an afterthought. I told him, not by name, but by the length of time I had known the man, that he was a guide from the Chopan community. The DIG asked no further questions and waved me away.

After a few days I took a long and convoluted route to see the lame man. Even though I did not seem to have a tail I wandered around in the market area beyond the lame man's *mohalla*, waiting in stalls, having *chai* at a stand, circling around the streets near his before going to his door, my head covered, a *pheran* shrouding me. We walked away from his house, separating to take different rickshaws to another *mohalla* and another *chai* shop.

No one had come to see him since our trip to Sonamarg. He had shown his identity card at each check-post we had gone through, so they could have tracked him down if they wanted to. They had not. I told him about the CID, Maqbool and the visit to the DIG. He wanted to know if any of them had asked for a bribe. They had not. He asked whether I knew how to judge when I was being asked for a bribe. It was a good question.

Do foreigners just miss the language of corruption sometimes and then find that obstacles have appeared to stop us from doing something? Or is it, as I replied to the lame man, that the majority of corruption is kept away from the foreigners so that it can be denied for lack of evidence? It is not in anyone's interest to ask a foreign journalist for a bribe, though that does not mean it does not happen. And when it does the response is usually outrage, an article, a volley from the media spokesman of the embassy or high commission of the foreign journalist's native country, and a sharp retort from the Ministry of External Affairs in Delhi. So the journalist leaves after a while, usually still outraged by their exposure to the corruption, but still without a real sense of its depth and all-pervading grip.

In the anonymity of a *chai* shop in an unfamiliar neighbourhood the lame man relaxed a little.

'Did you really understand that you were being trained as a *fedayeen* [a suicide fighter]?' I asked him.

He nodded and tapped the leg with the damaged foot.

'A waste of all their training. No use to them now. A *fedayeen* has to be fast.' He gave a thin smile, looking down at his foot. 'What is it they were training us for, all this talk of *jihad*? In the camp so often the commanders would tell us about *jihad*, and mullah-types were coming as well to tell us more things. Some of the others I was knowing there had a belief in these things we were being told. They would get excited and shout out about dying for Allah, things like this.' He stopped for a moment, looking up to see if I was listening. 'After some time I did not even hear any more what it was that was being said. It sounded all the same. I did not feel a *jihadi*. I had no job before and this was just work for me. I did not want it to be this way but they were paying me money for what I could do. Then this thing happened, so there is no use for me now.' He waved his hand at his foot again. 'Again I am without work, and with no way to earn money for me and my family.' He put his face into his hands.

When we spoke again it was not about the conflict, but

about easier things: of how he might be able to play cricket again some day soon, and that perhaps someone else could make the runs for him when he was batting.

Arshad, Mohammad's cousin, came to the boat again. He had heard about the problem with the CID. He wanted all the details.

'You know what we Kashmiris are like,' he said, settling himself in to hear the story. 'We like to work a little, spend time with our family a lot, drink tea, and gossip.'

He loved the story, stopping me each time he felt I had not fleshed it out with enough detail. Like the lame man he wanted to know if anyone had asked for a bribe. And like the lame man he was unconvinced when I told him that I had not been asked, suggesting that I had probably missed the hint. He thought that it would cause problems further down the line, that it would be a mark against me, that somehow a way would be found to exact some sort of payment from me at a later date.

'When I marry,' he said, 'it will become very hard. We try to hide from our wives and mothers how much corruption there is, and how many bribes we have to pay. You know how women worry about money. It would be a big problem if they knew how much went on, and how much we pay out. We men have to try and keep it from them.'

Over the years Arshad's eldest cousin, Mohammad, and I have had the same kind of conversation. We have talked of finding ways through the corruption and past the obstacles that are thrust up in the path of people who refuse to pay the bribes.

'We need a leader,' he said once. 'Someone who is so strong that he will make us feel again that we are strong and that we can face this corruption. Only when this thing happens will we be able to stop just accepting that this is the way it has to be. But where will we find this kind of leader? I do not see anyone like this here. Do you?'

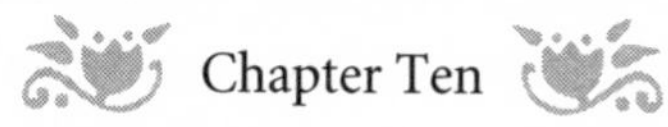

Chapter Ten

'WE WILL GO ON COVERING OUR HEADS'

ARSHAD, MOHAMMAD'S COUSIN, is going to marry Mohammad's daughter Zarina. Though they are only three years apart in age they are from different generations. Arshad is the son of Zarina's great-uncle, the brother of Sobra, and so he is first cousin to Mohammad, Imran, Ibrahim and Yusuf. Zarina and Arshad have been engaged since she was fifteen and he was eighteen.

When they do marry it will be a very religious occasion, and in many ways unelaborate, as befitting followers of Tablighi Jamaat, the movement that the family joined as the insurgency began. Tablighi does not encourage lavish weddings with extravagant shows of wealth. It suggests a quiet union between two servants of Allah. The movement often performs mass *nikaahs* (marriages), so encouraging poorer followers to be able to marry without the financially crippling weddings expected within their communities. The traditional weddings of Kashmir run for days, the whole contractual arrangement for months.

The intricate ceremonies of a traditional arranged marriage

begin with the *Thap*, a word that means to catch hold of somebody. For many it is the first time they see the person who has been chosen for them to marry. Sometimes the meeting is arranged at a local mosque, or in the more romantic setting of one of the Valley's Mughal gardens. The girl and boy see each other for the first time and they are allowed to talk, face to face, or face to veil. They decide whether they can spend their lives together or whether to part ways after the first meeting. This is why it happens outside the homes of the families involved, so that both can walk away without embarrassment if it is not a good match.

For Arshad and Zarina there was no *Thap*. They had grown up together. It was not required.

Once a marriage has been decided on, months of festivities follow. The actual wedding spreads across a minimum of four days, from the *mehendi* ceremony of the bride being decorated with henna patterning, to the parting day, when the groom asks permission of the girl's family before taking his bride away.

For so many who have left Kashmir since the insurgency, whether they are the Pandits like Nita Gigoo, cut off from Kashmir and living as refugees in their own country, or whether they are wealthy Valley Kashmiris who were able to chose to leave for, say, London or New York, the enfolding memories of Kashmiri weddings have the quality of connective tissue to the home that was left behind. They remember the panic of their relatives that some boy would not like their girl enough, and the celebratory relief when the *Thap*, that first meeting, was a success. Older women smile as they remember a young bride coming to them on the first day of her wedding celebrations, her hair in tight plaits, and of how they, her older and married relations, unbound her hair, releasing her girlhood with the plaits.

They tell stories of how many *wazas*, feast cooks, came to prepare for the great wedding *wazwan* of thirty-six dishes; of huge copper *majmas*, *thali* plates, mounded with lamb cooked so many different ways, from the crackling-fried rib meat of *tabak maaz*, to *gushtaaba* meatballs, the lamb ground smooth by stone-pounding, and glistening in thick curd sauce; of how everyone tried to have at least forty *wazas* preparing the food because to cut back on that was a cultural offence, a slight of hospitality; of how mothers would be unable to sleep for fear of running out of *roghan josh*, the rich red lamb dish so central to the *wazwan*, and to their position as a good hostess; and of the tempers of some of the great *vasta wazas*, the head feast cooks, as fiery as the spices they ground, as sharp as the huge cutting blades they wielded over carcass after carcass.

Arshad was unsure about all the paraphernalia of the wedding.

'In part I wish it was done already,' he said. 'This kind of attention is not comfortable for me.'

Zarina's face lit up at the idea of being the bride. 'Though it will be quite small, you know,' she said.

But still the thought of all the different outfits that she would need made her laugh excitedly each time the subject came up.

An ageing Valley woman in exile in a London suburb clapped her hands slowly as she talked of how the singing and dancing began at her own *mehendi* ceremony, and of how her female relatives had stopped her from joining the dancing for so long because the henna spirals and paisley patterning on her hands, arms, feet and legs had still needed more time to dry. She talked of how the intricate designs on her body had made her finally feel a woman rather than a girl, and of how they had stopped her being so afraid of that looming first night with her husband because she had not felt naked but adorned, decked out like a maharani, she said. She laughed as she remembered being bathed by her mother and aunts on the final day of the wedding, and how embarrassed and upset she had been when one of her aunts had said that her husband might not be so happy because she was bringing him only walnuts for breasts, but that at least she made up for this by having a melon of a bottom.

And then she showed photographs of a young couple, her husband and herself, she in an intricate wedding *salwar kameez*, the front heavy with embroidery, her husband smiling out with a lopsided grin, his *karakula topi*, his wedding turban, slightly crooked as well. Her expression was harder to read as she was looking down in most of the pictures, and to the side in another, towards someone beyond the edge of the frame. She said that her cousins had been trying to make her laugh while the pictures were being taken.

When she put the pictures away it was with the deep sadness of someone who has lived much of their life as an exile, cut off from the root that nourished and conditioned a way of being.

It used to be that weddings were performed at midnight, but the insurgency and the curfews that followed stopped that. For a while it seemed there were no weddings in the Valley, and that the idea of any kind of future had been entirely crushed by the ferocity of the military crackdown initiated by Governor Jagmohan in the early stages of the conflict. The *wazas*, the wedding feast cooks, were without work, scheming aunts and cousins no longer talked of matches and marriage plans. Even when the sadder rhythm of conflict took hold it could not entirely repress the human instinct for survival. It began to seep back, and so weddings returned, though in a much pared-down form.

While those who left the Valley cling to time-tinted images of joyous weddings, the rich spiked scent of *roghan josh* held in their sense memory, another reality of those long days of dancing and feasting fades with distance. For many poorer families the financial load of a wedding created debts that became impossible to repay, so creating a cycle of borrowing and impoverishment. With the insurgency this became even more acute as everyone had less money, the poor struggling for their most basic needs, the middle class trying to find ways to cut costs, and many of the wealthier Kashmiris leaving. It made the wild methods of extremists like Asiya Andrabi, the veiled leader of Dukhtaran-e-Millat, the Daughters of Faith, attractive to many for purely practical reasons. While much of her extremism was too radical for most, her rage against dowry was something that found wide support. Combined with her championing of remarriage for widows of the insurgency, and simple weddings, Andrabi, like the Tablighi Jamaat, found a wide audience hungry for the idea that marriage did not have to impoverish a family, and bind them to a life of debt; that in itself was a crime against the belief that money lending and charging interest are un-Islamic.

While these currents have not altered the traditional love of the whole wedding gamut, the result is that the tone of Valley weddings is now usually of a much lower key. Many richer families, particularly among the more devout, feel that they must set an example by keeping the marriage festivities to a minimum, reducing the days of celebration, the number of dishes in the *wazwan*, the public exchange of gifts between the bride and groom's families. This is what Mohammad wanted for Zarina and Arshad, a devout but pared-down marriage ceremony.

Whatever external restraints may be shown it is still mapped into the cultural DNA of the Valley to show largesse and extravagance, to prove to those around how well you have done, and your family's position within the community. To be understated about wealth and success is anathema to most Kashmiris, or it was until the insurgency. Whatever the cultural instinct, the advice of the religious leaders and teachers is what now calls the dance.

India's rapid economic growth means that more Muslims can now afford to go on the pilgrimage of Hajj, the fifth pillar of Islam. Officially there are about 150 million Muslims in India, including Kashmir. The overall economics of this greater Muslim community, twinned with the ease of air travel, mean that huge and increasing numbers of Indian Muslims are going to Saudi Arabia for Hajj, and for Umrah (the same pilgrimage, though taken at any period outside the time of Hajj).

Pilgrims return from Mecca over-awed by the enormity of a sea of the devoted advancing between the Well of Zamzam and Mount Arafat. They are moved to pick up habits and language more familiar in the Arab countries than in South and Central Asia, to show that they have been, to mark the impact of the huge pilgrimage in their life. They are also enormously impressed by Saudi organisation, the way the millions of pilgrims are guided and provided for by serried ranks of white-robed Hajj officials.

Mohammad speaks with awe of the arrangements.

'You cannot imagine how it is, the most beautiful thing you have ever seen. These special Hajj people are so helpful and giving everyone guidance about where to go and how to go about the acts of Hajj, no matter how small or humble a person it is they are helping. It is the same for all, the richest and most poor. It is so beautiful to see.'

When people return from Saudi Arabia they want to remind others, and themselves, that they have made the great pilgrimage. To copy something that has been inspirational for them is to keep the memory alive. Aspects of Islam shift within the culture of the Valley as the Saudi influence comes from so many directions, in an arc that reaches from the Hajj to the training camps in Pakistan-controlled Kashmir.

On the street Zarina and her female relatives could be mistaken for orthodox Muslim Arabs, completely covered in black *burqas*, moving through the alleys and markets, between the houses of relatives and friends in anonymous groups, separate from the more familiar open faces and simple scarves of other Kashmiri women.

In parts of the city the women are entirely covered, uniformly swathed in black in neighbourhoods under the influence of some of the more extreme mullahs, or militant groups that dictate how women dress. In other areas there is hardly a black *burqa* to be seen, the women in the more traditional *salwar kameez*, covered up in *pherans* only in winter, their hair tied back under scarves bright with flowers and colour, curls escaping around the edges, a long plait at the back. This was once the familiar look of a Srinagar street, another cityscape that changed as the insurgency began.

In marked contrast the more affluent centre of town, around Lal Chowk, along Polo View, Residency and Maulana Azad Road, has an easier dress code. Some girls are in jeans, their heads uncovered, their soft shapes visible under T-shirts. The police, paramilitary and men on the street stare as these girls go by. They have been starved of this kind of exposure for so many years. The confidence of the years after the successful election of 2002 brought with them a courage, a certain defiance that allows a girl from a less orthodox family to get away with wearing a T-shirt again. What it exposes will be watched, trawled over, drunk in, the girl left exposed by her exposure.

Who can judge them in this place where terror of the fighting meant that the streets became almost entirely male for so many years, and at a time when women scuttled to and fro in haste, covered, bowed over, rushing to get back inside for fear of assault or abuse, even in the richer, more relaxed parts of the city? Soldiers, policemen and paramilitaries will have been in postings for months on end. The women they see now on the more confident streets are the only ones they see, and so they stare, as do all the men on the streets.

While Zarina and her relatives may go out into the streets in black it is not just an Arabic import, though the Dars have adopted some of their more orthodox views and habits from their visits to Mecca, and from the guidelines of the Tablighi. Full black *burqas* are also a part of the Valley's tradition, and one that was not just confined to Islam. For centuries it was also the measure of a man's success. If he could afford to put his wife under the *burqa* when she was moving around outside the house it was a sign that the woman did not have to work, that there were enough servants in the house to fetch and carry, clean and cook, freeing the woman of the house to be fully covered, and therefore unable to carry loads on her head. Sikh Kashmiri women wore them, Hindus too, some of them black, but it was more common during the era of the *burqa* as a social statement to wear white and pale blue *burqas*.

The woman who made this point to me about how the *burqa* used to be worn is a Kashmiri doctor from Srinagar. She did not want to be named. She has been targeted by Asiya Andrabi's Daughters of Faith for her views about women in Islam. During the worst years of the insurgency she refused to cover up. She went to work in *salwar kameez*, her head uncovered, or in Western dress, as she always had, since she first qualified in the early 1980s.

She left the Valley and moved to Delhi so that she could go on working without being harassed, or attacked. She is in her early fifties now, slight and small. Her skin has the dusty quality of a smoker, the bags under her eyes are heavy and dark, her hair is cut short.

When I last saw her, a little over a year ago, we went to talk outside the hospital where she is now working in South Delhi. We found a bench and sat in early spring sun while she smoked. Patients walked to and fro, staring as they went. A Muslim family passed, the father out ahead of the group, his hands behind his back; his son came next, and two fully covered women in black *burqas* followed with a young girl in a pretty dress with lots of frills, her head still uncovered. She was only about five years old. As she turned to stare at the doctor she let go of the hand that held hers from beneath a *burqa*. The doctor blew a smoke ring at the girl who smiled and ran away.

'Hope I converted her,' the doctor said. 'You see so many of you foreigners just assume that the women wear the *burqa* because their husbands will beat them if they do not, or people like Andrabi will throw acid in their faces,' she said. 'This is there, both these things. But it is the women as much. They cover themselves, they teach their daughters to do the same, and so it goes. Sometimes it is because they are from this kind of family and there is no choice for them. Some of them do it because they know that all these men are just not able to control themselves. Women like this come to see me here with their problems, and they see my name and realise I am a Muslim. They ask me how I can move about without my head covered, and in these kind of clothes.' She pointed to the trousers and shirt that she was wearing under the doctor's white coat. 'They ask me if I am scared of being attacked by men. That is how it is with these women. They are too scared to take off the *burqa*, both for the shame that they believe it will bring on their families, and because they do not have any faith that men will be able to keep control of themselves if they all take off their *burqas*.' She brushed some ash off her knee and smiled. 'But you know I'm a grey-head now so they can't imagine how anyone would be interested in me as a woman now with this short hair, these clothes, smoking and all. Imagine if they knew I like to drink whisky as well.' She smiled again as another family stared as they walked past.

To Zarina and her female relatives someone like the doctor is as foreign in her views as I am to them.

'These kind of women are not really Muslims, are they?' Zarina said of women like the doctor: ones who do not cover their heads, those trying to take a stand against what they see as excessive restriction and, as in the case of the doctor, who regard many of these religious dictates, or diktats, as breaches of human rights.

Zarina was showing me around the new house that Mohammad and his large and extending family moved to in 2008, built on another part of the plot of land bought by her grandfather, Sobra. It is just a narrow garden plot away from the old family home where, until Mohammad and his family moved out, there were thirty-four members of the extended family: Sobra, his wife, the four sons, their wives, children and now grandchildren. It is a short distance between where the donga boat now lies, broken up and stacked beside the lake, and Mohammad’s new house, but it is a great generational and social stride for the Dars.

At the moment it is a relatively small crowd of twelve in the new house: Mohammad and his wife, his six children, the wives of his two elder sons and two grandchildren, so far. It is this house that Zarina will leave when she marries Arshad. They will live close by and Zarina’s bonds with her siblings, her mother and father will remain thick and tight. She will return often, the first time for a period soon after her marriage, and she will go back home again during her pregnancies, extending the maternity leave from her married home maybe for some months beyond the birth of her children. It will be a very porous dividing membrane between her married home and this, the newly built home of her immediate family.

‘You must forgive, it is a terrible, terrible mess,’ Zarina said as we moved upstairs to see the family bedroom suites. ‘We have been doing so much of unpacking and sorting, and now it is the time for the big spring clean. Everything you see will be all upside down.’

She took me first to her mother and father’s new room.

‘You know my father, he has to move all the time. If he is not on a plane going here, there and all places, if he is here for some time, even more than just a few days he has to be moving. When the snow was heavy he could not move around so much so he had to get us to change his bedroom so that he still felt that there was some kind of movement happening.’ She smiled.

Zarina loves her father. He is heroic to her, the builder of a new and modern home for his family, the symbol of success. He brings her back fragments of other worlds each time he returns with tales from Dubai, Saudi, London, Singapore, Shanghai, even from Delhi or Bangalore. He is her north and her south.

'See this mess now, imagine trying to make head and toe of all this,' she said, pushing the contents of a half-unpacked suitcase from one side of the bed to the other.

She pulled a long, soft grey chiffon *dupatta* from out of the pile, holding it up to the window and examining it against the light. Then she unwound the long scarf that was wrapped around her head and neck, discarded it onto the pile, and rewound the pale grey over her thick braid of glossy hair, and around her pale neck and throat. She moved to a mirror, sliding the scarf forward onto her forehead, and then back exactly to match her hairline so that not a strand or single hair could be seen. She patted it into place and then turned back to me.

'Better, no?' she asked.

I nodded.

Apart from the mirror the only things on the walls of her father and mother's new room were two framed verses from the Qur'an, their gold calligraphy matching the frame, and a picture of the Kaaba, the black-clothed heart of Islam, its structure turned to every day by billions as they pray. It is night in the photograph, the Kaaba floodlit, dark and solid amid a blurred swirl of pilgrims performing *tawaf*, the circumnavigation of the Kaaba, so integral to Hajj and Umrah.

'Now see this.' Zarina called me over to the glass door that led to a balcony beyond the room.

We stood outside in the afternoon sun, looking down the

garden towards the houseboats and the lake. Maqbool was crossing the meadow to the cook house, his hand raised to someone we could not see. Two *shikaras* slid across Nagin, their fine trails dotted by each dip of the *shikaris*' paddles.

On the floor above was her bedroom, as messy and mixed as that of any teenage girl, though she is in her twenties now. Clothes were scattered about, a basket of nail varnishes lay on her unmade bed. Zarina's toenails were painted blue, her fingernails candy pink. Some dolls were lined up on a shelf beside her bed, a small china pony and a kitten in a bonnet. But there is no music, none of the technology that is in almost every middle-class teenage bedroom in South Asia. Instead, the centrepiece of the room, beyond the bed, was a glass cabinet full of books on Hadith and Qur'anic commentaries. Beside her room was a small prayer room, its walls cedar-panelled like a sauna, a place where family members could go alone to contemplate, pray and reflect, away from the constant jumble of the family milieu.

'But you know it was so cold in winter we just could not go in and sit for any time at all without almost dying from cold,' she said, locking the door to the prayer room with a key from a collection that she carried. 'It is not the main place for prayer. That you must see, but come, see my brother,' she said as we crossed the hall.

Her elder brother, Asif, was sitting on his bed, his wife, the daughter of Mohammad's sheikh, sitting below him, their baby boy spread out in the crook of where her leg was crossed onto her knee – a perfect anatomical fit, close enough for him to be able to see his mother's face, but allowing her hands to be free. She was plaiting her hair under her black *hijab*. Her husband was lying propped on one elbow, a pair of sunglasses was pulled up onto his head, his full beard spread onto his chest, one trainer kicked off, the other unlaced under his plain white *salwar kameez*, his mobile phone in one hand, some photographs of a recent family outing in the other.

'Let me see, let me see.' Zarina grabbed the pictures from her brother.

They had driven to Pahalgam, the shepherds' valley high on the Lidder River. It had been on a recent Sunday, when the first of the warm spring sun was breaking through winter. The group had been Zarina, her two brothers, their wives, and their two babies. Zarina passed the photographs on to me as she looked at them.

'Look, look at this, how handsome my brothers are.' She passed one to me of her two brothers, standing on a rock in the middle of the river, bright sun, snow in the background, their hip sunglasses and trainers above and below plain white *salwar kameez*. Both boys are in their early twenties and both already have full, luxuriant beards.

'And this here.' Zarina passed another one.

It was of all of them, this time lined up on the edge of the river. The boys are carrying their children, the older of the two on his father's shoulders. The three women, Zarina, her elder brother's wife and her first cousin Sabeena, who is now also her sister-in-law, stand on either side of the men. They cannot be identified except by the tips of their shoes beneath their full black *burqas*, intense in bright sun beside the white of the men's clothing.

Zarina passed over another picture. It was of the two boys again, this time leaning on the front of Asif's car, its tinted windows dark in the sun, the back spoiler finlike in a place where it is rarely possible to go more than forty miles an hour on even the straightest stretch of road. Asif is draped over his car in the motor show style of a leggy blonde. He is very proud of his car. It was a wedding present to him from his father, Mohammad, discreetly given after the pared-down main ceremony was over.

Zarina snatched the rest of the photographs from her brother, and skittered out of the room, grabbing me with her free hand. Asif was laughing and shouting at her to bring them back. She called to her cousin, her younger brother's wife, as we shot down the stairs.

'Come, Sabeena, come, I have the pictures, I have them from Asif.'

Sabeena clattered out of the kitchen, with a bowl of baby food in one hand, the cousin who once spoke to me about wanting to be a lawyer.

'Show me, show me.' She reached out to take the pile of pictures from Zarina who waved them over the shorter girl's head.

'No, look at your hands, all over baby goo. Asif will be mad if you put so much of mess on them. We can all look in some moments after I have shown the prayer room.' Zarina skipped away, still waving the pictures at Sabeena.

As Zarina left the house she lowered her head and pulled her *hijab* further over her face as she called to one of the house servants to bring her the key to the main prayer room.

It was underneath the house, a prayer cellar, the whole basement, carpeted with Kashmiri rugs, one wall glassed in with shelves of books. Chandeliers lit the space, sparkly and gold in the plain surroundings. In this room, more than anywhere else, Mohammad's journey is manifest, both that of his success and his belief.

'We have such times here of teaching. Our sheik, he comes to this place and gives talks to us. It will be full up, no space for any more persons to come, and sometimes he gives talks just for women, just for us. It is a very great thing.' She picked at one of her candy-pink nails and turned to the bookshelves. 'Come, I have something for you.'

She sorted through a cupboard below the shelves and brought out two large pamphlets.

'You know I am teaching girls who come to the house, helping them with their studies of the Qur'an?' She turned back to me.

I nodded. I had sat at the edge of one of her classes during an earlier visit, listening hard but understanding very little as Zarina had talked to four little girls about the role of women in Islam. She had waved her index fingers in the air whenever she made a point, a sort of jive dance with her hands. It had made me smile as the little girls had looked on with wide eyes.

'Two of them were with me just before you came, small, small girls, one is eight, the other nine. These are not so much for them because as of now they are too young, but they are very helpful with older girls. They are very instructive.' She held out the pamphlets to me. 'These are for you from my side. They are made and printed here in Kashmir. I think you will find them very useful. You should become Muslim,' she said, turning back to close and lock the cupboard.

I thanked her as we went back up into the daylight.

'Come, now we must show these pictures to Sabeena, and you must say who is looking the best in the pictures.'

Zarina would not let me go into the kitchen with her to make tea. She wanted me to sit and wait in the formal sitting room, upright on a shiny velveteen sofa, the pamphlets in my lap. Her youngest eight-year-old brother was mildly torturing his toddler niece on the other side of the room, constantly running from the besotted baby every time she just managed to reach him, her arms outstretched to him. Zarina clattered pans loudly in the kitchen beyond, already teasing Sabeena about the photographs.

I began to read the pamphlets, published by Radiant Reality in Srinagar. One was titled *Sister, Mind Your Dress*, the other *Good Character*. They were mostly extracts from discourses given by various contributing Islamic teachers. At the back of *Sister, Mind Your Dress* was a section called 'Women abuse in America'.

'It is interesting, no?' Zarina said as she came back into the room, carrying a large tray.

There was an elegant little samovar of *kahwa chai* for me, two cups of milky *chai* for Zarina and Sabeena, and several plates piled high with biscuits, small seeded rounds of bread, honey cake and chocolate cake. Zarina poured *kahwa* into a delicate cup and passed it to me, offering plate after plate of everything else as well. Sabeena squatted down beside us, crumbling a *tsot* bread round into her mug, squishing it down and sucking at the rim before the tea spilled over the edge. Both girls focused on their mugs of tea-sodden bread until they were empty, a concentrated interlude of contented slurping that ended with Sabeena pouncing on the pile of photographs, having finished her tea just ahead of Zarina.

'Look at my husband, how handsome he looks in this one.' She pushed the picture at me, the one of the two boys, arms around each other's shoulders, balancing on a rock in the river.

'Both my brothers are looking nice.' Zarina snatched the picture away, wiping her hands on the front of her *kameez* as she did so.

'This one is not nice, I am looking fat in this. See how fat I look.' Sabeena passed another picture to me.

It was of her and one of the other two girls. I could not tell who was who. Sabeena tapped her finger on one of the black figures.

'The wind is blowing, look, it's billowing out your *burqa*. Of course it makes you look fat; it's not you, it's the wind.'

Sabeena took the picture back, peering at it again. She sniffed. 'Zarina is looking fine, not fat at all.'

Zarina is taller and slimmer than Sabeena. Whatever I said was not going to persuade Sabeena out of her insecurity. I concentrated on a piece of honey cake while Sabeena complained about not having been able to lose her pregnancy weight. Zarina remained silent, flipping through the pictures again without reassuring her cousin. Sabeena took a piece of chocolate cake and ate it purposely.

I studied the first of the pamphlets on my knee, scanning an article on marriage customs in *Sister, Mind Your Dress.*

> **Some important customs for Islamic weeding [sic].**
> In aping Western methods sheepishly, Muslims has adopted many customs which are un-Islamic and frowned upon. Some examples are:
> - Displaying the bride on stage.
> - Inviting guests for the wedding from far off places.
> - The bride's people incurring unnecessary expenses by holding a feast which has no basis in Shariah. We should remember that Walimah *[marriage blessing feast]* is the feast arranged by the bridegroom after the marriage is consummated.
> - It is contrary to Sunnah *[the way of the Prophet, the trodden path]* (and the practice of some non-Muslim tribes in India) to wish, hope for or demand presents and gifts for the bridegroom from the bride's people.

Almost every aspect of traditional Kashmiri weddings was contradicted.

'It disgusts me,' the woman doctor had said on the bench in the sun in South Delhi, cigarette in hand. 'They don't even know why they are covering up any more.'

I asked if she wanted them to be uncovered, if she felt that would be an advance.

'Only if they want to. They do not question it, this is what I find is the wrong of it. They just put it on, no challenge, no enquiry. Of course there are those who know exactly why, Dukhtaran-e-Millat, Daughters of Faith, those women, using it as a crude weapon against other women. Do you imagine they really think on this, though? Do you think they wonder how it will seem to other Muslim women around the world, or to non-Muslims who are sympathetic to Islam, and even to women who are not sympathetic, the kind who think that everyone with a beard is bad? How do they think they are helping Islam when their method is just to create more fear? The women of Islam are one of the great things we have to help us now in this time, but if they are arming themselves as well, if they are making the veil a weapon, this will only become worse.'

She looked across to what I was writing.

'You really will not use my name, will you? They know me, they know my feelings on this, but if my name is on it as well it gives them even more reason to make things very hard for my family in Srinagar.'

She leaned her head against the wall behind us, lifting her face into the spring sun.

'I did not always feel this way. When I was a young girl, in my early twenties and such, I used to cover my head. Not in this terrible way, but just a *dupatta*, a scarf, the prettier the better. It was a part of being a woman. It did not feel oppressive to me then. I was a young adult woman and we were all covering our heads, in part because we always had, a little because it was a sign of being grown up, a woman, and also because a woman without her head covered, well, then certain things would be thought about her, about her character. Of course there were some who did not, girls I was at college with, from well-to-do Pandit families, but most of us covered our heads on the streets, to fit in. And then all of this started and I went the opposite way.' She closed her eyes in the sun. 'You know some of those men think that the devil lives in women's hair, and that we do some kind of witchcraft with it. This is how foolish some of this is, like little children in the playground making up stories. So I cut mine off, what could they do then?' She laughed and reached for another cigarette.

During one of our conversations on the boat I asked Arshad, the bridegroom-in-waiting, if he expected his wife to have her head covered all the time. He did not answer directly.

'You know some women now cover themselves even in the bed, their heads as well, I mean?'

'But what about you?' I asked again.

He shrugged. 'I suppose she will have to because it is for her safety when she is outside of the house.'

I have asked Zarina if she had ever considered not covering her head.

'Why?' she asked. 'I would not be Muslim then.'

We talked about the wording in the Qur'an, the origin of *hijab* and how it seems to put the onus onto men to provide a veil of modesty or privacy to separate men and women, as it was in the family of Muhammad when men wished to speak to his wives.

'We will go on covering our heads,' Zarina said, closing down the conversation, and pulling the grey chiffon scarf that she had taken from her mother's bed further down over her forehead.

Chapter Eleven

ONE MORNING DURING RAMADAN

'I AM SO HAPPY in Ramadan,' Mohammad said. 'As the days go on each one makes me happy over again. But I am the most happy of all when I am with my family on Nagin Lake for the month of fasting. I can walk with my brothers and my sons to the mosque to hear *juz* [the evening recitation during Ramadan of one-thirtieth of the Qur'an. By the end of the month the entire text has been heard]. It is such a peaceful time.' He was in Delhi, struggling in the post-monsoon humidity, dreaming of cool evening air coming off his beloved lake.

It was just a week before Ramadan.

'The time cannot pass fast enough,' he said. 'Once I reach home there will be no more travelling for the whole of this time, only the quiet time of walking between the mosque and my house.' He paused contentedly. 'You know my youngest boy? He is, what, no more than five years at this time, but he is telling me, "Papa, I want to do *Sawm* [fasting] with you." ' His voice was full of his smile. 'Imagine this?' he said.

Children are not usually expected to fast for the month of Ramadan until they are twelve years old. The elderly, sick and pregnant women are also excused from going without food and water from sunrise to sunset. Some of the more orthodox do not even swallow their own spit during the fasting hours.

'I cannot think of any other thing that can bring me so much pleasure as the time I spend with my children, when we are resting a little after *Fajr* [dawn prayers]. There is so much peace, you can only imagine.'

The family wakes before sunrise to eat the meal of *suhoor*, the only food of the day until the fast is broken at *Maghrib* (sunset prayer). After this it is a quiet time; some sleep, others just rest; Mohammad calls his children to him.

He left Delhi the following week to get to Kashmir before the beginning of Ramadan on 4 October 2005.

It was to be unlike any other Ramadan of Mohammad's life.

On the first Saturday of the fast people were resting in the early morning. It meant that most were in their homes with their families around them.

At 8.50 a.m. on the Pakistani side of the Line of Control, and so at 9.20 a.m. on the Indian side, the earth opened up to a depth of ten kilometres.

It was an earthquake measuring between 7.6 and 7.7 on the Richter scale, the same level of ferocity as in San Francisco in 1906, the earthquake that changed building regulations in so many fault line areas of the world, though not all. The official number given for those killed in the 2005 earthquake, a few weeks afterwards, would have almost exactly filled the Olympic Stadium in Beijing in 2008, 80,000. That number continued to swell by further thousands throughout the winter. An estimated 3.3 million people were made homeless, and 8 million people's lives were affected. The destruction was said to have been intensified by the severity of the earth's upthrust, and by the poor standards of construction in affected areas. Little attention was drawn to the fact that the number of deaths was as high as it was since so many people were in their homes sleeping because it was the time of rest after morning prayers.

When he described it to me later Maqbool was standing with his legs wide, weaving from one side to the other. The whole houseboat was beginning to shift in the water as he swung from side to side.

'This is how it was, but not this, many times this. I was standing just somewhere near here, just there.' He pointed to the corner of the veranda. 'Sometimes when Ibrahim is coming down to see that all things are in order he likes to jump on the wires and this is making the boat rock, like a game.' He waved towards the thick, twisted wire cables that moor the houseboat to the bank. 'This is what I was thinking he was up to, except it was so much bigger, like whole of his family doing the same with him. I called out, "What is this?" and looked about to see what he was up to. I was confused by this thing as well because it was early, the time people are relaxing a little after prayers. But no one was there, and then it became so bad, the whole of the lake shaking about and things shooting up from the water. The others on the houseboats were calling out to me. We knew that this was not a usual tremble, that this was a very bad thing.'

In Kashmir, as in any fault line region, there are tremors all the time. The plates that collided to throw the sea into the sky, creating the Himalayas, and the Valley, continue to chaff and agitate.

People barely stop for what they call 'the shivering', and if they do it is just to look up to see if anything is crashing down from above: masonry, laundry, flower-pots from sills. People have been killed by things falling from the sky, not often, but it has happened, and so some people still look up before carrying on. There is a children's song that came out of the insurgency, a mother singing to her baby: 'May it be sweet flowers falling from the sky that takes you from me, and not the guns, and not the soldiers, and not the places beyond the mountains.'

If the tremors happen during the night people sleep through them, or, if they are awake they put out a hand to steady the glass of water beside their bed, or gather up a child who is not yet used to the fact that they have been born in a place that shudders.

On 8 October 2005 it was different. Even though the epicentre of the earthquake was seventy-seven miles away, the people of Srinagar knew that their world had ruptured again.

Muzaffarabad, the capital of Pakistan-controlled Kashmir, was at the epicentre. While many were resting in their homes, children were at school, Saturday being another full school day in most of South Asia. In engineering terms the city suffered total structural failure. The majority of its buildings were built of large unreinforced concrete blocks. It is one of the cheapest methods of building, and the Central Pakistan Government has always tried to save money in its administration of this part of Kashmir. Most of the government buildings, such as schools and hospitals, had been built this way. Sixty per cent of these buildings collapsed, causing the highest loss of life.

Srinagar managed to escape without large-scale destruction, because so many of the city's older houses had been built during a time of more careful craftsmanship that had made allowances for the shifting nature of the mountains. The Dars' old house escaped with just some cracks, while in Delhi, nearly 500 miles from the epicentre, buildings split and fell. In Kabul, 250 miles in the other direction, the shuddering was strong, though the shield of the high Karakoram ranges absorbed most of the shock before it reached the Afghan capital. In contrast the fault line runs down directly from Muzaffarabad into the plains and to the Indian capital. Tower blocks fell in Islamabad, the Pakistani capital, 200 miles from the destruction in the capital of Pakistan-controlled Kashmir. Whole villages in north Pakistan disappeared, flattened in the first upthrust, buried under landslides, or their cracks opened up more slowly in the wave of more than 1,000 aftershocks that followed, some measuring up to 6.2 on the Richter scale. Many of those trying to dig people out in the immediate aftermath were crushed under further collapsing buildings as the aftershocks came and came.

As those who had not been crushed emerged into the dust and chaos some thought at first that it had been a nuclear attack, that finally the fragile peace between India and Pakistan had broken. Pakistan's leader in the 1970s, Zulfikar Ali Bhutto, had boasted to the world that his people would eat grass in order to become a nuclear power. Governments had creamed money from the domestic budget to keep pace with India's nuclear programme. In both countries public building projects in some of the highest risk earthquake areas in the world had been put up without proper foundations and without reinforcement, undermined by both corruption and a lack of public funding. It was a natural disaster but the worst of its devastation was man-made.

Mohammad managed to get a message to me.

> Please come as soon as you can. We cannot make sense of why this thing has occurred at this time. We wait to hear from you in hope that you will be able to make people

> understand about this terrible thing that has happened here. With the help of Allah.
> Mohammad

As were so many others that morning, Mohammad had been resting with his family after the dawn prayers of Ramadan. At first he had not understood what was happening as he emerged from deep sleep. People were calling his name, a child was crying. He was not sure if it was one of his children. His youngest son was clinging to him, asking him over and over again what was happening. He tried to soothe his son but he did not have an answer.

'The most foolish thing is that no one was moving. It seemed we were not able. Even after so many years of knowing about these things, and of the way we are shaking so often, we did not know what was happening. It was as though we were waiting. When I came to know the full story it filled me with so much sadness for these people who were killed. For those who were not sleeping, if they did have some little warning, some shaking, I can only think that they were the same as this and could not find a way to move,' Mohammad said later.

Communication was hard in the immediate aftermath. The phone lines that had withstood the earthquake were constantly overloaded. Contact was random. Email was inefficient but it was slightly more reliable than the phone.

Another message came from Mohammad.

> With the help of Allah some local people and myself have managed to gather together three trucks of plastic and CGI sheets [corrugated galvanised iron] for the construction of shelters, blankets, and food supplies. These are being taken as I write this to you to Uri side *[the area most*

> *damaged by the earthquake in Indian-controlled Kashmir].*
> I will go with one of the trucks. May I humbly request that you help us to gather more supplies. We will need doctors, many of them. Please to contact all you know in the hope that they will be able to come to us in this terrible situation. In this sad time I greet you, in the name of Allah, the Merciful, the Compassionate.
> Mohammad

There was organisational chaos in Srinagar as local businessmen like Mohammad responded to the disaster, galvanising those around them to help as well. Local and international NGOs tried and failed to co-ordinate the relief efforts.

It was reported from India that many of the training camps in Pakistan-controlled Kashmir had been destroyed. As though to disprove this various militant groups continued to attack the security forces on the Indian side of the state. Some said that reinforcement units of the Pakistan Army were being sent up to the Line of Control because the leadership of General Pervez Musharraf believed that the Indian Government might use the disaster as an opportunity to attack. It was also reported that this movement of troops resulted in a delayed response to the disaster by the Pakistan military. The government tried to refute these reports, vehemently.

Much of the worst damage on the Indian side was centred on the Inner Line military areas because of the proximity of the epicentre to the Line of Control. It meant that the Indian Army was right there. The first rescuers that many of the people saw were soldiers.

'It was incredible, a thing I would never have imagined in my life. The army were like saviours for so many. People have been saying this thing to me, over and over,' Mohammad said of the Indian army's response to the disaster.

Three days after the earthquake he was on the road with the second convoy of relief supplies. The army and border roads units had already been able to clear many of the landslides that had blocked roads to villages that had been the most severely damaged, and they kept them open so that the relief supply trucks could get through. Mohammad was able to contact me again with what he was witnessing:

> It is with such a weight in my heart that I write to you of these things. For some of the time we were driving through these mountains that are of such beauty I cannot find ways to describe, and then we would reach another place where every building was collapsed, the people in so much shock that they were just sitting about on the sides of the road, some of them with a few of their possessions, but most of them with no more than the clothes they were wearing. Justine, these are poor people who have already been through so much during this time in Kashmir, and now they do not even have the little that they have worked for. Many of the people I spoke with were only able to cry while they were trying to tell me of how much they had lost. In the name of Allah, the Merciful, the Compassionate.
> Mohammad

For so much of the world this devastated place was a security tinderbox, a dangerous region that offered sanctuary to those claiming to have declared war on the West. And yet the Western countries responded in a way that amazed many people, from locals to world leaders.

Donations began to flood in as soon as the news of the earthquake broke, and agonising images from the disaster dominated the headlines. But Mohammad did not know any of this yet. News was limited in the Valley, and he was on the road all the time.

> Today I am just returned from Uri side to be with my family again on Nagin. How can I explain to you these things that I am seeing. We were there for some days. We drove with another delivery of CGI sheets and some medical supplies. These things had all been gathered by local persons here. Some are from business people who have the good fortune to be doing well, but others, even people from small villages with so little of all things, when they came to know where we were going they would give us some rupees to help. For some of these it was their money for the whole month. This thing will stay in my heart for all of my life. People who have nothing and so many difficulties of their own, they are giving to us to help. Allah is great.
> Mohammad

I flew back to India ten days after the earthquake. I was carrying money that had been given to me for earthquake relief work by people I knew, and by some I had never met, both in small amounts and larger ones too. Some was from people who had very little themselves. Several of the givers had gone to great lengths to get their donations to me. The night before I flew there was another message from Mohammad:

> We have a problem at this end that I am hoping you will be able to help us with. We have run out of supplies of hot

> bottles in Srinagar. Please find a way to bring some with you from England. This thing I know will be hard to do as we need large quantities, in the thousands. To people this is a foolish ask but it is this way, because the tents provided for people who are now without homes are thin and so they are keeping their *kangris* with them at all times. When they are sleeping the *kangris* fall over under blankets and coverings. They are then burning themselves and also tents are burning up as well. There is so much of sadness that people are sleeping much of the time. It is because they are very tired. It is also now getting cold in the nights, though the sun in the days is still quite warm. For this reason we need hot bottles. We have quite a good number of geysers in place now and so water can be boiled to fill them and there is not the risk of this burning that I speak about. I think perhaps I have not given enough time to you to arrange this thing so I am hoping that we will find another way to supply. In the name of Allah, the Merciful, the Compassionate.
> Mohammad

People had asked how they could help. They had rung, emailed and written. The request for hot-water bottles both surprised and pleased those I told. They were such a tangible thing. Bank details were sent – another act of faith because we were not yet an established NGO, and the nature of Kashmir's recent history meant that foreign donations were subject to the highest level of scrutiny. The enormity of the moment demanded great acts of humanity by governments, locally, nationally and internationally. But as the militants had, within days of the earthquake, continued to attack the security forces we, the outsiders rushing in to do what we believe we do so well, could only accept that the Government of India had a valid position in not allowing direct foreign donation, unless it was made through an already tightly vetted organisation. The transfer of money was an act of faith because it was going directly into my account. I was going to take it out in cash, and carry it to the Valley in cash.

The government's argument for not allowing foreign donation was very clear. Once the separatist insurgency had been hijacked from outside the Valley, money from Pakistan, Saudi, Dubai, Sudan, Egypt, Brunei and beyond was funnelled through various Islamic organisations to fund many of the Pakistan-based or -bred militant groups in their fight for 'the freedom of Kashmir'. In Pakistan there were collecting boxes at many mosques that clearly stated that the money was for one of the groups, say Hizb-ul-Mujahideen, and that it would be used in the fight for *Azadi* (freedom) in Indian-controlled Kashmir. The donations flowed in constantly. Across the fragile Line of Control the Government of India closed the route for foreign donations to Kashmir.

After the September 11 attacks in New York and Washington in 2001 General Musharraf, in his new role as an American ally, decreed that these collecting boxes be removed. In some places they were but in many cases word of mouth let people know where they could continue to make donations. The declaration of the war on terror acted as a donation trigger for many of the militant Islamic organisations as the world shifted into the ugly media tag of Islam versus the West.

While the Government of India's resistance to foreign donations to Kashmir was not without reason, it was profoundly unhelpful to the thousands who had lost homes: husbands, wives, children and parents, those who no longer had a way to earn money for food because their small tea stand had been crushed, their bicycle repair shop buried under concrete, their boss's sweatshop destroyed. The earthquake had sunk lives and small businesses across a mountainous arc where there is no insurance, with or without 'act of God' clauses.

The earthquake was still news, continuing to hold the front pages all over the world. As I travelled back to India the latest story was about the estimated figures for the loss of life, and how this would be compounded by the imminent arrival of the first snows. The projected statistics suggested that the fatality figures could as much as double, from 80,000 to 160,000, after the attrition of disease and a harsh winter following the earthquake.

It was still hot when I arrived in Delhi, which was heavy in the torpor that sits in late season humidity; people were wrung out by months of heat before the rains, and then suffocated by thick, wet air during the monsoon. There were collection boxes in shops all over the city for the victims of the earthquake.

I went to speak to shop-owners in one of the main markets, the ones that usually stocked hot-water bottles.

Though it was 32°C in Delhi the nights in the upper reaches of the Valley were already hovering around freezing. Rapidly erected shelters, with their corrugated-iron roofs and walls, became metal ovens in the sun during the day, and refrigerators at night. Blankets were being distributed from supply points along the roads that had been cleared. Those nearest to the roads were taking more blankets, while others further up into the hills were finding it harder to reach supply points. Some of the more remote villages were still inaccessible, their high roads blocked by the earthquake or, in some cases, by aftershocks that had triggered further landslides. Even though the Indian Army was creating supply lines to some of the most cut-off areas many had not yet been reached a week after the earthquake.

On the Pakistan side the army was being criticised for its failures while on the Indian side the worst-affected areas were receiving more disaster relief than any other Indian state had ever been given in the aftermath of a natural disaster, and the government was still maintaining Kashmir's fragile and special status.

Kashmir's rural wealth patterns were being played out again in the way aid was distributed after the earthquake. Those who lived closer to the main roads had a higher standard of living, in the tradition of ribbon development. After the disaster, aid and supplies reached them first. Blankets flooded in, the quantity allowing for three large ones per family. Those near the roads had as many as ten per family while their poorer neighbours, further from the road, had to wait longer to receive them, and were often given only one when they did arrive. Relief supplies log-jammed at Srinagar airport, piled to the height of buildings on the tarmac, while up in the mountains some remote villages still had not even been reached. It was the familiar theme of disaster relief: supplies pouring in, but a struggling delivery system on the ground.

In the heat of the Delhi market, among high-stacked shelves of everything and anything, the shopkeepers, their shirts limp, and with fans blowing directly in their faces, looked surprised by the request for large numbers of hot-water bottles. They would not be getting supplies in for several weeks, they said, as sweat tracked their tired faces. It was for the earthquake victims, I added. You should have said, they pointed out, making calls to suppliers, enlivened for a moment as they bullied people down crackling lines, their position made important as an agent of relief. But for all the noise no hot-water bottles appeared.

> My dear. Is there news of hot bottles? There is such great need. I am just now returned again from Uri-side. How to say this in some way that does not sound so bad? It is as though all things that I have done in my life to this point have been as preparation for this time. This is not meaning that I am without great gratitude for the good luck and blessings of Allah that I have had with my great travels in the world for carpet and shawl sales but, My Dear, this work is a new way for life for me at this time. As you know it is Ramadan and though we are moving around so much, travelling, helping with carrying of things, talking with people all the time, there does not seem even to be need for water. When the sun set it still did not even seem necessary to eat, though of course those of us who could came together to break the fast. My good wife had packed many dates and I was able to share these with the people I was with. But this aside it is as though this work itself is food, and all that we need. We are being guided by Allah in what we do. His work is Great. Please keep me informed of the situation with the hot bottles. We will meet soon, *Inshallah*.
>
> Mohammad

On the ground there was little divine intervention in the relief effort. The Indian Army's efficiency made some international aid agencies and NGOs chippy. The idea that the perceived occupying army had suddenly become heroic made them uncomfortable. The weekly aid meetings in Srinagar, instigated as an exercise in information sharing, often descended into petty bitching. Various NGO and agency representatives voiced their opinions loudly that it was inappropriate for the 'oppressor' of the Valley now to be spearheading the relief effort. When little local NGOs and relief groups raised their hands in protest, championing the Indian Army's speed and efficiency, they were stared down, or more usually shouted down by the international players. They, the people who had lived through the conflict, who had suffered under the worst excesses of both the military and the militants, were being told what was and was not acceptable by those who had just arrived on the scene from the outside world.

'We call them the photo-*wallahs*,' I was told over and over again by Kashmiris, local people involved in relief work, people like Mohammad.

'What else can we call them?' one of them said. He did not wish to be quoted, understandably. 'They will say I am biting off their hand, no? But look at them.'

Of course the world's press had also descended on the earthquake zone. The Delhi-based foreign correspondents flooded back to Srinagar and to the Hotel Broadway on Maulana Azad Road and Ahdoo's Hotel on Residency Road, as they had during the early days of the insurgency, sixteen years before. International news crews flew in and every local fixer was back in work, rushing about trying to find ways to get the news film teams they were acting for to the villages that were still cut off, or to Inner Line military areas that were off-limits. Representatives from the bigger international NGOs spent a lot of time checking with the hotels, the news teams, and seeking out fixers to try to establish where the news crews might be heading to next. If they did manage to find out, several large tips later, scenes of black comedy ensued.

A fleet of four-wheel-drive Land Cruisers and jeeps, variously emblazoned with the logo of the relevant NGOs, would jostle with unseemly haste along a road that had been predicted as a news crew route to a disaster-struck village or hamlet. They wanted to try to get there ahead of the news crew in question so that it would seem that they were already 'on the job', and so deserving of full media coverage and credit. Film crews would struggle over newly reopened roads in lesser vehicles than those used by the NGOs, only to arrive at a pulverised village to find a car park of four-wheel drives, and frantic activity among the NGO photo-*wallahs.*

A couple of news teams learned fast and even set red herring locations, having established from local people places that had not yet been served by the big international NGOs. While the film crew trundled to film somewhere undisclosed, the emblazoned jeeps sped to the aid of areas that urgently needed supplies, thinking they were heading to a mercy mission photo-shoot.

There is an odd method of madness in this sort of circumstance, added to by the fact that international NGOs fight hard for their share of the charity pound or dollar. They are heavily pressured by their marketing and PR departments to get the maximum media coverage. It is hard to try to justify this to a man on the road, his life and livelihood in ruins behind him, as the fleet of four-wheel drives speeds past without a sideways glance, intent on the road ahead and the village to be reached, where the cameras might be.

It was harder still to justify some of the bullying tactics used by international NGOs towards some of the smaller local ones, particularly as the performance in the field of some of the big boys was raising so many questions.

There was a recurring incident in the first few weeks that caused panic at the time. Mohammad was one of many to tell the same story. He explained how local lorry drivers were being contracted to deliver supplies to the villages that had been devastated. A driver and his helper would be despatched from one of the temporary supply depots, their lorry loaded with blankets, food supplies, tents, clothing, cooking utensils, basic medicines, all that was vital for survivors. Depending on which area they were heading to, an estimate was made of the time it would take the drivers to get there and return. This gave those at the depot an idea of how long they would have to organise another load of supplies for the next delivery. Sometimes it would take much longer than anticipated: a fresh landslide would have blocked a road; the driver and his helper perhaps had to spend hours on a dirt road, one side of the lorry propped up with rocks while the two of them heaved off a blown or punctured tyre, one that was likely to have already been bald and vulnerable on rubble-scattered roads. In contrast there were some surprisingly quick turnarounds, the empty lorries returning to the supply depot faster than even the quickest estimate. These drivers were applauded for their work. Some were paid bonuses.

Mohammad was getting reports from some of the disaster-struck villages of supply lorry drivers arriving, but while attempting to unload their cargo they were stormed by local people scrambling for supplies, clambering over each other, fallen bodies being crushed in the rush. The drivers were not NGO or aid workers. They had not been trained how to deal with crowd surges during supply deliveries. Many of them panicked, jumped back into the driver's cabin and accelerated away, supplies tumbling from the open tailgates, the view in the wing mirror of people falling over each other to chase down the trail of scattered supplies. Some of the drivers were injured in the crush of people. They frightened other drivers with stories of how they had been injured.

Other versions began to emerge of whole lorry supply loads being dumped in remote areas, nowhere near the villages or hamlets where they were needed, but under the cover of forests. The supplies were mostly unusable after they had been found.

It became clear that some of the drivers who had been paid bonuses for their quick delivery times had actually been dumping their loads, for fear of being injured, or worse, in the crush of earthquake victims.

'You cannot tell people these things,' one local NGO worker said. 'It will stop people from helping us. We will be abandoned.'

'You must tell what is happening here,' another said. 'People must know and learn for when this thing happens again. It must not be this way next time.'

Mohammad closed his eyes at the end of his version of the story. 'What can I say about this thing?' he said.

There was a sense of purpose in Srinagar, cohesion for the first time for a long period. Reports continued to come in from the more remote areas, detailing cruel statistics of relations lost in crushed villages. People hung around in crowds outside the offices and temporary headquarters of the local and international NGOs. They were waiting for news from villages that still had not been reached. The men pushed in around the doorways, the women sat huddled together in groups on the roadsides and pavements. It was a different kind of waiting, unlike when local women wait and wait to hear news of their men lost in the conflict, killed, arrested, blown up. The earthquake had equalised everyone, for a while. Soldiers coming back into the city from remote areas were being stopped on the street by women, fearless now as they asked for news from the hills of relations in cut-off villages that the army was trying to reach.

It was the middle of November, just over a month since the earthquake, and Mohammad had managed to find a hot-water bottle supply in Srinagar, just as the relief piles finally began to be moved from the airport tarmac. The bottles were neither given nor donated. In the end we had to buy them. The money for those bottles, and for all that came after them, was gathered together from around the world, tentative fingers of support in a nervous time, but still they reached from Boston, New York, London, Melbourne, Auckland and more, putting in place the first bricks of a human bridge. I handed the collected money to Mohammad. Again he closed his eyes and said, 'What can I say?'

Chapter Twelve

ONE EVENING

ONE EVENING DURING the following winter of December 2006, the first snows fell early in Srinagar. They came before the start of Chilla Kalan, the solstice of Kashmiri winter.

Everything was muffled, softened down, smoothed. The back canals, the old arteries of this water city, were veiled as, for a moment, the stagnant scum that now fills so many of them was painted away into white, until the heat of the fermenting waste beneath melted the snow. Garbage piles on street corners, where cows and dogs nuzzled among mounds of uncollected waste, disappeared under the first fall. All that was dirty, ugly, unfinished, hard-edged, every scar of war and corruption, faded.

Up in the mountains it was a much heavier fall in the villages where Mohammad and the members of our NGO team had been working since the earthquake. We were driving back from one of the highest villages, Kamalkote, right on the Line of Control. We were in a convoy of vehicles that pulled up to examine the depth of the fresh snow on the road.

As is ever the situation beyond Srinagar I was the only woman present, and, as the only one I am constantly confronted by the difficulty of trying to find discreet places to pee. As usual, when there is a random halt on one of the long drives, I was scanning for a rock, a tree, a scrubby bush. All was flattened out in the whiteness, though the land above us seemed to be a series of rocks and cutaways that, although now covered by snow, would allow enough privacy. I waved to the driver, a half salute that he had by now learned meant that I was once again heading off the road. He shrugged to show he understood.

The falling snow had the dry quality that made it puff up around me as I clambered up the slope towards the outcrop. I did not have to go so far to be out of sight. When I looked back towards the vehicles I could barely see them any more.

Ducking down, I surveyed the immediate landscape. It was almost entirely covered by the snow, but nonetheless there were indicators of what lay beneath.

I was among fallen timbers, bricks and masonry, not the rock outcrop that it had seemed to be from below. There had been a small house there and some outbuildings, perhaps other houses too, a little hamlet. As I stood the snowfall eased for a moment and a slide of sun lit the slope back down to the cars on the road.

All was covered by snow – the land, landscape, the destruction of the earthquake, the lives and livelihoods lost, all was equalled, the road back down into the Valley an exquisite path of refracted light.

Mohammad called up from the road. He was worried that we would get stuck in the snow. It had been a long day.

During the fourteen months since the earthquake the lives of many had changed radically. A huge number had lost everything, but for others something entirely new had begun.

Mohammad had become an aid worker, and the long drives up and down to Uri and Kamalkote, on the Line of Control, were as much a part of his life as flying to Dubai to show his carpets and shawls to a sheik or a princess.

In the initial surge of aid relief five crossing points on the Line of Control had been opened up between Pakistan and India to allow for the movement of supplies. The opening of these points also meant that some people had been able to meet with relatives they had been separated from since January 1949, when the UN Ceasefire Line, the demarcation that later became the Line of Control, had been established at the end of the first Kashmir war between India and Pakistan.

Amid the chaos of the disaster these openings had been seen as a sign of hope as men and women, stooped with age, took the hands of equally aged relatives across the border, the military of both countries looking on. General Musharraf, the Pakistani President, gave dramatic speeches, urging India to take this opportunity to resolve over half a century of dispute between the two countries. The Government of India, under Prime Minister Manmohan Singh, did not use such heightened rhetoric but played more of a watching game, promising the equivalent of $25 million towards the budget of $5 billion estimated for rebuilding in the areas devastated, most particularly Muzaffarabad, the capital of Pakistan-controlled Kashmir.

One of those five crossing points was at Kaman Post, just a few miles from Kamalkote, one of the places where we were focusing our efforts. After the immediacy of blankets, food, medical supplies and hot-water bottles came temporary shelters. Our team had become the Kashmir Welfare Trust and we began rebuilding damaged houses and building new ones, mainly in Uri and Kamalkote, as soon as it was possible to start laying foundations. Only a minimum amount could be achieved during that first winter after the earthquake. Snow and ground that was constantly frost-hardened throughout the winter meant that foundations were difficult to dig, and the weather was too cold for cement to dry. Our building work stopped during Chilla Kalan of December 2005 through to January 2006.

As the weeks passed the story slid from the newspaper front pages to the international pages. Increasing levels of insurgency in Iraq pulled the world's focus back to another part of the Islamic world while pneumonia and dysentery spread epidemically through the earthquake relief camps and shelters, the survivors' immune systems compromised by shock and grief. International medical teams struggled to treat tens of thousands of people with minimal supplies. A young American medic stared into a camera for a CBS news report, his eyes blown wide by the horror of what he was facing.

The interviewer asked, 'Do you have enough antibiotics?'

'No,' the young medic replied.

'Do you have enough anaesthesia?'

'No.'

'Do you have enough hypodermic needles?'

'No.'

'Do you have enough water?'

'No.'

'Do you have enough food?'

The young man rolled his eyes to the sky. 'No.' He paused. 'I don't think there is anything you could possibly list that could make it sufficient for a team of thirteen people to treat a valley of thousands, no, tens of thousands of people. Basically what we are doing here is sticking a band-aid on a wound the size of Texas.'

As the story slipped from international media consciousness security began to tighten up along the Line of Control again. It was no longer as easy as it had been to get into the Inner Line that mirrors the border. Even as a local Kashmiri it became harder for Mohammad. As a foreigner it became almost impossible for me. I had to have clearance from both the military and the bureaucracy, from the senior area army commander, and from the divisional commissioner in Srinagar, the most senior civil servant, permission that had then to be transmitted down the line, from district to district, military post to checkpoint.

We knew a senior officer, the one who had been spearheading the programme to rehabilitate militants leaving training camps in Pakistan-controlled Kashmir. He was already a hero to many of the local people at a time when the Indian Army was trying hard to repair its image in the Valley. Its earthquake relief work had only enhanced its own standing and that of The General. Each time I called him to say when I hoped to travel to Uri and Kamalkote next he would politely take the call, and assure me that all would be well once we had reached Baramulla, his headquarters.

It was more complicated at the divisional commissioner's office in Srinagar. First there was the checking and frisking, the smiling female officers who seemed confused that I was not accompanied by a man.

'Where is husband?' they asked. 'Why not with you?'

'But you don't have your husbands with you,' I said.

'We have not married yet,' they replied, and giggled.

'And I'm sure you won't bring your husbands to work when you do.' And we all laughed at the notion of brand-new husbands being brought to work in the women's frisking area at the gate of the divisional commissioner's office.

The laughter ended and the obstacles began after the smiling women at the gate.

The divisional commissioner is both a man and a position constantly lobbied by groups of people from all over the city, and the Valley. He is also very frequently 'out of station' in his other office in Jammu, the summer capital of the state.

There is always a shoving crowd outside the divisional commissioner's office, waving petitions, shouting their complaint to the door minders. Even if they know that the divisional commissioner is in Jammu, the crowds still come to wait, just their presence marking their protest. All will be noted and filed. The petitioners know this, though they also know that the noting and filing is probably as far as most of these things will get, unless there is lubrication along the way that will help ease the paperwork out of the file and onto someone's desk.

I am usually passed around these offices, partly for the amusement factor, and also because, in the absence of the divisional commissioner, the staff are unsure who exactly it is who should be explaining to me that what I require is very complicated, and not something that can be easily arranged – permission to travel to Uri and Kamalkote, a route now so difficult to take, bureaucratically.

It was a bitter day when I went. Mist in layered grey seeped into buildings. Blankets had been hung on the insides of doors, a second barrier against the pervading dank. People's outlines were now hunched over for winter.

At the divisional commissioner's office the petitioners were separated from the petitioned by dress, the men of the crowd in *pherans*, the men behind desks in Western clothing. On the ground floor, in the important offices most directly attached to the divisional commissioner, the men wore suits and blazers, individual heaters pulled close to their desks to preserve their sartorial statement of importance. Further up the building, in the lesser offices, the men did not take off their outdoor coats, scarves or hats, in cramped offices that had just one small stove in the centre of the room that people gravitated towards. They moved via its small circle of warmth on their way from one file-stacked desk to another.

The divisional commissioner was out of station. I was passed around and up the building, down through the ranks. It was my fault. I should have left, having established when the divisional commissioner would be back. The visit would have been noted and filed. I could have asked for a future appointment and returned with the male authority of Mohammad. The mistake was optimism, the hope that permission could be given that day.

In the attic of the building a man with an old overcoat, over a dirty anorak, over a jacket directed me towards the stove, and to a chair with one broken leg, the short end resting on a pile of files. It was the place of privilege and maximum visibility in the office in the eaves. As the men in their layers of clothing moved between their desks, via the stove's glow, they slowed to absorb the warmth and to examine me closely, this contradiction in their midst: cargo trousers, hiking boots, a dull grey thermal jacket beneath a pale pink *pashmina* shawl that covered my head. No *pheran* that day, not to the divisional commissioner's office. In this place the only chance of being granted permission by the bureaucracy was to be all that I am, irrespectively and respectfully: foreign, female, local NGO representative and journalist, head covered.

When one of the few female employees entered the long, low, cold room, the behaviour changed. It was as though a layer of sullenness lifted as the secretary, in her turquoise *salwar kameez*, purple cardigan and almost matching shawl, arrived, carrying a lightness of being with her bright colours. We smiled at each other, compared notes on the coldness of the day, as compared to the day before, and she offered me tea. She was interrupted by a tall man in a khaki ski jacket, his scarf still wrapped around his head.

'You came to see me?' he barked.

I had no idea who he was.

'Yes, of course, thank you,' I replied.

The secretary had gone with her colour. The man waved me to his desk at the far end of the room. He pushed past so that he would get there first, sitting down fast, as though it were important that he should be in place before I approached.

'What is it you want?' he asked, pointing to another propped-up chair beside his desk, this one balanced on an old dried milk tin.

I explained our situation and how, now that security had become much tighter again, I was seeking permission to go to the sites where we were working. I passed the folder to him of the work of the Kashmir Welfare Trust, a file carefully compiled with photographs of the damaged and destroyed buildings that we were restoring or building as new.

The man turned away and began to flick through the annotated lists of every household in the areas where we were working; a model borrowed from one used successfully during the relief work in the south of India after the tsunami of December 2004. Careful columns noted how many members there were in each family, what their monthly income had been, how it had been affected by the earthquake, a financial estimate of the loss they had suffered, and then a record of relief and aid received.

The low-ranking civil servant clumped together all the pages of photographs of our building work and fanned through them.

'We cannot give you permission. This work has been done without details being lodged with this office. All this work is illegal.'

'But we are lodging this work with you now, this folder is for you, all this information that has been gathered is for you.' I tried not to lean forward, or wave my hands about to emphasise my frustration. I sat still on the broken chair, my hands under my thighs, my face burning.

'So many of these buildings are mosques.' He thumbed through the photographs again. 'Why are you building so many of them?'

'Because a great many of them were damaged. After the earthquake it was the first place people went for safety and comfort. With so many of them damaged the villagers had nowhere to go. My colleagues felt that it was important to do this first, to rebuild the mosques so that people could gather there, not just for prayer, but for comfort.'

'Who told you to say this?' he asked.

Behind him the attic windows were crossed with tape, to hold the glass there in the event of a bomb blast. One window, behind the man's still scarf-wrapped head, had no glass, just a plastic fertiliser bag tacked into the frame. 'Best Ever Yield' it read.

'Would it be possible for the divisional commissioner to see this file?' I asked in a pinched voice.

'If this work was not lodged with this office we cannot help you. You should have done this through our office, then we would have told you what needed to be done. This is the way it should have been.' Again he thumbed through the pictures.

There was nothing to be gained by arguing or pointing out that we had been working on the ground since the earthquake, that we knew what was needed, that Mohammad was speaking to people every day, getting feedback from local *panchayat* councils, that we were not just passing through on official visits now and then, that no money exchanged hands in the name of bribery, that every rupee, pound, euro and dollar raised went straight to work, without middlemen, and without being side-tracked.

This man in the attic needed a victory.

'I am sorry about this.' I looked down at the floor.

'We cannot give permission.' The man slapped our file closed.

There was a long pause as the background noise of the room surrounded our silence.

'Would it be possible just to convey this folder of our work to the divisional commissioner, with our respects?' I asked.

The man looked up.

'I will see what can be arranged. This thing might be possible.' His voice sounded surprised, as though he had not expected me to try to ask for anything.

'Thank you for your help,' I lied, and bowed, and left the office.

The women at the frisking booth waved as I went past them at the gate. I raised my hand but could not smile.

By this time, in December 2006, the mobile phone networks in Kashmir were up and overloaded, their spread accelerated by the earthquake, and the need for people to communicate without having to rely on constantly disrupted, down or sabotaged land lines.

Mohammad did not answer his phone when I called. It was just before afternoon prayer. He has no message service. Very few do in Kashmir, or indeed in most of India. There is an almost cultural distaste for having to leave a message on a machine rather than with a human being.

Pushing miserably through grey streets filled with scuttling forms in *pherans* I crossed Lal Chowk and made again for Café Arabica on Maulana Azad Road, for its warmth, light, incongruous music and enthusiastic service.

At a table in the corner I was comforted by someone who understood, another journalist, also a foreigner familiar with India. He put his hand out to catch one of mine that was waving about as I raged pointlessly at the whole system that was crushing the future of Kashmir. The servers looked on from behind the counter and a table of men nearby stopped talking to listen to the outburst. They all stared. My comforter turned to stare them down but they ignored him and went on watching the show. The doorman I knew so well came in from out of the grey to see what was happening.

The frustrations of a year poured out, of the blind rules and bureaucratic bullying that we had been through since the earthquake. It was an extended show.

Mohammad was also upset when I told him later.

'Who is this man? How can he say these things about our work? I have been in contact so many times with the divisional commissioner's office and it has never been said to me at any of these times that we had to lodge information about how we are doing this work.'

We were sitting in what Mohammad calls the *hamam* room, propped against bolsters on the heated floor. I explained how it had been left, and that now I had 'lodged' the file of our work with the request that it be shown to the divisional commissioner when he returned from Jammu.

'I have never heard of this man in all the times I have been to the DC's office. I do not understand. Who is he?' Mohammad thumped the bolster and his youngest son hovered at the door, nervous about this unusual outburst from his father.

Mohammad waved the boy in and cradled him in his lap, stroking his hair, soothing him, while his own forehead was strained.

'These are not right these things that he is saying. Imagine how this thing would have been if from the very beginning, from the earthquake, each and every kind of building had to be lodged with the DC's office?'

We sat on the warm floor in silence, both of us knowing that the difficult man in the attic had based his argument on fine-print bureaucratic rules that could be used against us. Construction had to be cleared to be legal. Mohammad himself had lobbied for the removal of illegal buildings that encroached on Nagin Lake, his lake, pushing constantly further out into the shrinking water mass.

He crooned to his son as we sat, the boy floppy in his arms.

'But we are not doing this thing,' he said, the mutual thought process expressed. 'We are not doing any single thing except helping people to have their homes again.'

'And their mosques,' I added.

'But this is of course.' He looked at me in surprise.

'He seemed unhappy about the number of mosques that are being built.'

Mohammad raised his hands to the sky. 'We are just building again what was destroyed, *Al-hamdulilah*, with the help of Allah, why does he say these things? I am so upset.'

Mohammad and I returned to the divisional commissioner's office the following day. We were equipped for bureaucratic confrontation.

The divisional commissioner was still not there when we arrived but he was due imminently. So we waited, and when he appeared from beneath the shiny black hump-back of his official Ambassador, its blue lights flashing, we were the first to be ushered into his presence. He greeted Mohammad warmly, and welcomed me back to Kashmir courteously. An assistant passed him our folder and he moved to his desk, turning the pages, and congratulating us on the trust's work as he went. Even before he sat down to talk he had called in another assistant and ordered that letters of safe passage and recommendation be typed up immediately. While we waited we talked of the cost of building materials for the houses, the difficulties of haulage up to the villages, and of the weather, the depth of the day's mist and the chill of it.

As the first snows of December melted on the fermenting rubbish piles of the city, the obstacles thrown up by the man in the attic faded too. We did not complain about him. He had, after all, passed the folder of our work to the divisional commissioner, and he had not been bribed to do so.

Two days later, in the heart of a military camp, an officer sat in his office, his staff around him, a small man, neat, precise, powerful. He was wearing a suit while his hovering staff were in uniform. Mohammad, Ahsan, another of the trust's directors, and I sat on the other side of his desk in an upright row.

We had left Nagin Lake at dawn in order to reach The General by breakfast time on a Sunday morning, bringing cold air and carefully plastic-covered permissions from the divisional commissioner into his office with us.

After the to and fro of first greetings Mohammad asked The General if he would be able to accompany us on our journey to the high villages. He demurred, politely but firmly. He had a mess lunch that he had to attend. Mohammad looked down into his lap. I saw his hands clenching. He looked up again.

'Please, sir, it would be a great thing for the people in Kamalkote if you were to come,' he said.

The General represented power, Mohammad the people of the Valley. The presence of both men would be narcotic.

The General was in the middle of reading a document that had been passed to him by his ADC. He looked up.

'Excuse me for one moment,' he said.

He picked up one of the phones on his desk. While we examined the gallery on the wall of previous incumbents, moustached, bearded, turbaned and heavy with medals, The General cancelled his lunch appointment. When I turned back it was into Mohammad's smile, broad beneath his beard. He bowed his head to thank The General, adjusting his woollen hat as he came up, his hands shaking a little.

'I will be back in just a few moments. I will have to change if I am to join you, and a few arrangements will need to be made.' The General smiled and left the room, quietly issuing instructions to his ADC as he went.

Half an hour later we left the barracks, and Ahsan's car slotted behind The General's armoured jeep. Ahead of that were two more armed jeeps, and another two behind us, one with a manned gun turret. A few arrangements had indeed been made.

As we switchbacked further up into the mountains morning rain turned to sleet, blurring the stark, ragged lines of the ranges on either side, soaking all colours to shades of wet grey, but still the patrolling soldiers on the road could see the stars on The General's number plate, indicating the rank of the passenger. They turned towards the convoy, straight up and down, stamping and saluting as we passed. At the checkpoints soldiers and officers flanked either side of the road, saluting. We only stopped at The General's command: to greet a junior officer he recognised, or to clasp hands with a local man he knew on the side of the road. Each time the convoy slowed as heavily armed soldiers jumped from the lead and rear vehicles to run along the side of the road, shadowing The General's vehicle, and his every movement when he got out of his jeep.

At Uri we drank tea in another barracks, the Brigadier in command greeting The General on arrival at the head of a line of his own officers. The Brigadier had also cleared his day to be available for this last-minute outing.

Mohammad, Ahsan and I moved in a slight daze through the saluting, the issuing of orders, bodies snapping to attention, and polite tea-drinking.

The unofficial official visit began just down the road from the barracks, at one of the main children's schools that the Kashmir Welfare Trust had been helping to rebuild. A generous woman had given me handfuls of euros for our work. Her nephew had died recently and she asked that we do something in his honour. Mohammad had allocated the money for the rebuilding of the damaged school's toilet block. While The General talked to the school principal, Mohammad and I went to see the new building.

He stood proudly between two toilet doors, one marked for students, the other for staff. As I set up to take some pictures for the donor, wondering how best to portray the end result of her donation, Mohammad pointed earnestly to the plaque above the two doors. In gold lettering on black stone he had arranged the engraving: 'In Loving Memory of Jean'. He smiled and I took the picture. The donor understood the statement of these bathrooms. They represented progress, while also stopping the students from scattering into the alleys and hillsides during class times. They were not entirely progressive, being toilets just for male students, and teachers, in a male-only school.

We drank more tea at the school with the principal and some of the teachers. Below us a crowd of men gathered, their faces staring up to where we stood at the top of a raw concrete staircase, open to the driving sleet. Most of the external walls of the building were still being rebuilt.

There were no women. These crowds are inherently men-only.

The General, Mohammad and Ahsan posed with their cups of tea and I took pictures again. A photograph of Tower Bridge in London was their backdrop, pinned to a wall behind, one of the few in the building that had been reconstructed. Mohammad smiled shyly, his teacup to his lips.

The sleet began to get heavier as we left the school. The General stopped beside his jeep, surrounded by his runners, an umbrella held over his head by his ADC.

'Would you join us now?' he asked me.

I climbed in behind The General and the Brigadier, hunching low to sit behind them under a heavily reinforced roof. As we pulled away I had to duck low to avoid hitting the roof as we met each bump and pothole. Ahsan and Mohammad were reflected in the rear-view mirror, next to the Brigadier's eyes as he drove. They looked confused, peering towards the jeep, talking to each other at speed, unsure as to why I was now travelling with the officers.

The convoy moved on, hugging the narrow roads, the drivers looking up at most corners, watching for landslides as the shifting soil was made heavier still by falling sleet. Below us the army encampment outside Uri spread across the landscape, disappearing and reappearing as we clung to the mountain.

The conversation started lightly, on Hindi film. The General, the Brigadier and I compared notes on the most heart-wrenching love scenes, arguing the physical perfection of the Bollywood superstar Aishwarya Rai versus the more poignant acting and range of Tabu, the thinking man's beauty.

'The soldiers of course like Ash [the shorthand name for Aishwarya],' The General declared, as the vast camp below disappeared beneath a shelf of sleet and mist.

'Of course,' I agreed. Of course the lithe beauty was their pin-up girl. The Brigadier was smiling a quiet fantasy smile.

We did not talk just of Bollywood and who best filled a sari. There was the nuclear issue, and the threat in Pakistan of the fundamentalists getting too close to the centre of power for India's comfort. And there was the Indian Army line of how they felt encroached on by the heavy American presence in the region, on one side in Iraq, with NATO in Afghanistan on the other, and of how this created a sense of strategic encirclement.

The conversation was back on the arts, with The General's love of Keats and Tagore, when we were flagged down by a village elder. He was another Hajji Papa, veteran of Mecca and countless council meetings. The General leapt from the car, his ADC scrambling behind to open the umbrella over his head. The man in uniform and the old man in his sleet-sodden *pheran* embraced. The convoy halted. We went to take tea with Hajji Papa, following him up through thin winding alleys now gushing brown. We straddled the ground water to reach Hajji Papa's house, and then sat in rows in the temporary home with its roof and walls of corrugated galvanised iron. Though it was the practice of the house to take off your shoes on entering, Hajji Papa would not let his honoured guest remove his boots. The General tucked his feet carefully under the plastic chair that was brought for him, keeping them off the rug that covered the damp cement floor.

He asked questions about how the rebuilding programmes were going. Hajji Papa, in his role as *sarpanch*, the local council leader, talked of what they did not have, of what they were not being provided with, and of what the government was failing to deliver.

'Tell me, what you do have?' The General asked.

Hajji Papa smiled and talked about the success of a women's training programme that was teaching local women to be pattern cutters and seamstresses. The General had started the programme, I was told, one of many that he instigated. This small gathering of men talked about sewing machines while a daughter of the house was called for and instructed to take me on a tour of the women's project.

This pretty girl with her easy laugh was the only woman I was introduced to that day. She chattered as she led me through gushing mud to the women's centre, empty on a Sunday, the bright plastic chairs pushed in carefully behind each old hand-turned Usha sewing machine. The girl made a point of proudly showing off the attached ladies' bathroom.

'This is very important for them, you see,' she explained, pulling her flowered scarf off and re-tying it over thick dark hair. 'Many are still in temporary huts and tents. Many of these people have no bathroom. This is their bathroom now.' She smiled as she put the padlock back on the important door.

As we skidded back to the house she asked where my husband was. I tried to explain my lack of one.

'You can find a good husband here, and these soldiers, they are good men too. You can marry one of them.'

We stood on the small veranda outside the house as she pointed out the merits and physical drawbacks of the row of military men inside. I listened, enjoying the headiness of her laughter in this conversation about the Indian Army that I would never have believed possible in an Inner Line village in Kashmir.

The sleet eased as we left. Hajji Papa looked up at the sky. 'It will snow later,' he said.

Within an hour we had reached our highest destination, Kamalkote. It was a village of corrugated iron. Every house had been destroyed or badly damaged in the earthquake. Cloud and mist closed the village in from above and below, but still a silver light came from this place of temporary shelters. It bounced off the walls and roofs of rippled iron, these metal boxes made familiar by the doors that had been put into them, salvaged from the rubble, from the homes that had been lost.

The General asked if we could stop on the edge of the village.

'Come,' he said, helping me out of the back of the jeep. 'It will be better if we walk in.'

The armoured jeeps lined up outside the village and we walked in human convoy. As he had during the earlier stops The General discreetly despatched his protection team to the edges of the village, to shadow our approach from the higher ground rather than enter with us, heavily armed in full combat camouflage. Mohammad, Ahsan and I looked at each other, suddenly unsure of how we would be received in this village that we usually came to alone. Yet here we were now, arriving as part of a military convoy, flanked by soldiers with machine guns. As we walked towards the gathering crowd the elders came out to greet us, reaching out their hands to both Mohammad and The General. Both men smiled, thanked, clasped hands, but The General, the power, was the one towards whom the crowd surged.

It was again an entirely male throng. Every man of the village had come out to look at and to meet the VIP , this man who had built relationships with whole communities in a way that most people would never have thought possible for the Indian Army in Kashmir. They stood in the cold, huddled into blankets, the older ones with their heads wrapped around in shawls, some of the younger ones with baseball caps, a few of which were turned backwards, which was their way of covering their heads while proving that they were young – devout but cool.

It was a Sunday crowd. The lucky few who had secure government jobs were off for the day, shopkeepers had shut up to come and watch, shepherds were still up in the hills, but the majority were without jobs, their places of work either destroyed by the earthquake, or their unemployment another of the large statistics of the conflict.

As the crowd gathered we stopped under a spreading tree in the centre of the village, its broad girth still standing though there were the tumbled stumps around of others that had fallen during the earthquake. One of the junior officers produced more tea, served in ceremonial beakers, the colourful regimental insignia causing fascination among the village men. The beaker that I had been given was passed from hand to hand as men requisitioned mine rather than anyone else's because I was neither soldier nor man. The General called for it to be returned, smiling as his ADC rescued it from the multitude of hands.

Mohammad requested that The General come and see the progress being made on the rebuilding and restoration of the village's main mosque. A junior officer with a lush moustache rolled his eyes. The General stared at him very directly as we followed Mohammad and the elders up a steep and narrow path.

From the height of the path we could look down over the whole village. The General was just in front of me, his hands again clasped behind his back. He paused so that I could catch up.

'Now we can see who really lives here,' he said.

Below us were the houses of the village, the temporary huts and the tents that some people had been living in since the earthquake. Outside almost every home stood women and children, looking towards the crowd of men around the tree. A few had their faces lifted, looking up to where we stood. A gaggle of children was running down through the village towards the convoy of parked vehicles. One boy leapt into the air every few strides, his arms thrown up.

'I love to be with children,' The General said, tracking the progress of the leaping boy, his hand raised in a wave. 'I miss my own children so much. I was away so often as they were growing up, on all the postings here. I missed so much time with them.'

Several of the watching women below waved in reply. The running gaggle was moving too fast to focus on the uniformed man on the path above them. Mohammad laughed from the loop in the path above us.

'See how fast they are,' he said, his arm raised to the children as well.

Both men, hands lifted, continued to wave.

*

There is one particular photograph from that day, taken in Kamalkote, just before the snow began to fall.

Mohammad, The General, the Brigadier and I are standing at the front of the village's crowd of men. The General is smiling, one hand resting on the arm of a boy, the other around the shoulder of one of the village elders. Mohammad has half turned away, his bobble hat pulled down over his ears, his hands stuffed into the pockets of his overcoat. A red tartan scarf nestles around his hennaed beard. I am grinning, the only teeth showing in the crowd. The expressions around are a mixture of severe, a few wary smiles and a couple of warmer ones.

The photograph was taken with my camera by The General's ADC.

Whatever the nature of that day, and that trapped moment, it was still a crowd of Kashmiri village men being photographed by the Indian Army. This amount of military attention has a history to it, a pattern. For most of these villages an army presence still means crackdown, investigation or a house-to-house search.

Beakers of *chai* drunk among a crowd remain a novelty to be explored beyond the angry scars of a people who have so many reasons not to trust soldiers.

In the picture those immediately around The General are smiling, safe in their knowledge of him. They have seen his work, and somehow trust has managed to sneak in. Those who do not know him look on in anger or confusion. They cannot help it. They know that the army has helped them in this particular time of need and loss, and that its giant machinery has been able to bring some semblance of order back into their lives since the earthquake. But they do not know what will happen tomorrow, the day after, or how the army will be the next time it comes to the village.

Since this photograph was taken The General has been posted out of the Valley. This man, responsible for building so many bridges, has been shipped elsewhere, perhaps because he is needed elsewhere, and perhaps because he has ruffled a few too many feathers among high command as he got closer to people on the ground than many felt was necessary.

Mohammad and the other members of the Kashmir Welfare Trust continue to build for those who lost everything in the earthquake. It is more than the buildings now. The schools are expanding and there are orphanages too. On every visit to Uri, Kamalkote and beyond we discover how much there is still to be done.

We have had situations when we have realised that we are building a house for someone who is not from the village at all. They have turned out to be a relative of someone in the village, someone who has already had a house built for them. They have come from another village, or even from beyond the Valley. They have been told that houses are being built. And so they arrive and present their case of loss, and we believe them.

Grassroots work is so often to do with construction: building houses, schools, hospitals, clinics, temples, mosques or churches. We are beginning to understand that in war and conflict the real bricks are physical evidence of a much harder building process – the reconstruction of trust. When that is dented it is not the time to walk away but to examine methods, to check, learn and to push the energy of frustration in another direction.

Part of this kind of rebuilding means that trust will be

broken along the way, on both sides. There is that moment when you, the outsider, trying to find ways past corruption, overhear someone saying that you are not to be trusted because, well, you are not a Muslim.

I have cried into the darkness, through the night on the silent lake, asking why I am here, why I have become woven into the fabric of this tattered place.

The hope is that it is because Mohammad, his brothers, their wives, parents and children, accept that this outsider is a constant, that because I have returned again and again, with donated money to build and rebuild stuffed in my suitcases under clothes and books, that this is a bridge of sorts from the outside world into the Valley.

We work together. There are gaps, cultural voids that we fall into, sentences left unfinished, times when we have to turn away from each other.

When Mohammad and I walk to the school near the lake in Srinagar, a place that he started after the earthquake for orphans of the disaster, he walks a little ahead of me through the bazaar. My head is covered, my face lowered to the dirt road. But when we are away from the shops and the *chai* stalls he lets me catch up and we talk about things that are needed for the school. Sometimes he asks advice about something.

Our truth is that he and I know how different we are from each other, and we are trying not to challenge those differences.

Mohammad likes to sit facing the mountains when he is on the back of the houseboat. While we talk he looks out over the water, passing comment on the beauty of late light on the lake, a kingfisher's skill as an airborne fisher, the arrival of autumn, the retreat of winter as colour emerges again from the cold mist.

We were sitting this way when he and I last spoke beside the lake.

'I see now that our mistake at the beginning of all this trouble was to believe that people outside this place would hear the terrible things that were happening, and then they would come and do what was right. But all those appeals to the UN, this kind of thing, all was useless. There is no blame in this thing from my side. I see it a little differently now.

'I understand that the story is always changing. We people in Kashmir will be the story one week because of a bomb in our parliament building in Srinagar, or for the earthquake, or whatever else it is. Then there will be another big story, maybe a bigger one, somewhere else in the world, and people will forget us again. We have to make our own future from here, from this place, these people. It is hard at this time because of how so many people in the world are thinking of Islam in a bad way. All the time here new problems are happening. We will have to find another way of thinking. If we do not do this how will we make a future?' And Mohammad, the Muslim, Kashmiri, patriarch, house-boatman, carpet-seller and aid worker, looked out across the lake.

AUTHOR'S NOTE

A state election was held in Jammu and Kashmir over the course of a month, from 17 November to 24 December 2008. There is now a new leadership under a young man whose family has been inextricably involved in Kashmiri politics since the 1930s. Omar Abdullah, the new Chief Minister of Jammu and Kashmir, has brought with him an optimism that has not been felt in the Valley for a long time. The task he faces – of economic restructuring and trust building – is monumental.